Fin de Siècle

AND OTHER ESSAYS ON

America & Europe

Fin de Siècle

AND OTHER ESSAYS ON

America & Europe

WALTER LAQUEUR

TRANSACTION PUBLISHERS
New Brunswick (U.S.A.) and London (U.K.)

Copyright © 1997 by Transaction Publishers, New Brunswick, New Jersey 08903.

This book is printed on acid-free paper that meets the American National Standard for Permanence of Paper for Printed Library Materials.

Library of Congress Catalog Number: 96-33084
ISBN: 1-56000-261-1
Printed in the United States of America

Library of Congress Cataloging-in-Publication Data

Laqueur, Walter, 1921–
    Fin de siècle and other essays on America and Europe / Walter Laqueur.
        p. cm.
    Includes bibliographical references and index.
    ISBN 1-56000-261-1 (alk. paper)
    1. Radicalism—Europe—History—20th century. 2. Europe—Politics and government—1989– . 3. Radicalism—Russia (Federation). 4. Russia (Federation)—Politics and government—1991– . 5. Post-communism. 6. World politics—1989– . I. Title.
HN380.Z9R347 1996
320.9'049—dc20   96-33084
                                                                       CIP

Contents

Part IV: Writers and Fighters

Part V: Public and Private Affairs

Acknowledgements

"Fin de Siècle" reprinted from *Journal of Contemporary History,* January 1996 by permission, all rights reserved. The same applies to the following articles:

"Berlin and Moscow 1914" appeared originally in the catalogue of the *Berlin-Moscow Exhibition,* Berlin 1995.

"The Long Way to Europe" was first published as an introduction to W. Mommsen (ed.) *The Long Way to Europe,* edition q. Newton Conn. 1993.

"Public Diplomacy, Poor Relation" appeared first in *Foreign Affairs,* October 1994.

"Russian Nationalism" in *Foreign Affairs,* Winter 1992/3.

"Preparing for the Next Century" in *Partisan Review,* Winter 1994.

"Post Fascism, Post Communism" in *Partisan Review,* July 1995.

"Feuchtwanger and Gide" in *Partisan Review,* Fall 1992.

"Family Reunion" in *Commentary,* July 1994.

"Splendor and Misery of Sovietology" part one and two, *New Times,* (Moscow), August 1992.

"In Praise of Menshevism" in *Novoe Vremya,* 11 January 1992.

"Russian Nationalism" (1) was published in the *New Republic,* November 1990, part two appeared in Russian as a preface to the Russian edition of *Black Hundred,* Moscow, 1994.

"The End of the Cold War" appeared in German in H.P. Schwarz and K. Kaiser, *Die Neue Weltpolitik,* Bonn, 1995.

The essay on Sakharov is reproduced here by permission of Brandeis University Press.

"The Empire Strikes Out" *New Republic,* 15 September 1991.

The Essay on Maxim Gorky was not published previously.

"The Congress for Cultural Freedom" appeared first in *Partisan Review,* Spring 1996.

Introduction

On Victory in Europe Day General de Gaulle, in a pensive mood, went to the Arc de Triomphe to salute the Tomb of the Unknown Soldier and the chroniclers reported one of his famous asides: *"Comme ils sont obscurs les lendemains de la France."*

This ought to be the motto of the present book but for the fact that it refers not just to France. When the Soviet Empire collapsed and the cold war came to an end there had been a general rejoicing similar to the celebrations after World Wars I and II and, of course, for good cause. The walls dividing East and West had at last come down, the threat of nuclear war had been removed and the tyranny that had affected the lives of so many people had disappeared. New vistas opened up of peace, prosperity, and the pursuit of happiness.

The essays collected here all belong to the post-cold war period and if they have a common denominator it is of not joining the chorus of rejoicing. Not much foresight was needed even in 1989–90 to realize that Russia's and Eastern Europe's road to freedom would be, at best, protracted and arduous with many setbacks ahead. During the 1970s and 1980s Western scholars had engaged in acrimonious disputes as to whether the Soviet Union was an authoritarian or totalitarian state, a dictatorship qualitatively different from its predecessors. The prevailing consensus was that though it might have been totalitarian under Stalin, it had become more liberal in the subsequent decades. To some this seemed a scholastic debate—what did labels matter? But the aftermath of communist rule has shown that there was after all, an important distinction, for if the Soviet Union and Eastern Europe had indeed been authoritarian such as, for instance, Spain under Franco, Salazar's Portugal, and Chile under Pinochet, the transition to a democratic regime would have been much easier. Ten years after the reforms in the communist world, power, such as it is, is again in the hands of the communists, or of nationalists closely cooperating with communists. True, these are not old Stalinists;

most of them have undergone change, but their style is still authoritarian and no one can say for certain whether this conversion to democracy is lasting. The fact that the very word "democracy" has become a swear word in Russia does not augur well. Given the enormous problems facing them one should not be too harsh on the incumbents, for the alternative is even worse: the rise of a "red-brown alliance." Populism has emerged in Eastern Europe and the former Soviet Union and populist movements that can with equal ease turn to the extreme right and left, frequently combining the two traditions.

This trend is by no means confined to the former Soviet empire. Fundamentalism in the Middle East and North Africa as well as in other parts of the globe is heir to a militantly religious tradition. But in its practice, its monopolization of political power, terror, propaganda, its intolerance and aggressiveness, it has shown striking affinities with historical fascism. Has communism been defeated merely to open the door to a revival of that other abomination, fascism, or are we confronting a new phenomenon, a coalition of the two least savory political movements of the twentieth century?

Even in Europe the extreme right has reemerged in force—in France and Italy, in Russia and Austria these parties are among the strongest. And yet, as far as Europe is concerned (except perhaps the Balkans), there is reason for guarded optimism. Europe has been immunized to some extent to outright fascism, the new aggressiveness is directed inward. Europe's status in the world is very much diminished and will continue to decline as long as there is no greater unity. With all the extremist rhetoric, even European fascism is no longer militaristic, does not want to spend a large part of its GNP on rearmament. It wants to keep foreigners out but does not wish to risk aggressive war. Perhaps the fascists too have been corrupted by the welfare state, for what is fascism without great military parades and wars of conquest? If fascism still has a future, it is not in Germany or Italy or France but rather in the more advanced regions of what used to be called the third world.

There has been too much crying wolf since 1945 as far as a possible resurgence of fascism is concerned. The term has been used indiscriminately with regard to all kind of minor, transient political figures and movements that were of no consequence. And there is too little attention paid now. The fascism experts have engaged in theoretical debates about modernization, the role of the bureaucracy, about "functionalism" and "intentionalism" until in the end they quite often lost sight of the obvious features of fascism.

Western values and institutions have been attacked by the New Right as intensely as by the New Left, by patriotic environmentalists, Druids, radical feminists, Eastern and Western gurus, witches, ethnopluralists, and multiculturalists. There has been a longing for a leader to replace the present political system that seems not to work, and that has induced indifference towards public affairs among sections of the population. Only a few years have passed since the demise of communism and already there is nostalgia among many in Russia with regard to the good old days when vodka was cheap and order prevailed in the streets. In the West the positive aspects of Nazism and fascism are discovered, and eco-romanticism has turned against democracy.

The broad public associates fascism with Hitler's moustache, the image of brutal Gestapo officials in jackboots and uniform raincoats, with Mussolini's blackshirts and his unending speeches from the balcony of his Rome palace. This specific kind of "historical fascism" is gone forever, but fascism had many faces even in the 1930s and it could have even more in future, not all of them easily recognizable. It is also forgotten that fascism was never as monolithic as communism, the fine points of ideology never played such a central role.

Where fascism had its successes before World War II it was mainly due to the weaknesses of democratic societies, and this is the third theme of these essays. As we approach the end of the century and millennium, the cultural and social contradictions of capitalism have not become less acute. Since I was not affiliated with a university during the last decade I was not directly exposed to some of the higher lunacies that have found so many followers; it is easier to watch this scene with some amusement from a safe distance. But postmodernism and New Age are not the only aberrations of our time, nor perhaps the most threatening; the former will soon be forgotten and the latter, one way or another, like magic and astrology has always been with us.

The weaknesses and delusions of Western societies have not become fewer over the years. It should have been obvious that the end of the cold war would in many ways create even greater uncertainties rather than a new world order in international affairs. Instead, there has been an unmistakable trend towards isolationism, even though the label is still rejected by most of its proponents. On the domestic front, the idea that the automatism of market forces will solve our problems of health care and improve our educational system belong to the realm of fantasy, as does the belief that cultural life can exist without sponsors other than the occasional handout from the private sector. One of the essays deals with the problem of public diplomacy and cultural policy, or rather the belief, widespread in the White House and in Congress, that these are luxuries that America in its present weakened economic state cannot really afford.

How to explain such attitudes? Fierce individualism might be involved, but it is probably only a minor motive; in the final analysis it is a matter of priorities, of provincialism and naiveté. Despite the Marshall Plan, despite so many other instances of generosity, America had the reputation of being a materialist society with Mammon as its god, whereas in actual fact it has been more idealistic than almost any other country. But it is not certain that this is still true. With all the talk about the need to preserve the national heritage, America has been spending less for its cultural heritage than almost any other developed country. The cold war acted as a challenge; a major investment was made in education and technology in the 1960s since it seemed intolerable that the Russians should overtake America. Now this particular race has ended, and if American society is overtaken by others it seems not to matter, and many who should know better are not even aware of it. Dr. Johnson in a famous aside observed that nothing concentrates a man's mind as the knowledge that he is to be hanged in a fortnight. But if the hanging may be several years off, this does not help concentration, on the contrary, it befuddles the mind. This, broadly speaking, is the dilemma now facing America and also Europe; a price will have to be paid for the neglect as on past occasions, hopefully, it will not be too high.

W. L.
Washington, London
April 1996

Part I

The End of the Millennium

1

Fin de Siècle: Once More with Feeling

*"Morgen um die zwoelfte Stund Heia, geht die
Welt zugrund."*

—Felix Dahn, *Weltuntergang* (1889)

I

The phrase *fin de siècle* has meant and still means a great variety of
things. In France it signified being fashionable, modern, up to date,
recherché, sophisticated. It has also been a synonym for morbidity, decline, decadence, cultural pessimism. On occasion it has stood for symbolism, aestheticism, *l'art pour l'art*, narcissism. There was usually a
frivolous connotation—of fashionable dejection but not of total despair.
When Dorian Gray said (with a sigh), that life is a great disappointment,
replying to Lord Henry and his hostess who had invoked the fin de siècle
and *fin de globe*, the main underlying motive was, of course, boredom.
Ennui, was also the central element in the thoughts and actions of Jean
des Esseintes, the hero of Huysmans' *A rebours* (1884), the decadent
novel par excellence.[1]

The term fin de siècle first appeared in France in the 1880s. In a play
performed in Paris in 1888, Batchich, a Turkish banker, tells his interlocutors "you are decadent people, having the habitude of turning everything into a joke, incapable of that great enthusiasm which is at the bottom
of all great things.[2] If Jesus Christ, Muhammed, Charlemagne, or Napoleon were to reappear today they would last no longer than a week. Not
believing in anything anymore you will end up believing everything. Gogo
or Mercadet, this is France at the end of the 19th century."[3]

It is a fair description of what was believed to be a widespread mal-
aise, at least in the French capital. A great many pamphlets and books

7

appeared at the time with titles such as *finis Galliae*; there was genuine concern among French men and women that their country was going to the dogs. It was mainly (though not exclusively) a French phenomenon and it has been explained with reference to the lost war against Prussia, economic and demographic decline, the consumption of alcohol, the spread of atheism and of crime, the general decline of family ties, the deteriorations of morals. But by 1905–6 the mood changed even though there was no significant change as far as atheism, alcoholism, and general morality was concerned. Perhaps it was a generational problem, a young generation getting bored with the prevailing boredom.[4]

In Britain the fin de siècle mood had gone out of fashion even earlier; with the arrest of Oscar Wilde in 1896 the steam went out of the new movement. Aubrey Beardsley launched the *Yellow Book* in 1894, but within less than two years he was ousted from the editorship and in 1897 the periodical folded.

Did those who preached fin-de-siècle attitudes in art and literature truly believe that the world was coming to an end? Not really, many thought of themselves not as nihilists (whatever that meant) but as innovators, giving new impulses to a stagnant culture. There were a few purveyors of apocalyptic messages, but they were the exception. Leading German avant-garde journals were named *Die Gesellschaft* (society—rather than the individual) and *Der Sturmer* and the style of the times was called *Jugendstil*. These were not terms from the dictionary of the fin de siècle.

One of the messengers of doom was the wildly successful Polish author, Stanislaw Przybyszewski who wrote in German at the time, specifically his novel *Satanskinder*, published in 1897. This is the study of four anarchists, preparing the destruction of the world; one of them, Ostrap, is a gangster rather than a terrorist, but he joins the intellectuals anyway. Their immediate aim is the destruction of an unnamed town: all the buildings are burned down giving the anarchists an ecstatic-orgiastic feeling of happiness. To confound the confusion even more, the spiritual head of the Satanists is also killed by the terrorists. The reader is treated to endless reflections of an abstract nature about the right to kill and destroy. All this was designed to tickle nerves. There was always the impression that, having sown their wild oats, the "anarchists" would settle down to a normal bourgeois existence—as Przybyzewski did in subsequent years, writing in Polish.

Such a novel—and it was by no means the only one—lacked authenticity, it exuded cerebral terror, the desire to shock. It was about as remote from true apocalyptic fear as a Bela Lugosi horror movie from a presence in Auschwitz.

There has been an apocalyptic-eschatological tradition in Christianity (and in many other religions) since time immemorial: the idea of a final catastrophe as the result of an earthquake, a great flood, or the heavens and the skies falling down. Equally frequent is the vision of a general, all-consuming conflagration, or a great freeze or total darkness, or a final, decisive battle (Armageddon). However, there is no total extinction, a few humans survive who ultimately bring about a renewal, a better world. Christianity, with its stress on sin and fear was the religion preoccupied in greatest detail with the last judgment. As the Antichrist (whose reign was to precede the coming of Messiah) did not arrive in the year 1000, alternative predictions were made for 1184, 1186, 1229, 1345, 1385, 1516, and countless dates more recently.[5] Among Orthodox Jews, *Habad* (the Lubavich tradition) announced "without any shadow of doubt" the coming of Messiah in 1991. First it was a matter of years, later of months, later yet of weeks. It was implied that "Ramam," Menachem Mendel Shneerson, the head of the sect, was the Messiah, and when he died in 1994 without having brought redemption this created serious problems for his followers.

The idea of a cosmic disaster was not uncommon in literary circles at the turn of the last century. Richard Jefferies' *After London* is quite typical; a naturalist by vocation, Jefferies had written before about wildlife and gamekeeping. In this book he envisaged an ecological catastrophe as a result of which London was submerged in a flood of mud. The most emphatic predictions of doom were provided by the Germans and Russians, with Jakob van Hoddis short poem *Weltende* (1911) as the classic example.

> Dem Bürger fliegt vom spitzen Kopf der Hut
> in allen Lüften hallt es wie Geschrei.
> Dachdecker stürzen ab und gehn entzwei.
> Und an den Küsten—liest man—steigt die Flut.
> Der Sturm is da, die wilden Meere hüpfen
> An Land um dicke Dämme zu erdrücken
> die meisten Menschen haben einen Schnupfen
> die Eisenbahnen fallen von den Brücken.

Poems of other early expressionists such as Georg Heym ("The Demons of the Cities" and "War") and Alfred Lichtenstein ("Prophecy")
contain the most emphatic visions of cities vanishing, great fires, the
thunder of earthquakes, and a great slaughter.

II

There was one country in which pessimism and a fin-de-siècle mood
seem to have been more warranted than in any other—Russia. The Russian intelligentsia had frequently gravitated towards pessimism, the alien-
ation between it and the government was proverbial. Discontent was
widespread also among other sections of the population; among Old Believers and some of the sectarians the coming of the Antichrist was expected hourly. The last work of Vladimir Solovyev, the greatest Russian
philosopher of the nineteenth century, was a *Short Tale of the Antichrist*,
published in 1900—the year of his death. True, this was a rather gentle
affair—an attempt by an ecumenical Council in Jerusalem to smuggle
through a new Christian understanding—disregarding Jesus Christ.
Solovyev did believe towards the end of his life that the world was coming to an end and Vyacheslav Ivanov, the great theoretician of symbolism, even gave an exact date—the year 1900. Even before the turn of the
century one finds in Russia Satanism and the image of burning cities
(Konstantine Balmont); contempt for the barbarian multitude, Schopen-
hauerian pessimism, and a general feeling of melancholy (Fyodor
Sologub). The cult of religious mysticism and the second coming flour-
ished in the salon of Zinaida Gippius and her husband Dmitri
Merezhkovsky in St. Petersburg. Andrei Belyi's *Petersburg*, the latest
and most powerful fruit of this trend was a mixture of Przybyszewski
and Jefferies in its themes of political terror and catastrophism.

But the period, roughly speaking, between 1895 and 1914 was also
the Silver Age of Russian culture. Symbolism was the prevailing trend,
but was it decadent? Its theoreticians emphatically rejected the label;
Merezhkosky in an influential essay published in 1893 stated that the
new movement was a reaction against the decline that had taken place
before. Serge Diaghilev in another programmatic announcement derided
the decadence of classicism and romanticism; others blamed the "epigones
of academic art."

The Russian Silver Age covered so many groups and individuals that
one can find evidence for almost any tendency, including decadence. Valery

Bryusov and Nikolai Gumilev studied the tracts of the various schools of occultism, the young Balmont was a decadent in the French style, so was the painter Konstantin Somov. Andrei Belyi became a follower, first of theosophy and later of anthroposophy. But for most of them this was a transient stage.[6]

Nikolai Ryabushinsky, a very wealthy playboy and one of the most important supporters of the arts, inaugurated a competition in 1907 for the most striking depiction of the devil, which must have made the heart of the Satanists beat faster. But the prize was not awarded in the end. And it was precisely in the periodical financed by Ryabushinsky, *Zolotoe Runo* (Golden Fleece), that the purely aesthetic view of art was criticized.

At the beginning of the Silver Age there was Dmitri Fofanov, a poet now largely forgotten, reporting that he and his generation were cold, tired, and despondent with nothing to guide them but a row of darkening graves near the hillside. But this was written in the 1880s and Fofanov's younger colleagues were far from tired. Instead they went on expeditions to exotic places to gather new inspiration and impressions—Balmont to Mexico, New Zealand, and Samoa, Ivan Bunin to India, Belyi to Egypt, Kondratiev to Palestine, Gumilev to Ethiopia. They studied the Bhagavad Gita, the Upanishads, Zend Avest, and Lao Tse tung. In brief, they were not world-weary but enterprising, "conquistadors" in Gumilev's phrase. True, at the bottom of symbolism was a belief in the central importance of mysticism, but a surfeit of this cult, led symbolism into a crisis, a split, and eventually to its disappearance.

The Russians seldom believed in *l'art pour l'art*. They thought they had a message for Russia and the world—namely the renaissance of Russian culture and ultimately of Russian life. *Mir Iskusstva (The World of Art,* 1899–1904) was one of the most important periodicals in Russian (and European) cultural history. Edited by Diaghilev, it preached all along that the public should be educated for a cultural revival, that the past should not be negated but closely studied. There was no contempt for those who were not supermen. If Nietzsche was embraced by some, he was still criticized for his purely negative role, for not replacing the values he had destroyed by new ones. In brief, the Russian fin de siècle was different in its beliefs, aspirations, and ultimately its achievements from the French and English. It was influenced by a Russian tradition going back to Fet, Tyutchev, and beyond. These traditions were equally obvious in the case of Stravinsky, the *Ballets Russes,* and some of the contemporary painters.

Symbolism and fin de siècle was a European phenomenon but the differences in various countries were as striking as the common features. Some critics later argued that the idea of the fin de siècle had originated in Germany with Schopenhauer, Nietzsche, and Wagner who had decisively influenced French cultural life.[7] But one should not overrate the interest and the receptiveness of the French in German culture in 1880s; they had their own traditions going back to Nerval, Gautier, and Musset. The Russians were admittedly looking to Paris for recent fashions; the early issues of *Zolotoe Runo* (1905–1909) appeared in French and in Russian. However, but for the domestic traditions, to which reference has been made, there would have been no Silver Age in Russia.

In Russia pessimism had receded well before the outbreak of World War I with the arrival of a new generation of Acmeists and Futurists, brash, enterprising, anything but *früh gereift und zart und traurig* (Hofmannsthal's phrase). When Gumilev, Akhmatova's husband, went to study in Paris, the fin de siècle was a thing of the past. Among his contemporaries, the Russian futurists, like the Italians, were interested in modern life and above all, technology, a thought that had been anathema to the St. Petersburg decadents. If the typical figure of the French, and even more of the British fin de siècle had been the world of the weary dandy with the cult of the self, he was succeeded within ten years by a very different prototype. It was fascinating to see how Maurice Barrès and D'Annunzio managed to transform themselves from hyperaestheticism to a superpatriotism that came close to fascism. Within five years of the publication of a trilogy entitled *Le Culte du moi,* Barrès progressed to his new trilogy that he called *Roman de l'energie nationale.* The first volume (*Les déracinés*) referred to the French intellectuals. Even in retrospect the rapid change in mentality and outlook is amazing.

III

It is tempting to dismiss in retrospect the fin de siècle as a short-lived fad, a posture by a group of dandies. The Marxists interpreted it as yet another manifestation of the crisis of bourgeois society; moralists regarded it as immoral and corrupt; for psychologists it was a rich quarry to mine material for a variety of theories. Compared with the fear and trembling of the Middle Ages, the fashionable apocalyptic mood appeared little more than a fraudulent imitation. Christianity, more than any other major religion had been based on the belief that the world belonged to Satan (*campus diaboli*) rather than to God, that, being a valley of tears, human life was nothing but misery and pain, of short-lived joys and eternal suffering, that worldly goods were there to be discarded. As Cardinal Segni, the future pope Innocent III, wrote in his *De contemptu mundi*: Man is born for work, for sorrow, for fear and for death. Among the many temptations that of the flesh was indubitably the greatest and the most dangerous. Before the fall, mankind had been asexual and that remained the ideal—the ascetic, the monk, and the nun. But this proposition had no appeal to the London dandy and the St. Petersburg spiritualist, for them sex was a central issue. They held the bourgeois (and the multitude in general) in contempt, and the possession of material goods was by no means frowned upon.

But the anxiety and the despair was not always a pose; there is nothing fraudulent about Edvard Munch's famous painting, *The Cry,* (1893). (The Norwegian painter was a friend of Przybyszewski of whom mention has been made earlier on). Nor would it be correct, as some contemporaries did, to interpret this picture as a manifestation of nervous excitement; there is no convincing evidence that nerves were weaker in 1900 than fifty years earlier.

Max Nordau's famous *Degeneration* was first published in German in 1893, in English in 1895. It was a violent, intemperate attack against modernism by a leading critic, widely read at the time, forgotten after a decade. Nordau has not fared well, he was derided as a philistine, daring to question the work of geniuses, Beckmesser attempting to sit in judgment of his betters. But as Israel Zangwill predicted at the time of Nordau's death (1923) in an essay entitled "The Martyrdom of Max Nordau," "whenever art goes crazy and letters lose touch with life, men will remember the prophet of *Degeneration.*"[8]

There were sinister imputations: Nordau's central concept of degeneration (*Entartung*) was said to have a fatal resemblance to Nazi strictures against "*Entartete Kunst.*" Reading Nordau today another aspect obtrudes—his strictures against the haste and nervousness of modern big city life (and of modern means of transport) sound like a precursor of the Greens even though they have so far failed to pay homage to him. What Nordau wrote about Nietzsche's ignorant conceit, intellectual perversion, and insanity, has struck generations of admirers of Nietzsche not just as pedestrian but as ludicrous, the illiterate attempt of a *Kaffehausliterat* to debunk one of the greatest geniuses of all time.

Rereading Nietzsche towards the end of the twentieth century about cruelty, about the destructive urge, advising his brothers against loving their neighbors, about being the highest authority concerning decadence (and everything else), one feels more hesitant to dismiss Nordau. With time the dark side of this genius has become only too obvious. In a letter to his sister Nietzsche wrote in June 1884 that he was "terrified by the thought of the sort of people who may one day invoke my authority." Nietzsche's misgivings were only too justified. He cannot be made wholly responsible for the use made of him by misguided disciples, but can he be wholly acquitted? In politics, Nietzsche was as much a disaster as Heidegger and Sartre.

One hundred years after it first appeared *Degeneration* is once again in print, in contrast to many other fin-de-siècle writings.[9] Describing the fin-de-siècle mood, Nordau defined it as the impotent despair of a sick man, who feels himself dying by inches in the midst of an eternally living nature, blooming insolently forever; the envy of the rich, hoary, voluptary who sees a pair of young lovers making for a sequestered forest nook. Nordau summarized several newspapers stories typical, in his view, of the fin-de-siècle spirit—a king selling his sovereign rights for a check, a newly wedded pair taking their wedding trip in a balloon, a prince of the church behaving like Barnum, the circus king, a schoolboy proud of his father imprisoned for embezzlement.

The stories have a common feature—contempt for traditional customs and morality, disdain of any consideration for fellow men. And, as a corollary, confusion among the powers that be and the rise of false prophets. A physician by training, Nordau is not satisfied with the common (philistine) explanation, that fin de siècle is no more than a passing fashion, an eccentricity, or affection. He looks for deeper causes and finds them in degeneration and hysteria (or neurasthenia). He describes in considerable detail moral insanity (a term coined by Maudsley) emotionalism, pessimism and despondency, *ennui* and the general abhorrence of activity. The degenerate is tormented by doubts and inclined towards mysticism; he lacks balance and harmony; he is exceedingly impressionable. The constitution of his (or her) brain and nervous system is affected by a number of negative trends—poisoning by the rising consumption of alcohol, tobacco, drugs, and tainted foods and, above all, residence in large cities, unhealthy in almost every respect.

As a result of steam and electricity the pulse of life has quickened as never before in history. In consequence, these new activities, even the simplest, involve a strain on the nervous system and a wearing of tissue, fatigue and exhaustion. According to Nordau the statistics show that crime, madness, and suicide have increased; people age more rapidly than before. The stress and high pressure make people need glasses at an earlier age than their ancestors; the same is true with regard to tooth decay and premature baldness. There follow some reflections about the connection between the constant vibration undergone in railway travelling and the twilight mood engulfing modern society.

Two main sections are entitled "Mysticism" and "Egomania." Nordau is an admirer of the Enlightenment and the classics; he has little use for the romantics who for all their talents were regressive, except perhaps the French romantics who gravitated towards the Renaissance rather than the dark Middle Ages. He makes short shrift of the Pre-Raphaelites; Ruskin was the "Torquemada of aesthetics," a turgid, fallacious, wildly eccentric mind. Nordau discusses Verlaine at length, and his impressions are not favorable: a repulsive degenerate with an asymmetric skull and Mongolian face; an impulsive vagabond and dipsomaniac who was jailed under the most disgraceful circumstance; an emotional dreamer of feeble intellect who painfully fights against his bad impulses; a mystic whose qualmish consciousness is flooded with ideas of God and saints; and a dotard who manifests the absence of any definite thought by incoherent speech.[10]

Next a chapter on Tolstoyism. Nordau does not deny that Tolstoy is a great writer, even though he regrets his long-windedness. However, he is mainly preoccupied with Tolstoy as a theologian and philosopher and notes in this context that Tolstoy wrote (in his *Confession*), "I felt that I was not mentally quite sound."[11] What would Nordau have made of Dostoevsky who does not appear in his book? Dostoevsky embodied everything Nordau abhorred. He had been translated into German since 1863, but European fame came to him only at the turn of the century.

Nordau's chief *bêtes noires* are Nietzsche and Wagner on the one hand, and Ibsen and Zola on the other. Nietzsche was an insane megalomaniac, the fact that he should be regarded as a philosopher and founded a school is a "disgrace for Germany." Wagner's high musical talent is not disputed, Nordau likes the "Venusberg" music and the "Weia! Waga!" of the Rheinmaidens but regrets that it is repeated 136 times. But all this is compatible with an advanced state of degeneration; not for nothing did

Wagner become a fin-de-siècle idol. Nordau dislikes his graphomania as much as his eroticism, his chauvinism and hysterical anti-Semitism.

True decadents such as Baudelaire and Huysmans get less attention than Ibsen and Zola, perhaps because their roots go back to an earlier age. Nordau pays tribute to Ibsen's poetical talent, but he is bothered by Ibsen's philosophy; his excursion into medicine (and heredity); his views on marriage and religion; his obsession with original sin; and his vague anarchism, the right of the individual to live in accordance with his own law. As for Zola, "the fact that he is a sexual psychopath is betrayed on every page of his novels." His works are not based on observation, nor are they human documents nor experimental novels, nor a reproduction of the milieu. Zola is a decadent because of his pervasive pessimism, because he sees every phenomenon monstrously magnified and weirdly distorted.[12]

Nordau's faith in scientific certainties was partly misplaced, his literary judgments were one-sided and often crude, some of the trends he criticizes were by no means identical with the fin de siècle; few, but the experts, remember Tolstoyanism now. What became of Nordau's other targets? Nietzsche, despising the vulgar masses, has made a triumphal comeback as a cultural hero of the left, as an atheist, the great destroyer of all bourgeois values. He has even become a liberator for the radical feminists for debunking the masculine principle of reason and the hierarchies of power (patriarchy). Zarathustra's whip has been hidden in a feminist closet.

Zola and Ibsen have become classics, but there is a cure for syphilis which makes *Ghosts* redundant. The film version of *Germinal* (despite Gérard Depardieu) seems far more outdated than *Cyrano de Bergerac* (also with Depardieu). There is no anthology of French poetry without Baudelaire, Rimbaud, and Verlaine.

A look at medical statistics shows that tooth decay has dramatically declined, so has, of late, the incidence of coronary disease, at least in developed countries; fewer people are now detained in mental institutions. The consumption of nicotine and hard liquor has gone down and the theory of the physiological roots of degeneracy seems no longer tenable. Whether these statistics are a true yardstick for the health of society is another question.

The cultural revolution that took place after the turn of the century was in many ways more radical than Nordau had feared—in music and the plastic arts it was even more pronounced than in literature. The world became ever more fragmented. The wholesome harmony of past ages could not be restored.

IV

Hans Delbrück, a leading German historian, published a long, learned essay that also appeared in the year of *Degeneration*.[13]

> We certainly live in a time of evil: Discontent, decline, disintegration everywhere. Even thirty years ago people would have been ashamed to confess to open atheism, today it is done with great emphasis. This is the road to the abyss, by way of liberalism, Jewry, Mammonism, socialism, pessimism, anarchism and nihilism. Virtue and morals are outmoded, art has acquired a monopoly of being mean, schools convey knowledge but not character, the sanctity of marriage is not what it used to be, justice opens the criminal the door for escape. Brutish Semitic features are believed to represent the face of our age.

Delbrück then goes back in history, generation by generation, and finds complaints about moral deterioration in all ages. In 1869, Wolfgang Menzel had written in apocalyptic terms about the *Zeitgeist*, and the organ of the Protestant church had stated that "mad sans-cullotism" was celebrating an impertinent carnival. Mammonism, eroticism, general demoralization had been denounced in near despair in 1847; the alarming rise in the crime rate and alcohol consumption had been observed with great concern in 1836. In 1827, the educated classes were attacked for their general negativism. Fichte had written in 1807 that the contemporary era was one of complete sinfulness, and his colleague Niethammer had regretted the perishing of idealism and spiritual value. The British ambassador at the court of Frederick II had reported in the 1770s that one could not find in Berlin a single *vir fortis nec femina casta*, neither a honorable man nor a virtuous woman.

Delbrück traces further back the search for paradise lost, and he encounters at all times the same warnings about the loss of faith, moral deterioration, about drinking and whoring; about discontent, anarchy, confusion, and exploitation; about general putrefaction—back to the early Middle Ages and beyond, Byzantium, the Roman Empire. Even Nestor, Homer's aged hero had complained that in his day young people had been better. Beyond this point documentation is no longer available.

Like most critics and moralists before and after, Nordau had idealized the past; the heritage of the classics that he admired had been taken over by a generation of epigones. Nordau was uncomfortable in an age of innovation when a break was occurring with the values and concepts of beauty and morals that had shaped European culture since the Renaissance. This led to a crisis with all the well-known consequences such as the growing distance between the artistic avant-garde that manoeuvered itself into isolation from the public at large. It led, of necessity, to problems that remain unsolved to this day.

Benedetto Croce, a little younger than Nordau and a more astute observer, noted that fin de siècle was more than a literary and artistic fashion. Something fundamental had changed during these years—the decline of religion. Neither Croce nor Nordau were religious believers, but Croce could not fail to notice that secular humanism only incompletely filled the void. In any case it, as much as religion, was under attack by the likes of Nietzsche. Hence the "irrationalism and debauchery" of a whole age.[14]

How important was all this? In the very beginning of his book Nordau had observed that only a small minority found pleasure in the "new tendencies,"

> but this minority has the gift of covering the whole visible surface of society, as a little oil extends over a large area of the surface of the sea. It consists chiefly of rich, educated people, or of fanatics. The former give the *ton* to all the snobs, the fools and the blockheads; the latter make an impression upon the weak and dependent, and intimidate the nervous.[15]

It was a shrewd observation. The representative literary figures in England in 1890s were Thomas Hardy and Henry James, Joseph Conrad, Rudyard Kipling and Arnold Bennett, Bernard Shaw and H.G. Wells, not the contributors to the *Yellow Book*. And the bestsellers were written by A. Conan Doyle and A.E.W. Mason. As for the long-term consequences of the break in tradition, they concern, of course, far wider issue than the fin de siècle.

V

If pessimism was one of the chief hallmarks of the age, how pessimistic were the educated classes and the general public? There were no opinion polls at the time and there have always been optimists and pessimists, but there are enough indications to convey a general impression. As the old century ended, many balance sheets appeared relating to the past century and the hopes and expectations of the contemporaries for the next. The 1890s had not been a good decade. The panic of 1893 and the ensuing depression was still vividly remembered in the United States; many businesses had failed, employment had been shrinking, and in the ensuing turmoil the Democratic party had split. In Britain too, the growth rate declined; British industry was steadily falling behind its competitors; exports decreased and agriculture suffered from food imports. Germany faced an economic crisis in the 1890s; the French were confronted with major corruption scandals and, of course, the Dreyfus affair. The Russian famine of 1892–93 in which thousands perished and many more starved, became a major European scandal. It was followed by a famine on a smaller scale in 1898. The growing political ferment that led to the revolution of 1905 was casting an enormous shadow.

And yet, rereading the editorials at the end of the century and the beginning of the new, one is struck by the optimistic note struck everywhere. Mankind had never had it so good and progress was bound to continue.[16] "Twentieth Century; Triumphant Entry" read the page-one headline of the *New York Times* (price one cent). The subtitle was "Welcomed by New York with Tumultuous Rejoicing. City Hall Gorgeously Decked. Brilliant Illuminations and a Pandemonium of Music, Song and Noise—Wedding at Midnight—Great Crush Almost causes Panic."

Lights flashed, crowds were singing, the sirens of the ships in the harbor screeched. There were two thousand flags on City Hall and two thousand bulbs in red, white, and blue emblazoning a giant "Welcome 20th Century." Sousa's band was playing; Randolph Guggenheimer, president of the New York City Council was seen to move his lips but no one could hear him, such was the noise of the giant crowd. (He wanted to say—the newspapers reported—that the advance of New York had been such that it would become soon a city without par in the world.) There were fireworks such as never seen before and enormous choirs were singing "Sea, Mountain and Prairie," "Ring Out, Wild Bells" as well as *"Der Tag des Herrn"* and *"Aus der Heimat."* In a fifteen-part editorial in the *New York Times*, the nineteenth century was called a glorious century of marvels, the flower of all centuries. Liberal institutions had advanced everywhere, scientific progress had been enormous, and there had been just recently an unprecedented revolution in medicine with the new method of anesthetics. Countless great inventions had been made, most recently by Mr. Edison.[17]

The theme was taken up by a writer at the *Washington Post*. What was there left to discover? Seven hundred thousand inventions had been patented in the U.S. during the century. The writer noted that in the field of electricity the possibilities of the future were beyond human comprehension:

> In every department of scientific and intellectual activity we have gone far beyond the wildest dreams of the workers and the thinkers of 1800. In everything that contributed to human comfort happiness and luxury and convenience we have progressed to an extent that would not have been imaginable a century ago. Scientific invention has obliterated time and space.[18]

Even in more restrained London the consensus was that humanity was firmly convinced that the nineteenth century was unprecedented, that no one had done anything to speak of before it, that there was something exhilarating in the thought of a new century. The idea that the future was open was a tremendous moral stimulus[19] and all that despite ruinous floods and abnormal snowfall in the last week of December that stopped trains in Britain, carried off buildings and bridges, and isolated villages.

In all the major capitals there was quiet (or loud) satisfaction about the nation's position in the world. The American press noted that the U.S. had become a great power, England's achievements were said to "stand apart from the efforts of other nations, surpassing them in unity of purpose and the scale of magnitude." Happiness about the tremendous progress achieved since 1800 was particularly striking in Berlin, not only among the conservatives but equally among liberals. "We have truly gone far," said the editorialist of the *Berliner Tageblatt*.[20] One hundred years ago Prussia had been a small agrarian state. Now Germany was the biggest commercial and industrial power but for England, the army was the most disciplined in the world, its merchant fleet the very biggest. (In fact, German industrial production had overtaken the British in 1895.) The Emperor had just announced that the building of a much bigger war fleet was his most urgent assignment. But there was a danger of self satisfaction, and there were reactionary forces, especially the *Junkers*, who preferred the "good old days" to the present. A people that did not want to rule was bound to be the slave of another. Hence the need to conduct *Weltpolitik*, a global policy: "As long as there are devils among human beings and robbers among nations, we ought to increase our power wherever we can do so."[21] Not to go forward would be tantamount to retreat, and this at a time when the changes of the last century had opened for Germany wonderful new opportunities and challenges.

And so it was everywhere, great contentment with past achievements, great expectations for the future. As the *Petit Parisien* put it mankind could legitimately greet the coming century with cries of gladness.[22]

Le Petit Journal said it is sweet to think that during the past century France remained at the head of civilization, the French genius, worthy of the French revolution had expressed itself magnificently in the arts and sciences. It had earned the gratitude of all mankind as the century drew to its close. French soldiers too, despite some setbacks, had upheld the Napoleonic tradition of Marengo.

Le Journal de Debats reminded its readers that on January 1, 1801 it had reported that French generals, having prevailed over their external enemies, had danced in the streets of Poitiers. The hit of the season of 1801 was a parody of Haydn's *Creation*, performed by the Opera Comique. *Le Temps* interviewed Prince Roland Bonaparte who said that politically France had only one enemy Britain. (*Le Petit Journal* agreed.) *Figaro* thought that the most remarkable aspect was scientific progress and that important advances had been made towards the promotion of world peace even if some belittled it. Anatole France published an essay on how to celebrate gaily the new century. There were banquets given by the president of the Republic and the *maire* of Paris, there were processions, illuminations and a mass at Sacré Coeur.[23]

This mood was by no means limited to the ruling classes; the left was equally confident that its progress would continue, though against considerable resistance on the part of reactionary elements. Everywhere the forces of progress were growing stronger and it was only a question of time until the working classes would take over and establish a new society based on freedom and justice.

A document typical of such optimism was Edward Bellamy's *Looking Backward*, first published in 1888. This is the story of Julian West, a young native of Boston who after an uncommonly long sleep wakes up in the wonderful world of the twenty-first century, in a society in which credit cards have replaced money, and all social problems been solved. The book was read by everyone, was translated into twenty languages (an astonishing figure at the time), and sold millions of copies.[24]

There were, as always a few dissenting voices. Archdeacon Farrar preaching in Westminster Abbey[25] reviewed the situation with sorrow and gazed into the future with a gloomy prescience. The last hundred years (he said) had brought no change in the passions, the cruelties, and the barbarous impulses of mankind. *The Washington Post* commented in a similar vein: "Rapine, cruelty, greed, and persecution animate the nations of today just as they did the nations of the Middle Ages—there was no difference in the matter of inhumanity, no change from savagery. We enter upon a new century equipped with every wonderful device of science and of art. But our primeval appetites and passions are untouched."

However, the Archbishop of Canterbury, the superior of the Dean took a more moderate line. In his New Year sermon he said that he was far more impressed by the promise and potency of the active conscious effort to change present conditions for the better than by any prospect of an unconscious degradation into evil, or of an outbreak of purely destructive nihilism.

A great many people, famous and less famous, were quoted by the media on the eve of the new century. One of the most interesting contributions came from an elderly writer, living in virtual seclusion in Putney, a London suburb. A poem entitled "1901" began

> An age too great for thought of ours to scan
> a wave upon the sleepless sea of time and it ended
> We cry across the veering gale
> Farewell—and midnight answers us, Farewell.
> Hail—and the heaven of morning answer Hail.[26]

It was signed Algernon Charles Swinburne, widely thought to be the grandfather of the English decadents, admirer of Baudelaire, friend of the Pre-Raphaelites. Whatever his earlier views, Swinburne must have felt that his share among the congratulations should not have been missing.

VI

Paris before the turn of the century was not only Verlaine exclaiming *Je suis l'Empire à la fin décadence*—he loved the word which, he wrote, was *un coup de genie*.[27] It was also *La Belle Epoque* with Yvette Guilbert singing *"Le Fiacre"* and *"La soularde"* and dozens of other performers whose chansons survived almost as well as Verlaine's poetry. During the very years (1886–1889) that the periodical *Le Décadent* was published, the Eiffel Tower was constructed in record time, by a small crew on a tiny budget. Very few people read *Le Décadent,* but every Parisian saw the Eiffel Tower every day, a symbol of French industry and technical know-how. This was the France of the jubilee exhibition of 1889 and the world exhibition of 1900, of Madame Curie working in her laboratory on radium, of the brothers Lumière showing the first of their films in December 1895, in a cellar on the Boulevard des Capucines. The first permanent movie theater opened in Paris in 1897 and the first showing (by Georges Meliés) of a film of the Dreyfus affair (1899) and *Jeanne d'Arc* (1900) which lasted all of fifteen minutes. It was the time when Baron le Coubertin conceived the idea of reviving the Olympic Games and people were dancing in the streets on July 14. Daring spirits were experimenting with aircraft and only three more years were to pass until Blériot would fly over the Channel. In brief, it was not really a "triste epoque" as Barrès called it, but a period of considerable achievement and great optimism.

Romanticism did not always lead to despair but to extolling *elan vital,* idealism, and the enjoyment of life as the German *Wandervogel* was showing. Founded in Berlin in 1897 it rapidly spread over the German speaking countries—young people in groups hiking and singing at their campfires. There was, in fact, a tremendous appetite for enjoyment all over Europe— not the hectic desire to make up for lost time following a great disaster but a seemingly natural appetite based on the realization that life was getting better not just for a happy few but for people in general.

The history of popular song and of the operetta and its tremendous popularity is as good a yardstick as any. The eighties had been the golden age of the Vienna operetta which conquered Europe. Both Johann Strauss and Karl Millöcker died in the last year of the old century, but their junior rivals were still going strong—Richard Heuberger's *Opernball* (with the famous song about the *chambre separée*) and Ziehrer's *Landstreicher* (1899) with its immortal *"Sei gepriesen du lauschige Nacht"* survive to this very day.

The second golden age was already dawning with Franz Lehar and Oscar Straus in the front rank. Mistinguette was singing at the Paris *Eldorado*; 1898 was the year of *Lily of Laguna*, in the music halls of Mile End they were singing "The Man Who Broke the Bank of Monte Carlo" and "Goodbye Dolly Gray" (1900). The Germans went mad in the year 1900 over *"Susanna, wie ist das Leben doch so schön,"* not a pessimistic song as the title indicates. The great craze in Berlin was Paul

Lincke (1866–1946) with *Frau Luna* (1899) extolling space travel. It was shown six hundred times in a row at the Apollo theater; considerably more people went to see it than read Przybyszewski's *Satanists*. Melies' film of 1902 was also concerned with space travel: *La voyage dans la lune*. Paul Lincke, needless to say, was not in the class of a Beethoven or Brahms or a Richard Strauss. He had trained at the Folies Bergére. But a hundred years after the event not many in Germany can remember a single motive from *Elektra* and perhaps only one from *Salome*, the great heroine of the fin de siècle. But Paul Lincke's hit songs are played to this day by the Berlin Philharmonic Orchestra under Daniel Barenboim; they have become the unofficial anthems of Berlin. They are not high art, but they reflected the mood of a basically optimistic, forward-looking age (Lincke's *Lass den Kopf nicht hängen*) and they kept their appeal through all the disasters that followed.

VII

Fin de siècle, decadence, and symbolism have been used in the foregoing without sufficient distinction. There were important differences between these phenomena quite apart from the fact that the terms had a different meaning in different places during different periods. The main emphasis here is on pessimism; at a distance it seems that there was not remotely as much despair as some contemporaries believed. There was nostalgia for the past and a feeling that the modern world debases everything—men, women, children, love, the cities, the nations, the race—even death (Charles Péguy). But there was also Victor Hugo having written earlier *"Le dix neuvième siècle est grand, le vingtième sera heureux!"* The great majority of Europeans agreed with Hugo despite the strains and stresses of modern city life, despite loneliness and insecurity, despite social unrest and economic setbacks.

If there was less religion in 1900 than in 1800 this process had got under way much earlier, and, in any case, Christian religion, even in its modern version, was not that cheerful and optimistic, whereas material progress during the age was startling and helped to imbue among many a feeling of satisfaction. Simply put, most people were better off than they had been a generation before.

Theologians and avant-garde artists would disagree, but they usually took a contrary position. It was also the age of increasing nationalism and imperialism, and the anti-Semites were ruling Vienna. The political extremes became more extreme. This is even more true for the right, part of which moved beyond conservatism towards an ideology that paved the ways for fascism and Nazism. The left on the whole became more moderate. While its official doctrine and phraseology was still revolutionary, it had in fact, embraced evolution and reformism. Violent anarchism had been a short interlude in the 1890s, and the truly revolutionary left was small, with its stronghold in underdeveloped countries such as Russia.

There were plenty of warning signs, referring to a collision with Halley's comet and also voices prophesying war. In retrospect we tend to single them our for their perspicacity—because of World War I and its consequences. But there were more indications that peace and progress and the spread of civilization and of wealth would continue.

Those advocating violence would not have had their chance but for the First World War. But for the war, the prophets of doom would have been false prophets.

VIII
Fin de Siècle, 2000

One hundred years ago the fin-de-siècle mood expressed itself mainly in books, plays, and paintings. In the 1990s the action is not among writers and artists but among teachers of English literature, linguists, and also among members of quasi-religious movements and millenary sectarians. Despite dire predictions there is little fear of an impending cosmic disaster; even ardent environmentalists are more concerned with long-term rather than immediate threats. But "objectively" (to use a discarded Leninist term), the dangers are far greater than a century ago; weapons of mass destruction are available that did not exist then.[28]

In the academic field fin de siècle manifests itself in the shape of postmodernism and poststructuralism which includes deconstruction, postcolonial studies, American studies, the new historicism, cultural studies, and gender studies. This movement has generated great enthusiasm among its members and ridicule among its opponents; it is certainly of fascination for the outside observer. The term postmodernism has been used with regard to trends in painting since the 1880s, among architects since the 1940s—in a polemic against the Bauhaus.[29] According to Arnold

Toynbee, writing in 1938, the postmodern phase in European culture began about 1875, and the German writer Rudolf Pannwitz referred to it in 1915 as the "great decadence of the radical revolution of European nihilism," a remarkable definition considering the date.[29] In the 1960s American literary critics such as Irving Howe and Leslie Fiedler used it but it acquired its present connotation only in the late 1970s, probably following the publication of Jean Francois Lyotard's *La condition postmoderne* in 1979. The other French thinkers thought to be the founders of the movement did not refer to themselves as post-modernist. However, even before Lyotard's book appeared the *New Yorker* announced (in 1975) that postmodernism was out.[30]

The task of the onlooker is not made easier by a lack of precision. It is by no means clear what the inherent differences are between postmodernism (or structuralism) and its predecessors, except that chronologically they came after. Seen in this light, postmodernism is an extreme, subjective species of modernism. As far as substance is concerned the differences are often not visible to the naked eye. Postcolonial theory, to give but one example, has little to do with events in the periods since the great and small empires dissolved. Instead, it means the belief that imperialism had, and continues to have (America!), a negative impact on the colonial world. Thirty years ago the term "anticolonial" or "third world studies" might have been apposite. But with the disintegration of the third world, mainly as a result of the economic success of the countries of the Far East and the failure of others, the term African studies would be more correct. However, North Africa does not want to belong to this entity nor does South Africa, and on the other hand some academics in Canada and Australia wish to be included.

A leading theoretician of postcolonial (and postmodern and gender studies), Dr. Gayatari Spivak, a professor of English literature of Indian origin, calls herself a "third world person." But few in India (or China or the Far East) follow her example. It has been the misfortune of the postcolonials to appear on the intellectual scene when even those in full sympathy with third worldism had admitted defeat. In the 1960s and 1970s Gunder Frank, Samir Amin, and Immanuel Wallerstein had developed their theories about "dependence," "unequal exchange," and a "new socialist world system." In the 1990s it was accepted that the third world had disintegrated, and that the attempts to build state socialism had failed. In retrospect it seemed that the very attempt might have been an optical illusion—it had never been tried.[31]

The activities of gender and postimperialism studies were preoccupied with their own cause to such an extent that they had no wish to cooperate with others. They believed that gender (or racial) oppression was the most important thing in the world; hence their lack of enthusiasm for issues of class, or the philosophies of the postmodernists. They strive for the solidarity of women—sisterhood—or of colored people but not for solidarity of human beings. As a result, a recent widely discussed post-Marxist author has reached pessimistic conclusions about the feasibility of an international rainbow coalition because of the stress on divisions of gender and race.[32]

A recent survey of the postmodern tradition lists fifty key contemporary thinkers.[33] Disregarding Freud, Nietzsche, and other dead white males, one is left with the living who, with a few exceptions are French, or live in France. Their impact in France (and in continental Europe) has been less than in English-speaking countries.[34] But these French gurus of postmodernism are of little concern to postcolonialists. A few Westernized Africans or Asians may embrace Althusser but these are rare exceptions.

The migration of ideas from France to England and America is an intriguing phenomenon. In earlier ages the English-speaking world imported its philosophy from Germany and Austria, but this became unfashionable in the 1930s. In any case, these countries had less to offer of late, except perhaps Heidegger—and Habermas, who was however, too much of a rationalist for the postmodernists.

Postmodernism is mainly preoccupied with (literary) criticism and theory, with semiotics and narrative, with metacriticism, narratology, and theories of the grotesque. All this would be less noteworthy if those involved would confine themselves to their field of study—English literature (or as they prefer—texts). But their ambitions go well beyond it, their aim is to provide the key to a transformation of society. Following Derrida they believe in the identity of politics and linguistic analysis— language and literature determine the nature of society. Thus, one finds in a *Cultural Studies Reader* essays about shopping centers and advertising; a case could no doubt be made that these subjects should not be wholly left to economists and sociologists. Many postmodernists believe that philosophy and sociology are dead, or nearly dead, and that they have the right, nay the duty, to deal with subjects outside their profession! This expansionism tends to take strange forms. *The Post-Colonial Studies Reader* in a twenty-page bibliography, lists countless articles from *Social Text, Critical Inquiry, Cultural Critique, Modern Fiction, Boundary, Ariel, Discourse, Transition, New Foundation, Novel, Feminist Review,* and other journals concerned with the theory of literatures but not a single one from a periodical specializing in African or Asian politics, economic, or social conditions. A *Feminist Reader* deals not with political, social or economic issues but with subjects such as sexual linguistics; among the authorities most often quoted are Helene Cixous, Julia Kristeva, Luce Irigaray—French students of linguistics, semiotics, psychoanalysis, novelists and literary critics. One would expect to find in a postcolonial studies reader at least passing references to issues such as tribalism, nation building, poverty, starvation, AIDS, genocide, that is to say contemporary Africa's real problems. Instead the emphasis is on subjects such as "Contamination as a Literary Strategy," "Toward a Theory for Post-Colonial Women's Texts," "Jameson's Rhetoric of Otherness and the 'National Allegory.'"[35]

Once one reaches the New Historicism the situation gets truly confused because those represented maintain almost without exception that they really have nothing in common with each other; the best-known figure in the field (Stephen Greenblatt, a Renaissance scholar) argues that the New Historicism had no doctrine at all. True, an attempt was made to find a common denominator of sorts ("subject-positioning," "power-knowledge," "internal dialogism," and "thick description"). The first of these common features is derived from literary theory, the second from Foucault, the third from Bakhtin, the fourth from anthropology, none, it would appear, from the study of history. New historicism is heavily preoccupied with such works as George Eliot's *Daniel Deronda* and *Adam Bede,* Thackeray's *Henry Esmond*, Henry James' *The Bostonians*—all important works of literature but only part of the evidence most historians normally use in their work.[36]

Outside observers might be struck by this positive, idealistic belief in the all-curative propensities of literature. But this, alas, is not the case, the relationship of many postmodernist practitioners to their texts, is more like that of a pathologist to his corpse. Their attitude to great literature is egalitarian, not elitist, for the reader is as important (if not more so) than the author, and for some of them the difference in importance between *Hamlet* and *Dallas* is not always obvious. In fact, at least some students of gender and postcolonialism display a positive dislike of literature, which they regard as a tool of exploitation, oppression, and discrimination. It is not so much love of great literature that inspires them but the conviction that deconstruction may provide the key to the most important questions of the age, of society, politics, the economy, and how to change them, a feeling that mankind may be on the eve of a breakthrough comparable to Newton and Einstein, Marx or Freud. And, as unkind critics would put it, they tend to forget that their endeavor, like their own field, is essentially parasitic, in the sense that art and literature can exist without interpretation, just as history and science can manage without a philosophy of history and science but not vice versa. To paraphrase an old French textbook—No text, no deconstruction.

Where does the main support of postmodernism come from, how far has it spread and why has it provoked such vociferous protest? Its main support came from students of English language and literature, it has fellow travellers in geography, philosophy, anthropology and architecture, where however, postmodernism has, by necessity, a different meaning, namely a mixture of styles. Among the main body of psychologists, historians and social scientists it is largely unknown or considered irrelevant.

Attempts have been made in some quarters to develop new milestones on the road to a postmodern sociology and political science. Postmodernists claim with some justice that these professions are in a state of crisis, theory having reached a dead end, being of interest only to fellow theoreticians. What do the postmodernists propose to revitalize the field? "Social narrative with a moral intent" which means the politicization of the field; but this is not exactly a revolutionary idea.

The main strength of postmodernism is in America, with considerable backing in Britain and some pockets in Scandinavia and the Netherlands. Outside the West it is virtually unknown. In France, whence most of the original inspiration came from the intellectual debate takes place not in *Tel Quel* but in journals such as *Commentaire, Esprit, Debat, La pensée politique, Philosophie Politique* that have little interest in postmodernism and do not even polemicize against it. To some extent it is a provincial phenomenon even though Yale was its main cradle in America. Just as the postcolonialists endeavor to "provincialize" Europe, British provincial lecturers—where most of the postmodernist action is seem to want to downgrade Cambridge, Oxford, and London which have shown somewhat less enthusiasm. There seem to be more women than men in this movement. This may have to do with the prominent part played by feminist activists in the academic world, it could also reflect the increasing number of women in subjects such as English literature. However, there could be deeper reasons: In the New Age movement (the other major manifestation of fin de siècle on which more below) there has likewise been a strong representation of women both as gurus and followers. Among the advocates and practitioners of postmodernism there are excellent specialists on traditional English literary subjects as Milton and Richardson, but few are at home in more than one period let alone one culture. Some seem to imply that this may not be necessary, since, as they see it, the borders between disciplines have become blurred.

These students of English literature like to refer to "late capitalism," but they are not experts in economic history let alone physics, advanced mathematics, and molecular biology. Yet some of them have been writing on these topics confidently, distributing praise and blame and demanding revolutionary changes in these sciences. The earlier fin de siècle also suggested a break with past traditions, but it had no scientific ambitions, and it was cosmopolitan rather than provincial in outlook.

Sometimes the impression is created that postmodernism is more a language than a theory. Everyone who knows the difference between difference (Saussure) and *différance* (Derrida), between phallocentrism and phallogocentrism, who is familiar with Foucault's "space" and "power," who has heard about discourse displacement and interpellation, about binary opposition and margin, about intertextuality (Barthes), champ (Bourdieu), ideologeme, hegemony, and essentialism, about classeme and misprision can, in principle, participate in the new critical theory debate. The feminists have made their own contribution with gynesis, selfsame, symbolic contract, relational interaction, mothering, and much more. The postcolonialists have given us "subaltern," "Western mathematics," "hybridity," and other terms with their specific meaning. Fortunately, some of the postmovement texts carry glossaries and there have been several encyclopedias covering the terms of contemporary literary theory.[37]

Since the middle 1980s postmodernism has been in slow decline, its adherents have been unable to agree on many things. To the extent that the movement has had an effect outside the university it has been the reverse of what was intended; it contributed to the conservative backlash in America. Radical policies with regard to crime led to a new upsurge of law and order slogans, feminist attacks on the traditional family helped to bring about the reassertion of traditional family values. Allocations for the arts and humanities and for headstart operations were cut. The balance sheet is not encouraging.

Has the reaction against the "postmovements" been excessive? The defenders of liberal education were concerned about the onslaught of obscurantism at a time when intellectual standards were declining anyway. They were worried about the apparently successful efforts to propagate cultural and moral relativism. They were shocked by the cult of irrationalism and the attacks against science, the idea that there are no truths, only perspectives.[38]

Whereas in the past the left (including Marxists) was the party of almost blind belief in science and its progress, their successors have turned against it, partly because it is Western in origin, partly because of its elitist character, its not being accessible to everyone. If it were true that there are certain objective laws in science this would make it exceedingly difficult to press successfully the claim for African mathematics or feminist astronomy.

The critics in turn have been criticized for singling out certain particularly nonsensical statements made by radical feminist or postcolonialist spokesmen. Was it really justified to see the barbarians at the gate, about to destroy all that has been achieved for centuries in Western culture? The critics would argue that the outcry against nihilism and destruction towards the end of the nineteenth century concerned individual works of art and philosophy, intellectual fashions which after a few years passed. The nihilism of the late twentieth century, on the other hand, is bound to have a longer life span because it has made inroads in higher education, become institutionalized, changed the curricula, and affected the whole intellectual climate in certain fields. Those who subscribe to it have tenure, will remain in their positions for many years, will appoint likeminded spirits, and are also immune to change.

All this could be true, but there still is the tendency to overrate the impact of the postmovements and to underrate the rapidity with which they are likely to vanish or transform themselves. The perspective from inside the university is a limited one; few outside the campuses ever heard of the Modern Language Association. Negative features have taken root only in some fields in some universities in a very few countries. If America has been more strongly affected, the rest of the world has been much less so, or not at all. A dialectical process is at work; movements of this kind expand up to a certain point when they come to a halt and then recede.

Absurdities do not last; if it should appear, that the attack against science has a direct effect on educational standards and on the economy, the backlash is bound to be quick and severe. If the field of literary studies is hardly affected by the backlash, this merely reflects the feeling, right or wrong, that whatever happens in a field like this is of no interest to other disciplines and of no consequence to society at large.

The postmovements are to some extent a product of generational revolt, and the attempt to make the insights of one generation the new orthodoxy is bound to fail: indoctrination always generates opposition and at best indifference as compulsory teaching of religion (and atheism) has shown. In the contemporary world it fails even quicker than in the past.

The revolutionary movements of the nineteenth and early twentieth centuries offered or were believed to offer, political, social and economic alternatives to the established order. The postmovements have no such alternatives, nor do they seem to be interested in them. There is the feeling that one should do away with the market and frequent references to "late capitalism" but no ideas about what could or should succeed it. Some have characterized it as a movement of the left, attempts to refurbish what is left of Marxist ideology. But Nietzsche and Heidegger are not signposts pointing the way towards a left-wing revival. The philosophy of Lyotard or a Baudrillard, to name but two recent influential thinkers, is pessimistic in outlook which has annoyed their radical followers. There will be no new flowering on the scholastic cemetery left by Althusser.

Where does it all lead to? The attack against reason, "intellectualism," and humanism in general, is reminiscent of the precursors of fascism; the moral relativism preached was typical for the totalitarian movements of the first half of the century. Among feminists it has been customary to embrace the thinkers (Bachofen's *Mutterrecht*) who influenced National Socialist philosophy. The radical feminists dislike Judaism because the Hebrew Bible helped to destroy the earlier matriarchal order and replace it with a patriarchal system. According to their anthropological image, females—in contrast to men—are beautiful, good, and harmonious whereas males are alienated from the deepest sources of nature. The "essential male" element then turns into the "essentially Jewish"—rationalist, intellectualist, and pioneer of capitalism. This in turn leads to the Goddess cult, neo-paganism, modern witchcraft. There is even a belief that German women were victims of Nazism rather than collaborators, that Hitlerism and fascism do not really concern them.[39] The retreat from reason is unmistakable but there is a long way from these ideological constructions to true fanaticism such as inspired the Nazis and the early Bolsheviks.

The postcolonialists despise European culture; at the same time they wish to prove that blacks (by way of Egypt) created it. They have no particular wish even to visit Africa. They attack the English language as an instrument of oppression, but continue to use it rather than returning to tribal languages. They ignore antiblack feeling where it is strongest, such as in the Far East, and concentrate instead on the most liberal societies. All this points to a lack of seriousness, an *épater le bourgeois* mentality reminiscent of the fin de siècle of 1900.

The ideological confusion of the 1990s (the "nutty nineties," in English colloquial language) is a halfway house unsuitable for a prolonged stay. What will be the next station on this pilgrimage? Should the present ferment end, there will still be the remnants of a radical feminist left and the "anticolonialists" will still press their complaints, justified or not. Where will they turn? There is an unlimited number of possibilities, including a return to reason. But there is also the possibility of new creeds appearing. It is to the world of esoteric cults and the practices of New Age that we shall turn next.

IX   *Occultism*

Throughout the annals of mankind, religious cults, sects and prophets have prospered in times of material and spiritual crisis. Necromants, haruspices, magicians, inspired oracles purveyors of amulets and elixirs have known good times and bad, the worse the state of affairs, the more frightening the future prospects, the greater the chances that the message of prophets promising salvation would fall on fertile ground.

The history of modern occultism begins with the *Naturphilosophie* of the romantic age. This was followed by a decline which lasted roughly speaking, until the 1890s, the fin de siècle. The aftermath of the First World War with its material and spiritual ravages saw another upswing, followed by yet another decline. The great explosion of esotericism came in the 1970s and 80s. Marginal traditional sects and new creeds within a few years grew into movements of millions of people with a considerable impact on the *Zeitgeist.* Whoever felt the urge in 1975 to know more about Shamanism, alchemy, witchcraft and similar topics had to read the classic studies by Frazer, Dürkheim, von Lippmann, Levy-Brühl and perhaps a handful of more recent books by Mircea Eliade. Twenty years later there are thousands of books on each of these subjects and several dozens of other topics of which outsiders have not even heard. This whole field is, in the words of one of its gurus and practitioners, a "facet of the cultural trend commonly known as Post-Modernism"; on the other hand, one could also view postmodernism as a facet of occultism:

> Walk into any occult bookshop and you will find a vast array of magical and mytho-logical lifestyles available with yet more being rediscovered or rewritten each year. Postmodernism is a cauldron seething with styles and fashions, where icons and products from all world cultures and epochs can be found nestling among advertise-ments and highstreet supermarket shelves. This is an age when esotericism thrives, as magical thinking permeates all levels of society from economics to art.[40]

The journal *Chaos International* repeats on the bottom of each page its slogan Nothing is true, everything is permitted, ascribed to Hassan Ben Sabah, the founder of the sect of the Assassins, the Old Man of the Mountain.

If the journals of the academic postmodernists circulate in 2- to 3,000 copies, the publications of the New Age sell hundreds of thousands, some-times millions of copies, not counting the numbers of tapes and video cassettes. The world of the occult [41] covers astrology, hermetism, Nostradamus, Kabbalism, various kind of magic, holistic medicine, al-chemy exorcism, witchcraft, cards, geomancy, fetishism, and a hundred other practices that usually escape the purview of historians, sociolo-gists, and even most psychoanalysts because they are not thought to be "serious": For the last two hundred years the miracles of science had outshone the miracles of spiritualism.

Esotericism had a certain impact on the fin de siècle of 1900; the first theosophical associations were founded in Britain and the U.S. in the 1880s and 1890s and Rudolf Steiner's Anthroposophical groups devel-oped just after the turn of the century. Occultism had a strong influence on symbolist poetry and on some precursors of fascism, in particular Julius Evola (a Dadaist turned fascist), the German Ariosophists and the *Thule* society.[42] So manifold are the manifestations and ramifications of this world that multivolume encyclopedias are needed to do them justice; in the present context we are concerned only with the most recent up-surge, particularly in its New Age apparition.[43]

Some established religions have also experienced a revival in the form of fundamentalism, notably Islam (and, to a lesser extent in Protestantism and Judaism). Other congregations such as the Mormons and Jehovah's Witnesses (who have millions of members) have consolidated their influence, while *Christian Science Brahamism,* the *Forum* (Erhard Seminary Training), and probably also scientology have declined. Some have merged such as the "I am"—"Ascended Masters" (founded by the Ballards in the 1930s) with the *Church Universal and Triumphant* (CUT) launched by Mark and Elizabeth Prophet in the 1960s. They claim to have millions of members (probably an exaggerated claim) but show great missionary activity from Sweden to Ghana. Many Indian cults which at one time had a considerable following in the West have disappeared.

Some such as Meher Baba and Bhagwan Shree Rajneesh can now be found under the general umbrella of New Age, which is not a church or a congregation but a network of groups believing in personal (spiritual) transformation, monism and a universal religion for all people, reincarnation and Karma: each person chooses a *sadhana,* a "road to growth and spiritual development." For most believers God is the "Ultimate Unifying Principle," for others God and the universe in one reality. Worship is by way of meditation as taught by gurus. Other important elements are Holism, a biological perspective—all systems constituting the universe are connected—"earth consciousness," astrology, and the belief that the Aquarian age—Aquarius being the eleventh sign of the Zodiac—has dawned or is dawning. Since each such age lasts two thousand years, this means that a wholly new era with a new cosmic worldview is about to prevail. The New Age movement came into being in the wake of the counterculture of the late 1960s, succeeding the psychodelic fashion. Its birthplace was a Boston macrobiotic community and it quickly spread throughout the United States and subsequently to Europe.[44] Since the New Age, not being a monolithic movement has absorbed or rallied many old and new spiritualist movements including the Church of New Jerusalem (the Swedenborgians) the various offshoots of theosophy (Blavatsky et al.), anthroposophy (Rudolf Steiner), various groups of shamaism (including Castaneda) and above all a great variety of Indian teachers including Maharishi Mahesh Yogi (at one time the personal guru of the Beatles), Kirpal Singh, Swami Kriyananda, Baba Ram Dass and others. Some of these are reborn Westerners; Ram Dass, a friend of Timothy Leary, had been Richard Albert, a Harvard professor of psychology prior to his conversion. Ram Dass-Albert was the central spokesman of the movement during the first decade (author of the bestselling *The Aquarian Conspiracy* 1980) together with David Spangler, who commuted between America and Scotland to become the principal advocate of self-discovery and self-development. Fritjof Capra, a physicist is probably the most important link between modern science and the New Age.[45]

In contrast to other earlier spiritualist movements the New Age appeals to well-educated upwardly mobile people and aims at a synthesis of science and its metaphysical insight. The New Age has generated communities, directories, publications, seminars, even self-styled universities and it has been very active in the field of psychology and (holistic) medicine. Transformatorial techniques and therapies are taught in thousands of courses all over the United States and elsewhere. New Age shops sell organic food, macrobiotic cook wear, incense, Ouija boards, tarot cards, rune sets, healing stones, crystal balls.

The great success of the New Age movement has to be explained against the background of dissatisfaction with established religion which has become too impersonal with no regard for the emotional needs of the individual. New Age, on the other hand, is undogmatic, catering to all tastes. Much of the stress is on healing, helping people with their complaints. It is an optimistic, quasi-religious belief in the imminence of a brilliant future. Among its advocates and ardent followers have been famous stars from the Beatles to Shirley MacLaine, including leading rock singers, Steven Spielberg, David Carradine (of Kung Fu fame). If the appeal of New Age was not even wider, one of the reasons was that it is an expensive religion. Only people with some means could afford to buy the paraphernalia, participate in all the right activities on the road to self realization[46] develope their psychic ability, and facilitate spiritual "unfoldment." Nevertheless, within a decade the New Age had become a major market, multibillion dollar business. According to some estimates more than 10 percent of all books in America and major European countries belong to esoteric literature.

With commercialization there came corruption. Many of those selling their goods, material and spiritual, were business people rather than true prophets. Some of the eccentric guests from exotic countries and some of the native prophets were clearly frauds, exploiting the credulity of their public.

Another weakness of New Age was the fact that many of those interested in one of its activities did not necessarily want to embrace it as a

Weltanschauung and a way of life. Thus it became fashionable to participate in a few weekend workshops, but this did not of necessity lead to full commitment and spiritual transformation. Just as the New Age was profoundly eclectic, those subscribing to it also prefer to pick and chose from its rich menu.

Like postmodernism New Age has been strongest in America, but it has also found followers in Europe, more in the northern than in the southern part of the continent. Given the long tradition of sects in Britain and continental Europe their revival during the last third of the century did not come as a surprise. In some countries there has been an upsurge of neopaganism with the reappearance of Druids and Celtic priests and priestesses, Arthurian mystic cycles, and Nordic runes from the Elder Edda. In Germany American Indian faith healers, fire and sun dances have been popular. There are introductory seminars and retreats for those wanting to know more about Shamanism and reincarnation, intuitive breathing and (male) Yang and (female) Yin thinking and their dialectical relationship.

The Findhorn Foundation in Scotland, a New Age community, managed through collaboration with *devas* (nature spirits) to produce vegetables of huge size in sand or poor soil. The magic of crystals, and their healing propensities are studied all over Europe and Asia. "Dowsing," the ability to discover underground water and minerals, is practiced by means of a pendulum. The *Egyptian Book of the Dead* is studied as intensely as *Bardol Thodol,* the Tibetan Book of the Dead—to chart expectations in afterlife. While spiritualist seances with the guidance of a medium seem to be on the decline there has been a strong upsurge of "channelling" which has the advantage that a state of trance is unnecessary and that contact can be established not only with the dead but also with the living. A search for the Messiah has gone on everywhere (the twelfth Imam of the Shiites, Khidr of the Sufis, Kalki of the Hindu). Benjamin Crane, a Scottish artist, has found Maitreyah, the great Buddhist world teacher (aged 95,000 years), in the incarnation of a Pakistani boy in London. The New Age faithful have gathered in harmonic convergence on Mount Shasta in California as well as in Glastonbury, the magical capital of Britain. On any given day in any major European or American city those interested can enroll in courses in which they are taught how alchemy could change their life, on the Dolphin Dream time experience, on holistic Kinesiology, on Reiki and Qi gong, on Cranio-Sacral Therapy and out-of-body experiences. Similar activities have been going on for a very long time; what matters in this context is that infinitely more courses, seminars, and workshops are now offered to more people.

Catalogues of occult and New Age literature in print list 10,000 publications and more, not counting hundreds of journals and video and audio cassettes. While there are no exact statistics on membership and sympathizers, there has been an enormous, perhaps hundredfold, growth in interest.[47] There are thousands of books in print on subjects such as meditation (New Age, New Thought, Jewish, Guided, Instructural, etc.) consciousness expansion, Goddess and feminism, and astrology. Authors such as Joseph Campbell (thirty-four books) E. B. Szekely (twenty-eight), Chogyam, Trungpa, and Tarthang Tulku have probably more books in print than any other writers of nonfiction even though these are not household names as far as the general public is concerned. Thirty-six compact discs of Louise Hay are available, forty-five of Dick Suthpen, which would be the envy of even very famous musicians.

The explosion of esoteric activities has been nowhere more striking than in Russia after communism. There was in Russia a long tradition of belief in magic, faith healing, demons, and every kind of superstition; Rasputin was only the best known of many such practitioners, some outside the church, others within. Even under communism clairvoyants were in great demand. Madame Dzhuna was consulted by Brezhnev and again by Yeltsin's White House. Other such figures in the recent past were Tyazhelnikov and Baibakov. Some of them even tried to combine parapsychology with dialectical materialism and Dr. Kashpirovsky, the television hypnotic dealer, was at one time[48] probably the most popular figure in the former Soviet Union. Books on astrology, tarot, and meditation, publications by Christian and Buddhist sects topped the bestseller lists in Moscow. As the official ideology evaporated, there was a great thirst for teachings of this kind. The "party" of sectarian believers was indubitably greater than any political movement and even Japanese sects such as Aum (Supreme Truth) of chemical warfare fame had more adherents in Russia than in Japan when it was dissolved in April 1995.

More than in the West, Russian believers subscribed to faith in satanic conspiracies. This tradition of ascribing demonic, almost unlimited powers to the "satanists" goes back to the nineteenth century and even before and the part of the Orthodox church in it is unmistakable.[49] After 1988 it had a substantial revival. As one of its propenents wrote:

Mankind has only one enemy—Satan and his army, consisting of demons and biorobots. Demons instal themselves in human souls and murder them, transforming people into zombies and helpers of Satan. The demons can even resuscitate the dead, these are the most horrible zombies.[50] Or as the Metropolitan of Petersburg, Ioan, one of the highest princes of the Orthodox Church, said all demons are democrats, they killed Jesus and their main assignment now is to kill Russia.

In the past views like these had provoked misgivings among the church hierarchy, but in the 1990s there was hardly any protest or disavowal on the part of the supreme church leadership.

In contrast, paranoia has been infrequent in the New Age movement which, on the whole is positive and optimistic in outlook, like theosophy and anthroposophy before—but unlike some of the extreme fundamentalist churches for which Satan and conspiracies were crucial elements. However, in the 1990s there appeared on the fringes of the movement a bestselling literature according to which the Vatican, the Trilateral Commission, the Elders of Zion, orthodox religion, and other groups were engaged in a giant conspiracy, in which "aliens" (by way of UFOs) also played an important role, scheming with the U.S.government.[51]

From this kind of belief it is only one step, and not a big one, to prophecies that not only the end of the century but of the world is at hand.

X

Apocalyptic predictions played a certain role in the 1900 fin de siècle and they figure *a fortiori* now, at the end of a millennium. Both fascism and Communism were in some ways, millennial movements; the *Internationale,* after all mentions a last, decisive battle between the forces of darkness and light; Armageddon in earlier language, and Hitler's Reich were to last a thousand years. But the religious or quasi-religious concept of a cosmic disaster rests on different grounds. Inasmuch as Christianity is concerned the Book of Revelations is the main text ("there was a great earthquake and the sun became black as a sackcloth or hair, and the moon became as blood, and the stars fell unto the earth"). To a lesser extent the prophets Ezekiel and Daniel are quoted. The year 1000 (the date mentioned in Revelations) came and went but doomsday did not occur. The subject continued to intrigue Durer and countless other contemporaries; "Millennium" had to be redefined.

For some considerable time the end of the world has been predicted for the year 2000. Among the prophets were Nostradamus, the most important seer of all time, Edgar Cayce (1877–1945) a famous clairvoyant from Kentucky, Sun Bear (a Chippewa medicine man), Alice Bailey, Fatima, the Irish seer St. Malachy (1094–1148), the Pyramid prophets, the Warsaw prophets, Seventh Day Adventists and a great many others.[52] These are the leading figures in the field of prophecy, but they do not agree on the exact day; some have opted for the 1990s, others for 1999, yet others for 2000 or 2001; to be on the safe side, some give a vaguer, later date. Nor is there full agreement about the exact circumstances; some refer to natural environmental catastrophes such as a giant flood or conflagration, others to epidemics such as AIDS and starvation, yet others to a third world war. Some think that "Armageddon" should be taken literally, that is to say, that it will occur near Megiddo, between Haifa and Jenin. Others opt for another site in the Middle East; a war between Russia and China has also been mentioned, so have a series of major civil wars and nuclear terrorism.

According to Nostradamus the reign of the Antichrist (which will precede the coming of Messiah) will last a mere twenty-seven years, but most others (including Revelations) foresee a much longer period of tribulation. Nostradamus believed that about two-thirds of mankind will perish in the disaster, but he could not make up his mind whether Satan would make his appearance in China or the Black Sea region. According to some prophets Satan has already made his descent (in the 1950s or 1960s), according to others he will still come, and yet others think that the major earth changes may, in fact, occur without his participation. As for the Four Horsemen of the Apocalypse, also known as the hell riders of doom, their character has changed since the days of St. John. There is now much emphasis on ecology, including the ozone layer, global warming (but also a new glacial age), the exhaustion of water resources (but also floods inundating California and half of Europe). Publications of the U.S. Department of Agriculture and commerce are quoted side by side with *Ragnarök*, the ancient Norse Prophecies. Some of the divinators have not taken their own prophecies too seriously because they realize that their calculations could be slightly wrong, by fifty of a hundred years or more.[53] Others have no doubt at all: Mark and Clare Prophet, the leaders of the CUT cult who claimed to be in direct contact with Jesus Christ, advised their followers to sell all their property and to move to the Montana mountains, where they have been digging deep air raid shelters.

In the meantime political prophesying has been continuous. Edgar Cayce predicted a world state, whereas Bhagwan has announced the fall of democracy ("mobocracy") and the rise of meritocracy. A variety of sages have made it known that Russia still has a great future if it succeeds in overcoming its present difficulties. Some predict a resurgence of spiritual Communism, others the disappearance of God, the nuclear family, and nationalism.

All this is predicated on the emergence of *homo novus,* the birth of a new humanity. As Bhagwan wrote in 1986, the new man is an absolute necessity. The old is dead or dying and cannot survive long. And if we cannot produce a new human being, then humanity will disappear from the Earth.

This is the relatively painless eschatology of the New Age—the end of the age of Pisces (Christianity) and as the song from *Hair* proclaimed: "this is the dawning of the age of Aquarius," a radical tranformation of consciousness:[54] Few astronomers agree with these calculations, but this has not dampened the enthusiasm of the believers. They are not bound to any specific date, the dawn could be metaphorical rather than literal. All that matters is that with the rise of consciousness there will be a planetary transformation, resulting in great harmony and happiness.

A much grimmer view has been taken, not unexpectely, in Russia concerning the circumstances of the Second Coming.[54] The reign of the Antichrist which began in 1917 and the end of which cannot be foreseen, was bound to bring horrible suffering to Russia. The country is surrounded by enemies, not to mention the foes within—foreigners, Christians of other denominations, Orthodox believers belonging to rival churches, Jews, Satanists, freemasons, Russian unbelievers. These are the emissaries of the devil, laboring day and night to destroy the country and the Orthodox church. This eschatological tradition is reinforced by pre- and anti-Christian elements such as astrology, magic, and other fields. and while the prophets of doom maintain that the righteous still have a chance, the odds cannot be rated high considering the strength of the forces of darkness.

XI

Throughout modern history there have been cults of the irrational with a great variety of artistic, intellectual, and above all, quasi-religious manifestations. This tradition seems to gather momentum towards the end of the century, which is probably quite accidental. In 1900 the Franco-Prussian and Crimean Wars had receded into the past, most of those alive in the 1990s knew the Second World War from hearsay only.

There are an infinite number of major economic and social problems facing Europe and America but not of the dramatic, immediately threatening kind. Established ideologies have suffered eclipse and the appeal of the established churches, despite the fundamentalist resurgence is also declining. In these circumstances, on top of the perennial desire for change and new ideas, there is the additional longing for new causes to believe in.

What certainties emerge from the belief that "Nothing is true"? The contradiction may be more apparent than real, for if nothing is true, everything is, at least to some extent. As the Egyptian banker (of fin-de-siècle fame) put it—those who believe in nothing well end up accepting anything.

The young Benedetto Croce commenting in later years on the Italian fin de siècle of 1900, for which he felt (in his own words) a wholehearted loathing, noticed some of the dangers. The kaleidoscope of teaching and fashions—including occultism and theosophy with logical restraints removed, the critical faculty, enfeebled, the responsibility of rational assent brushed aside—presented itself as something easy and attractive. But in fact, the new irrationalism was a mixture of antiquated theological speculation and modern decadence, combining the style of the moderns with the language of the ancients.[56] Writing under fascism Croce was not in a position to dot all the i's, but having referred to Nietzsche, d'Annunzio, Barrès, Maurras, and the Action Française, it is obvious that he had fascism in mind, the political consequence of "anti-liberal ideas of war and dictatorship." Taken one by one, Croce's targets were little more than fads that would not have survived unless the political stage had been set for them.

One hundred years later fin de siècle does not connote a titanic struggle of ideas. Either there is no serious ideological challenge or no new messages of salvation that have not been known before. But even if the world will not come to an end in the year 2000, there are bound to be disasters of various kinds, enough to sustain the faith of those believing in the imminence of the apocalypse or similar calamities of a lesser kind. Intellectual fashions that would normally disappear after a few years may be given a new lease of life because of a political, social, or economic breakdown. Although a second coming of fascism as we knew it still seems unlikely there is still a great variety of chaotic possibilities. And since nature abhors a vacuum, there could still be a future for ideas, ideologies, and quasi-religions which in the normal course of events would be forgotten by the year 2000, or soon after.

Notes

1. The literature on the fin de siècle is immense and still growing. Among recent contributions the following ought to be mentioned: M. Teich and R. Porter (eds.) *Fin-de-Siècle and Its Legacy* (1990) dealing with the often neglected scientific and technical aspects; S. Ledger and S. Mc Cracken, *Cultural Politics and Fin-de-siècle* (1995) postmodernist in inspiration dealing with England only; S. West, *Fin-de-Siècle* (1994) with the emphasis on the history of art; E. J. Chamberlain and S. Gilman, *Degeneration* (1985); J.Stoken, *Fin de Siècle, Fin de Globe* (1992).
   The standard works on England are Richard Gilman, *Oscar Wilde* (1988), Richard Gilman's *Decadence* (1979), as well as Holbrook Jackson's *The Eighteen Nineties* originally published in 1913, reprinted in 1988. On France see Eugen Weber, *France, Fin de siècle* (1986). A.E. Carter, *The Idea of Decadence in French Literature 1830–1900* (1958), and Koenraad W. Swart, *The Sense of Decadence in Nineteenth-Century France* (1964). On Austria see Carl E. Schorske, *Fin-de-Siècle Vienna* (1985).
   There are excellent monographs on Germany and Russia but no general works. Nearest perhaps are Renato Poggioli, *The Poets of Russia 1890–1930* and R. Hamann and J. Hermand, *Deutsche Kunst und Kultur von der Gründerzeit*, 4 vols. (1959–1969).
2. The play by Micard, Jouvenot, and Cohen was first performed in April 1888 in the Theatre du Chateau d'Eau in Paris. (The name of the third author was later deleted.) Even earlier, in 1886 the journal *Voltaire* had defined fin de siècle as the passive submission under the (hated) prevailing social conditions, acceptance of the general corruption.
3. F. de Jouvenot and H. Micard, *Fin-de-siècle* (1888). Gogo was a simpleton in French folklore, Mercadet is an artful financier in one of Balzac's novels.
4. Boredom is a neglected subject in cultural history. Eugen Weber mentions one French dissertation. I do not know of others. The major exception is Heidegger's famous lecture on metaphysics in Freiburg in the winter of 1929–30. On this occasion Heidegger talked at great length about "deep boredom" as the inevitable state needed to understand the abyss of human existence and to feel the *horror vacui*. Once this boredom had been experienced human beings could regain their freedom by deciding to act—thus putting an end to boredom. It will be recalled how Heidegger put an end to his boredom through his decision in 1932–33.
5. The depth of the great fear of the year 1000 has been debated by European historians since the late nineteenth century. According to one school of thought the great fear was largely mythical, an invention of a later age; the title of Ferdinand Lot's study *le mythe des terreurs de l'an mille* (1947), is indicative. According to this school violent anxiety was limited to some overwrought monks

and, generally speaking, the more backward elements in society. According to other historians the eschatological fears were not limited to specific sections of society and went much deeper. For recent surveys of the evidence and the state of the discussion see Johannes Fried, "Endzeiterwartung um die Jahrtausendwende" in *Deutsches Archiv fuer die Erforschung des Mittelalters*, 1989; Richard A. Landes, *Relics, Apocalypse and the Deceits of History* (1995); Ted Daniels, *Millenialism* (1992); Stephen O'Leary, *Arguing the Apocalypse* (1994).

Eschatological fears were expressed as the eighteenth century drew to its close. Thus Hölderlin reports strange portents such as inundations and other disasters indicating the end of history. (*Die Christenheit oder Europa*); for some Napoleon was the incarnation of the Antichrist. But these were exceptions rather than the rule.

6. Vadim Kreid (ed.) *Vospominanya o serebryyanom veke* (1993); *Serebryanyi Vek* (1990).
7. This was the belief of, among others, Walter Binni, *La poetica del decadentismo* (1949).
8. Quoted in George Mosse's introduction (1968) to a reissue of Nordau's book.
9. In a paperback edition published by the University of Nebraska Press (1993).
10. P. 128.
11. Tolstoy's views on modern art were not that remote from Nordau's but Nordau could not know this for Tolstoy's *What is Art?* was published five years after *Degeneration*.
12. P. 491.
13. *Preussische Jahrbücher* 1893, "Die gute alte Zeit," pp. 1–28.
14. Benedetto Croce, "Gabriele D'Annunzio," *La letteratura della nuova Italia* (1922). See R. Drake "Towards a Theory of Decadence," *Journal of Contemporary History*, January 1982.
15. Nordau, p. 7.
16. The German emperor decided that the century ended on December 31, 1899; elsewhere after protracted debate the occasion was celebrated a year later.
17. *New York Times*, 1 January 1901.
18. *Washington Post*, 1 January 1901.
19. *The Saturday Review*, 5 January 1901.
20. *Berliner Tageblatt*, 1 January 1901.
21. The editorialist interpreted the emperor's aim as "economic world policy and peaceful competition" and he asked for more democracy at home.
22. Quoted in Eugen Weber, *France, Fin de Siècle*, p. 243.
23. "Fin-de-siècle," *Le Petit Journal*, January 1, 1901; "Bon Siècle" *Figaro*, 1 January 1901. "La Mission du vingtième siècle," *Temps*, 31 December 1900; "Conte pour commencement gaiement l'année " *Le Figaro*, 2 January 1901; "Au jour le jour; la fin de l'autre siècle," *Journal des Debats*, 2–3 January 1901.
24. S. E. Bowman, *Edward Bellamy Abroad*, (1962).
25. Frederic William Farrar (1831–1903) was dean of Canterbury at the time, he had been archdeacon of Westminster in the 1880s. He is best known for his *Life of Christ* which went through many editions and his opposition to the church dogma of everlasting punishment.
26. *The Saturday Review*, 5 January 1901.
27. Baudelaire, on the other hand detested the term and called it "a word for the lazy."

28. There was an attack of mass fear in the late 1970s and 1980s underlying the stationing of long range NATO missiles in Western Europe, which passed however, even before the cold war ended, even though many of the missiles had not been removed.

29. Jacques Le Rider and Gerart Raulet (eds.) *Verabschiedung der (post) Moderne?* (1987).

30. Joseph Hochmut, "The Post Modern House," *Architecture and the Spirit of Man* (1949).

31. Quoted in Jacques Le Rider, "Le Post-Modernism," *Commentaire*.

31. Ernesto Laclau, one of Lechter's most important contemporary thinkers. *Reflections on the New Revolutions of Our Times* (1991).

32. John Lachte, *Fifty Contemporary Thinkers* (1994).

33. A recent work on temporary French culture mentions neither Lyotard nor Baudrillard, neither Althusser nor Bourdieu, neither Dumezil nor Le Doeuff, all of whom are among the chief postmodern thinkers and figure prominently in Lechte's book mentioned above.

34. Malcolm Cook (ed.) *French Culture Since 1945* (1993). See also Antoine Compagnon, *Les cinq paradoxes de la modernité* (1990).

35. Frederic Jameson, a leading Marxist, postmodernist critic at Duke University. The works mentioned are C. Belsey and J. Moore, *The Feminist Reader* (1989); B. Ashcroft et al., *The Post-Colonial Studies Reader* (1995); S. During, *The Cultural Studies Reader* (1993).

36. H. Aram Veeser, *The New Historicism Reader* (1994). Steven Seidman (ed.) in *The Postmodern Turn: New Perspectives on Social Theory* (1994), p. 126.

37. Such as, for instance I. Makaryk (ed.) *Encyclopedia of Contemporary Literary Theory* (1993).

38. Paul R. Gross and N. Levith, *Higher Superstition* (1994). For the impact of postmodernist thought in Germany, Dietrich Bohler, "Die Zerstörung des politisch-ethischen Universalismus, über die Gefahr des heute (post) modernen Relativismus und Dezisionismus," *Forum für Philosophie: Zerstörung des moralischen Selbstbewusstsein* (1988).

39. Carol Christ, *Woman Spirit Rising*, Mary Daly, *Pure Lust*, Maria Gimbutas and Elizabeth Schüssler-Fiorenza in the United States; Christa Mulack, Hannah Wolf (a Jungian) and Gerda Weiler in Germany. For a critical survey Philip G. Davis "The Goddess and the Academy," *Academic Questions,* Fall 1993; for a critique of anti-Jewish elements in radical feminist thinking Charlotte Kohn and Ilse Korontin (ed.) *Sündenfall? Antisemitische Vorurteile in der Frauenbewegung* (1994), in particular the contributions by Susanne Heine and Anita Natmessnig.

40. Phil Hine "Chaos and Culture" in *The Occult Observer,* vol. 2, no. 4., 1993, p. 16.

41. The term "occultism" first appeared in French in the 1860s or 1870s, in English during the subsequent decade.

42. Alain Mercier, *Les sources esoteriques et occultes de la poésie symboliste 1870–1914,* 2 vols. (1969–74). On occultism and Nazism, N. Goodrick-Clarke, *The Occult Roots of Nazism* (1985) as well as the books by James Webb and Ellic Howe.

43. Lynn Thorndike, *A History of Magic and Experimental Science,* 8 vols. (1923–58); for the most recent period, I. Shepard, *Encyclopedia of Occultism and Parapsychology* (1991); George A. Mather and Larry Nichols, *Dictionary of Cults, Sects, Religions and the Occult* (1993).

44. J. Gordon Melton (ed.), *The New Age Encyclopedia* Detroit 1990. See also *The New Age Catalogue* (1988); M. Satin, *New Age Politics* (1978). For critical reviews D. Groothuis, *Revealing the New Age* (1986) from a Christian viewpoint and C. Manes, *Green Rage* (1990).
45. The books of Judith Skutch such as the multivolume *Course in Miracles* (1975) have also been influential and were widely read.
46. The U.S. *Gnosis and Green Eggs,* the U.K. *Starfire,* the German *Hexenzeitschrift,* the Dutch *Wiccam Rede,* and other periodicals sell at about $8 to $12 per issue.
47. The high-level magazines include *Lyre* (pagan) published in Ohio, and the German-language *Anubis. Fenrir* is a journal of Satanism, *Pagan Dawn* is the mouthpiece of the Pagan Federation "Europe's foremost Pagan Body." *Chaos International* has been looking for a "post-structural stance in modern Magic" (*Chaos International,* 18, 1995).
48. On Dzhuna and Yeltsin's White House, *Komsomolskaya Pravda,* 15 February 1995; on sects in general, Korolev in *Nezavisimaya Gazetta,* 28 April 1994; Viktor Kuznetsov, ibid., 12 August 1992 and countless other publications
49. S. Dudakov, *Istoriya odnovo Mifa* (1993).
50. Valeri Khatiushin, "Satanism demokratii" in *Molodaya Gvardiya* 9, 1994, and ibid. 3, 1995, "Esli poimem—spasemsiya."
51. "Conspiracy hysteria running deep," *Psychic News,* 22 April 1995 referring to David Icke, *The Robots Rebellion* (1994); William Cooper, *Ride a Pale Horse,* Arthur Findley, *The Curse of Ignorance*; on the other hand Alan Morrison, *The Serpent and the Cross* (1994), a fundamentalist minister sees the New Age movement as a plot of the devil.
52. According to the *Millennial Prophecy Report,* at least 350 organizations in the United States and many more abroad believe in an apocalypse of sorts. *Guardian,* 8 April 1995. There is a substantial millennialist literature. Perhaps the best introduction is provided by A.T. Mann, *Millennium Prophecies: Predictions for the Year 2000* (1992) and his earlier *The Future of Astrology* (1987).
53. At least seventy different dates have been given for the beginning of the Age of Aquarius with a range of fifteen hundred years. N. Campion, *The Book of World Horoscopes* (1988).
54. M. Ferguson, *The Aquarian Conspiracy* (1981).
55. For a review of Russian prophecies see S. Fomin (ed.) *Rossiya pered vtorym prishestviem* (1994). This is the second edition of an anthology originally published by the Troitski-Sergiev monastery.
56. Benedetto Croce, *A History of Italy, 1871–1915* (1929), pp. 242, 261, 268.

2

Berlin and Moscow, 1914

Berlin and Moscow had more in common in 1914 than is commonly believed. Compared with St. Petersburg, Moscow was the city of business, of technology, of urbanism, just as Berlin was. It was certainly no coincidence that futurism emerged in Moscow and symbolism in St. Petersburg. St. Petersburg was a town of form, of (relative) order, whereas Moscow was amorphous. The same applied, *mutatis mutandis*, with regard to Berlin, the bigger city by far at the time; from one million inhabitants it had grown to 3.5 million within less than two generations. Of course, it was not altogether formless, which would have been unthinkable in Wilhelminian Germany. Nor was the *savoir vivre* wholly absent. It was fashionable to have breakfast at Habel (*frühstücken* meant something different from what it means today), the Cafe Bauer and the other fashionable places were still open late at night after the theatres had closed. There was the Apollo Theater and the *Chat Noir* and, on a higher level of sophistication, Richard Strauss was conducting at the Royal Opera House, Arthur Nikisch at the Philharmonic, Max Reinhardt presided over almost 300 performances of Gorky's *The Lower Depths* at the Deutsche Theater. There were about one hundred daily newspapers in Berlin, not counting the weeklies and monthlies; there were 300 cinemas in the city. It was an international city with Indian tearooms, American roller skating rinks, countless Italian ice cream parlours and thousands of permanent Russian residents. It was an efficient city, famous (or infamous) for its hectic pace, (*Keine Zeit, Keine Zeit*, no time, time is money); a Rohrpost letter took between one and two hours to reach the addressee. It was, all things considered, an inexpensive city, *Berlin hör ich den Namen bloss, da muss vergnügt ich lachen, wie kann man da für wenig Moos den dicken Wilhelm machen*). A room in the Adlon and the Kaiserhof could be obtained for five marks (fifteen with bath).

less distinguished

How much culture was there in Berlin? In 1900 the answer would have been unenthusiastic, it was the era of the epigones, there were no new impulses, and, inasmuch as the plastic arts were concerned, there was *pace* Max Liebermann and Max Slevogt, more in Munich and western Germany than in Berlin. In 1914 those following contemporary trends would have been less categorical in denigrating Berlin. There had been the New Secession and in 1911 Ernst Ludwig Kirchner moved to Berlin and with him virtually the whole Brücke; they occupied Otto Mueller's study in Steglitz. In 1910 the first issue of Herwarth Walden's *Sturm* appeared, in 1911 Franz Pfemfert's *Aktion*. Berlin had become the world capital of expressionism. What Russian painter would have dreamt of moving to Germany rather than Paris twenty years earlier? After 1910, more Russian painters were living in Germany, or at least exhibiting there, than in France. While the Russian Ballet conquered Paris, the Russian painters became part of the German artistic scene. There was less enthusiasm for the great Russian composers of the day, and when the Moscow Art Theater visited Berlin first in 1906, the reception was initially unfriendly. But this soon turned to enthusiasm. It took longer for the Russian writers of that age to be accepted in Germany and this for obvious reasons. They were predominantly poets, difficult to translate and thus Gorky and Merezhkovsky's historical novels were more widely read than Blok, Bely, and Bryusov. The cultural traffic in the other direction was similar—Gerhart Hauptmann's plays were all performed and so was Frank Wedekind and even Hermann Sudermann, but the important German poets of the period became known only much later and only in part.

How important was Moscow as a cultural metropolis? It had an important university and the Moscow theaters were, of course, preeminent. In addition to the Arts theatre there were the Maly, Vera Komissarzhevskaya's Dramatic Theater, the Alexandrinsky, and Alexander Tairov's Kamerny, to mention but a few. The literary salons were, above all, in St. Petersburg, but most of the rich Maecenases buying up French impressionists and post-impressionists were Moscow Old Believers—Schukshin, Ryabushinsky, Morozov, and others. It was the Silver Age of Russian culture but it was also the famous "dance on the volcano." Everyone knew that something horrible was about to happen—a world war, a general cataclysm, the destruction of society and culture. Alexander Blok called his generation as well as those slightly older "the children of Russia's horrible [or dreadful] years," whose slogan was *tryn-trava*—couldn't-care-lessism. The smell of burning and blood was in the air, at least according to the avant-garde poets; the pan-Mongol hordes in the East were grouping for an invasion to culminate in ruin à la Genghis Khan. Russian painting and music (Scriabin excepted) were less apocalyptic than Russian writing, the composers and painters were more robust, more earthy, they read fewer newspapers and less philosophy and theology. The notion of the Russian writer as prophet is not an easy subject to write about: later on it was claimed that they had uncanny forebodings of the catastrophe that was about to happen, that they had already heard the apocalyptic horsemen well beyond the horizon. But how deep was the perception of living on the brink, on the edge of an abyss? How horrible were the horrible years? Not very much in retrospect, certainly not in comparison with the decades that followed. The mood of the Russian avant-garde during the years before the First World War was not that different from the mood elsewhere—except that it came a little later and was a little shriller. It was part of the fin-de-siècle feeling, of decadence and symbolism, of protest against a life that was too orderly and too calm. It was the same feeling and suffocation of which the generation of 1914 complained all over Europe, the same boredom and the search for a new faith. In France it had begun earlier, following the lost war against Germany in 1870–71, and ended earlier; in Germany early expressionist writing had been dealing with the same motifs—visions of chaos, tidal waves of destruction, damnation of life in the big cities, announcements of war's imminence (*"Aufgestanden ist. welcher lange schlief...,"* Georg Heym, *Der ewige Tag*, 1911). All these motifs could be found among Russian writers of the day such as Blok and Bely. In Jakob van Hoddis's poems, railway trains fall from bridges, in Alfred Kubin's *Die andere Seite*, the dream city is as utterly destroyed. The mood extended to those who were not expressionists at all, such as Gerhart Hauptmann's *Atlantis*; the great ship *Roland* sinks as the *Titanic* was to go under the year after.

The breaking of sexual taboos was more dramatic in Russia than in Germany, perhaps because the reins of censorship had been loosened in Russia more suddenly than in other European countries. But Mikhail Artzybashev's *Sanin* had appeared also in German translation and my explanation could be wrong. Perhaps Russian sexual mores had always been freer than German. Moscow incidentally was the first European city after Budapest in which a psychoanalytical institute was founded—

there was much less resistance than in Vienna and more interest than in Berlin.

There had been literary and artistic fashions in modern Europe before and all had been transitory. The French fin de siècle was over well before the outbreak of the First World War. Almost from one day to the next decadence was out and all kinds of positive, "normal," healthy trends became the vogue—manifestoes to the young generation, sport, even militarism. By 1912 Russian fin de siècle was also petering out, some of the symbolist writers and painters turned to futurism or other varieties of modernism. Even the leading journals of the Silver Age had ceased to appear. In German expressionism there had always been a strong element of action—even of frenzied action. Its main mouthpieces were called *Der Sturm, Die Aktion*, and there was, of course, *Der Blaue Reiter*; it was unthinkable that they would be called *World of Art, Golden Fleece*, or *Scorpion*, as the Russian ones were. I do not of course want to argue that the Russian *Weltschmerz* was entirely fake, that those who predicted the end of the world were mere poseurs—though there was a strong theatrical element in Russian cultural life. Rather the cultural pessimism in Russia as elsewhere did express a *Zeitgeist* that was changing by 1910 and turning in different directions. It was quite true that, as Nikolai Berdyaev wrote in his autobiography, "our misfortune lay in our isolation...I cannot help realizing that we were living in an ivory tower where mystical discourse was pursued, while below the tragic destiny of Russia took its course." But the same is true for writers and artists in most countries, most of the time. And it is by no means clear whether their artistic predilection would have differed to any significant degree if they had been in the midst of the social and political struggle of the time.

Why was mass culture during that time so much more optimistic than the avant-garde? To a large extent it always was and is, but seldom was the discrepancy as pronounced as in Berlin and Moscow before the war. It had to do, of course, with stormy technical progress and the resulting improvement in the standard of living, though not necessarily the quality of life. During the early years of the century electricity became the new miracle; Lenin's famous formula of communism as Soviet power plus electrification was by no means original, it had appeared in even more striking terms as the *Elektro Kultur*, the paradise of the future in August Bebel's *Women and Socialism* (English edition, 1909). This optimism was shared by many millions. Everyone knows Paul Lincke's *Glühwürm-chen Idyll*:

Führe uns auf rechten Wegen
führe uns dem Glück entgegen.

Few are aware that the reference was not to glowworms (*Lampyridae*) but to the streetlighting in Berlin. In Paul Lincke's *Frau Luna* (1899) the mechanic Steppke preempts what seventy years later became reality—space travel and a visit to the moon. What matters is not the prescient character of *Frau Luna*, but the fact that the optimism of *Das ist die Berliner Luft* and *Lass den Kopf nicht hängen* expressed the *Zeitgeist* more accurately than the visions of Georg Heym and Jakob van Hoddis.

The same is true, *mutatis mutandis*, with regard to Russia, a backward country, to be sure, but in a process of rapid development. Stanislaw Govorukhin's famous documentary *The Russia We Lost* with Eliseev's food shop well stocked, the new Trans-Siberian Railway, well-nourished peasants working in the fields, and young men and women skiing in the suburbs of Moscow and St. Petersburg is of course overdrawn. There were many dark sides. But it is also true that in 1913 the output of coal had grown sixfold over the previous twenty-five years and the production of wheat had doubled. According to official statistics (probably exaggerated) 70 percent of the population was said to be literate, and it was thought that by 1925 illiteracy would be stamped out altogether. According to demographic projections (including one by academician Dmitri Mendeleev), some 348 million citizens would live within the borders of the Russian Empire by the late 1940s. Russian social legislation (for instance with regard to the length of the working day) was more advanced than such laws in many West European countries. The technical craze had reached Russia: Tsiolkovsky and his friends were drawing up blueprints for rockets; when war broke out in 1914, the Russian air force was the only one to have a multiengine bomber plane (the *Sikorski*,) and Nicholas II had twenty-one private motorcars, including two Rolls Royces, more than Brezhnev had fifty years later.

The German entrepreneurial record before 1914 was mixed. The crucial inventions in motorcar production had been made by Germans—Daimler and Benz, Diesel, and Bosch. But German willingness to take risks and to make the most of it was not outstanding in the field of motor transport. In 1913 there were thirteen times as many cars in the US as in Germany (70,000); even France had more. But in the key heavy industries, in the chemical and electrical industries (the latter largely concentrated in Berlin), German progress had been quicker and more substantial than elsewhere in Europe. Worldwide, Germany was as competitive as America.

If so, what of the "dance on the volcano"? Was the First World War really inevitable? Was the Bolshevik Revolution unavoidable? And what would have happened if these two events had not taken place? Such speculations are called "counter-factual history." It is a perfectly legitimate endeavour; history makes sense only if the various alternatives are considered. Can the outbreak of World War I be explained against the background of conflicting imperialist economic interests? Between Russia and Germany, between Germany and France, there was little competition. If these theories had been right, the First World War should have been fought between the United States and Great Britain, because between these two powers there were indeed major conflicts of economic interest.

The mainsprings of the First World War were, of course, quite different: the German wish to expand, the tensions between the Slavs and the Austrians, the struggle for the succession of the Ottoman Empire, which was in a state of advanced decay. But noting these facts does not provide a satisfactory explanation. There have always been conflicts between nations, there have been war parties and peace parties since time immemorial, and in 1914 a majority of people in all major European countries did not believe that a major war would bring great benefits and involve no risks. In other words, if there had been stronger , more farsighted rulers in Russia, Germany, and Austro-Hungary, a world war could have been prevented. There would have been no Bolshevism and fascism, the development of Europe would have proceeded on more peaceful lines.

Some historians have told us that a war was still inevitable because the great internal tensions increased the likelihood of an explosion. There was in Russia a resurgence of political opposition and social ferment. After the Lena goldfield massacre in 1912, in which two hundred workers had been killed by the police, there was a wave of strikes such as Russia had not witnessed since the Revolution of 1905. But there had been mass strikes on an even greater scale in France during the years before 1914 and even in England. In Imperial Germany the Social Democrats, then considered a dangerous revolutionary party, had emerged as the strongest single force. They had steadily grown for thirty years and after the *Hottentotten Wahlen* of 1907 (with 28.9 percent of the total), they scored even higher in 1912 with 34.8 percent.

When Raymond Poincaré, the French president, went to St. Petersburg in July 1914, 200,000 workers were on strike. But if Poincaré had gone to Italy that summer, he would have encountered half a country in revolt, with whole provinces such as Emilia Romagna in the hands of the insurgents.

If there was much tension in Russia, the same was true with regard to the rest of Europe. And yet there is no reason to believe that but for three years of war and heavy losses there would have been a revolution. Even the Bolsheviks realized that the strike of 1914 would be defeated, and it is interesting that those most fearful of the situation in Russia were on the right rather than the left. A commentator in Moscow compared the situation to the building up of pressures in a hermetically sealed boiler, and Durnovo, one of the ministers closest to the Tsar, in a memorandum that later became very famous, warned of a social revolution in case of war.[1] As he saw it, a social revolution rather than a political one, was the greater danger: the Russian masses, whether workmen or peasants, were not looking for political rights, which they neither wanted nor comprehended. The peasant dreamt of obtaining a gratuitous share of somebody else's land; the workman of getting hold of the entire capital and profits of the manufacturers! Tikhomirov, the terrorist turned monarchist, wrote in 1914 that Russia's tranquillity was lifeless and the nation no longer believed in itself; as Stolypin had put it a few years earlier, Russia was dissatisfied with herself.

Those in the center and on the left were more optimistic. They thought that social processes were in motion that were irresistible in the long run: Russia was on the path towards a modern democratic state. Most foreign observers who knew Russia well, academics with no particular axe to grind, shared the belief that Russia was not doomed to perdition. They included Otto Hoetzsch, the leading German Russologist of his generation, Anatole Leroy Beaulieu, Bernard Pares, Mackenzie Wallace, and Maurice Baring.

True, the immediate prospects for a Western-style political system in Russia were less than brilliant, but this is not tantamount to saying that Lenin and Stalin were the only alternative. At almost every juncture in Russian history up to 1917, events in Russia could have taken another turn. In 1905, Russia had moved from autocracy to pseudo-constitution-alism (*Schein Konstitutionalismus* in Max Weber's well-known phrase). But this, too, was progress of sorts. The powers of the Duma could be whittled down, but the Tsar could not simply return to the old way of ruling.

When war broke out in 1914, there was neither a political nor a social revolution, but on the contrary, as elsewhere in Europe, a great patriotic upsurge. Even most of the intellectuals who had seen impending doom, sickness and decay, forgot their cultural discontents for a while and rallied around the flag. And it will be recalled that Lenin in his Zurich exile thought as late as January 1917 that the revolution was far off. In brief, there was *Anagke*, no inevitability of a Greek tragedy unfolding.

This takes us back to the starting point, the stupidity of the rulers. Wilhelm II was a vain and arrogant man, whose weakness of character would have mattered less but for his constant interference in politics. Nicholas was charming, had nice manners, was unpretentious and loved his family. But he was a weak man, isolated from realities, manipulated by his entourage. Menshikov, the brilliant political commentator of the extreme right, wrote in 1918 that almost anyone else could have saved Russia. This is a sweeping statement; Sergei Witte, one of the most talented statesmen of the late tsarist period, disagreed. Once he was asked, "What if Alexander III had been succeeded by Mikhail rather than the inept Nikolai?" (What if the German Crown Prince, Friedrich Wilhelm—later Friedrich III—had not died of cancer in 1888 but ruled for another twenty or thirty years?) Witte believed that even a talented, statesman-like monarch wold not have been able to do more than prolong somewhat the existence of the autocratic system. The tsarist regime was doomed (just as the Wilhelminian), just like others in history that had outlived whatever usefulness they had once possessed.

But it still does not follow that war, civil war and many years of brutal, and ultimately inefficient, dictatorship were the only alternative. There was the possibility of a (relatively) peaceful transition in Russia from autocracy to a constitutional regime, and in Germany from a Wilhelmian-style monarchy to a modern, more liberal one. It could have taken two or three decades longer. It might have come (the best case) as the result of a more liberal successor to kaiser and tsar. It could have occurred following a court cabal, a military conspiracy, growing political and social unrest, perhaps an old-fashioned revolution. It is possible, but unlikely, that the Hohenzollerns and the Romanovs would have voluntarily abdicated. But the inexorable pressure would have compelled them to surrender their political power. The German aristocracy, which still maintained most key positions in the state and the army in 1914, would have adjusted itself to changing circumstances, managing its rural estates, selling luxury cars and champagne, which in the end it did anyway. The obstacles to reform in Russia were greater—how could rural misery have been eliminated? How would industrial growth have been achieved without rapid success in agriculture? Hence the belief of some historians that the cause of freedom was bound to fail in Russia. But it is impossible to accept the notion that everything in Russia was programmed—the fall of tsarism, the February and October Revolutions of 1917, and eventually also the fall of the Soviet regime.

Such inevitability does not exist in history. If it had depended entirely on Russia's economic development, there is reason to believe that, but for the war, considerable progress would have been achieved under almost any regime. There is reason to assume that under a non-Communist regime, Russia would have recovered fairly quickly after the world war—every other country did. Perhaps a military dictatorship of the far right would have been established in Russia. It would have meant a painful reversal, but it would not have lasted long, and it would have caused less damage than the Bolsheviks, if only because the ambition of the right was not to create a radically new social order. The transition after Franco to democracy in Spain, as well as the example of other countries, tends to show that the peaceful transition from authoritarian to democratic regimes is possible even in not highly developed countries.

What would have happened to Berlin and Moscow if the cataclysm had not occurred? Both cities were about to become *Weltstädte* in 1914; Berlin was still considered a parvenu city compared with Paris and London. But it attracted more foreign visitors every year (more than 2 million in 1913). The University of Berlin was the leading one in the world, so were the hospitals, and the museums were among the most important. It was the "greatest factory in the world" (Walther Rathenau)—7 percent of Germany's industrial production was created there. It was not a "poetical city" (Theodor Fontane in a letter to Theodor Storm) and Rilke wrote that it "oppressed him like a nightmare"; Rilke in fact preferred Moscow to Berlin. But Berlin became more important and had more to offer every year. But for the First World War it would almost certainly have become one of the political and cultural centers of the world; rather than a *Frontstadt* with an excellent cabaret called *Die Insulaner*. In Russia Moscow again became the capital, de facto in 1918, de jure only in 1923. Moscow in 1914 had some 1.2 million inhabitants, no one knows how many there are today, what with the presence of so many *limitchiki*, but ten million seems a reasonably safe estimate. Like Berlin, it is an industrial city—15 percent of Russia's industrial output is produced there. The growth of Moscow as a showcase city was promoted under Lenin, Stalin, and their successors, and the cultural position of Moscow vis-à-vis the rest of the country has been infinitely stronger than that of Berlin vis à vis other German cities.

But Russia's isolation from the rest of the world over more than seventy years effectively prevented its growth as a true *Weltstadt*. It is not so long ago that visitors called Berlin and Moscow big villages, or collections of big villages, and there is much to be said for the olden days, of Moscow, modest and perhaps even insignificant (V. Bryusov) before the turn of the century. But as another poet (Okudzhava) said, the chances that we shall meet Alexander Sergeevich (Pushkin) walking the streets of Moscow are small, no greater than encountering Fontane or Raabe in the Sperlinggasse. Old Berlin, like old Moscow, for better or worse, has vanished and the two cities, capitals of great countries, are doomed to become *Weltstädte*. Under the circumstances they should try to make it a success.

Note

1. Hans Rogger "Russia in 1914," *Journal of Contemporary History* 4, 1966, p. 95 et seq.

3

The Long Way to Unity

Americans have watched Europe's long road to unity with attention and sympathy but also with considerable irritation; it is taking very long and no end is in sight. Full unity seemed to be just around the corner. At the present time it appears to be much further ahead. In most European countries the Euroskeptics and Europessimists have uttered dire warnings and succeeded in watering down the Maastricht blueprints. The obstacle race to European unity resembles the famous pilgrimage somewhere in northwest Germany where three steps forward are invariably followed by two steps taken back—and sometimes even three.

Americans tend to believe in continents, they are impatient with small countries. Quite often, after a return from Europe to Washington I have been asked what Europe thought of a new president or a new political or intellectual fashion. My answer, that such generalizations were impossible because there was no Europe, and certainly no European consensus, was always met with disbelief or even dismay: when would the Europeans at long last get their act (and their opinions) together? Americans tend to forget that their country too was quite small at one time and that it took a long time to unite Italy and Germany (three wars, Bismarck, and many decades) and that even the United States, like Rome, was not built in a day: secessionism had not been an unknown phenomenon in American history.

Once upon a time Europe was united and it was a beautiful brilliant time as Novalis pointed out in a famous essay.[1] But then division prevailed and it was only in the eighteenth century that the European idea found new advocates among some philosophers, writers and, of course, Napoleon. At that time it was generally thought, at least by the intellectuals, that only Christianity could unite Europe, even Victor Hugo, a republican, shared this belief which was somewhat unreal, for how could Protestant Europe accept the leadership of the Pope? But there was also the beginning of a new vision of Europe, of common interest, best expressed by Saint Simon and Thierry in 1814 in a book about the reconstruction of a Community of European States in which even a European parliament was envisaged. In contrast to Novalis they thought that the golden age of Europe did not belong to the distant past—it was as yet to come.

To what extent was America an ideal for those in Europe dreaming about unity? There were a few looking with interest and even enthusiasm to America; Goethe ("America du hast es besser") was one of them, so was Chateaubriand, and Victor Hugo expected an infusion of warmth, vitality, and youthful spirit from the new continent to the old.[2]

But on the whole America was a very distant and savage country about which even the educated knew very little and which hardly intrigued them.

Curiously, simple people, the huddled masses, were far more attracted, and millions of them emigrated to the country of freedom and economic opportunity. There is an intriguing disparity between elite attitudes and mass culture in the nineteenth century as much as in the twentieth. The year that G.B. Shaw wrote that a 100 percent American was a 99 percent idiot, European emigrants were queueing in the European ports to get a place even in the most miserable conditions to cross the Atlantic. In the second half of the twentieth century when cultural anti-Americanism was the great fashion in Western Europe, American mass culture was winning hands down the battle for the hearts and minds of Europe. It became difficult to watch any movie in Berlin, Paris or London that was not of American origin.

Among the European countries most interested in America in the nineteenth century was Russia, and the first Russian to provide a detailed and systematic account of how the American system of government worked (the term democracy was used at the time with some hesitation) was a distant relation of mine, Alexander Borisovich Lakier.[3] He was sanguine about America's future:

Young, active, practical, happy in their enterprises, the American people will have an influence on Europe, but it will use neither arms, nor swords nor fire, nor death and destruction. They will spread their influence by the strength of their inventions, their trade and their industry. And this influence will be more durable than any conquest.

Lakier's prediction was correct as far as it went, but incomplete. On two occasions America did have to intervene in Europe with sword and fire to redress the political balance, and for many years after the Second World War the American presence in Europe was taken for granted.

II

Some Europeans and many Americans reached the conclusion years ago that America has outstayed its welcome in Europe, and the slogan "Yankee go home," was heard on both sides of the Atlantic. At the same time there has been a tendency in Europe to exaggerate America's vital interests in the old continent. America could not possibly surrender its positions in Europe, it was frequently argued in the 1960 and 1970s, because of its massive investments; but those in Canada and Mexico were even more substantial. In any case, foreign trade was less important for the U.S. than for the major European nations. But America could not possibly surrender Western Europe to Soviet pressure, it was argued. This, too, was not quite convincing, for whatever the Soviet Union might have done in Europe, America was not on the frontline, whereas Germany and the other European nations were. Cultural ties and ethnic kinship were invoked as the cement of the alliance. This too, was correct as far as it went, but no massive American military presence in Europe was needed to preserve these ties; in any case, New York had became the world's most important art market as well as musical center.

Many Europeans are not wholly familiar with the depth of the American isolationist tradition and American ambivalence towards Europe. They seem to have forgotten that the early settlers in North America did not come because life was so good in Europe, to paraphrase a Russian saying. They came because of religious persecution, famine, and lack of prospects. The very first American major literary document, William Bradford's *History of Plymouth Plantation*, written between 1630 and 1651, included dire comments on that "gross darkness of popecy" that the pilgrims escaped. George Washington admonished his fellow countrymen to evade at any cost entanglement in the quarrels and intrigues of Europe, *The Federalist* spoke of the arrogant pretensions of certain Europeans, claiming that everything was salubrious in America—even the dogs stopped barking having breathed American air...

Through American intellectual life in the nineteenth century suspicion of Europe runs like a red thread. If European visitors from Frances Trollope to Dickens were shocked by the uncivilized American natives, American writers reacted with bitterness and sarcasm such as in James Kirke Paulding's *John Bull in America* (1825) where in British eyes every third American was drunk by nine in the morning, pigs were about to be given the vote, and the inhabitants of New York consisted of three classes, beggars, thieves, and those who made debts. Ferdinand Kurnberger, a liberal German novelist wrote a book, *Der Amerikamüde* (1855), very famous at the time, that contained all the stereotypes of anti-Americanism prevailing to this day, above all the basic tenet that Americans had only one god—Mammon. Heine, who had never been to America, subscribed to the idea, so did Knut Hamsun and Maxim Gorky who made their way to God's own country in later years and came to regret it. There is the famous exchange between Oswald Spengler and Harvard University which had invited him to attend some celebration. Spengler who had never been to the United States declined with thanks; he feared that the shock would be too great, and he might be compelled to revise some of his views as a result of the exposure to American realities.

American judgment on Europe for all the suspicions and reservations was less disdainful. Americans continued to attend Europe's leading universities up to World War I and even after because they were superior to their own and a few settled in Europe, either because they found Britain's aristocratic society more congenial or the social and cultural freedom of Paris in the 1920s more attractive. But like Sam Dodsworth, they did not feel at ease in Europe; the snobbishness and arrogance of the aristocracy made them uncomfortable. While they were often painfully aware of their own lack of sophistication they decried the insincerity and the frivolity of the upper-class Europeans they met.

There were knowledgeable and sensible people on both sides of the Atlantic concentrating on the admirable rather than the negative features of American and European ways of life. But there was not that much love lost between the continents.[4] In retrospect it still is not quite clear why America entered the First World War. Economic interest was certainly not a decisive factor; if economic rivalry had been the main motive, America should have made war against Britain rather than Germany. Ethnic and cultural kinship did play a certain role but it cannot account for everything; pro-British sentiments were counterbalanced by anti-

Russian (or rather antitsarist) feelings. In the final analysis American idealism did play a role, specifically the belief that the Kaiser was up to no good and that he might win unless the Yanks were coming.

The role of idealism in American foreign policy has seldom been fully appreciated in Europe perhaps because it has been such a long time since important decisions in the foreign policy of the major European states had been motivated by idealistic consideration—or at least by disinterest. Everyone knew that in foreign affairs there was no room for friendship, only for interests and ambitions. Why should America be different? American preoccupation with human rights in the 1970s again caused considerable annoyance in European foreign ministries; this surely was not the right way to promote peace between nations and international coordination. There were some exceptions such as Holland and (within limits) the Scandinavian countries, but in the foreign policy of the major European countries human rights were far from the top of the political agenda.

American policymakers, on the other hand, complained of European reluctance to resist aggression, be it on the part of the Soviet Union or in the Middle East. Part of the explanation was, as Kissinger said on more than one occasion, that only America was thinking in global terms, of *Weltpolitik*, whereas the horizon of even the major European countries was continental, regional. European statesmen did not like Kissinger's observation, but in retrospect it cannot seriously be contested.

III

America's involvement in European affairs was quite limited prior to the First World War. True, American presidents helped to make peace between Russia and Japan (1905) and they were prominently involved in the establishment of an International Court at the Hague and the peace conferences around the turn of the century (1899 and 1907). But America's impact on Europe was primarily that of an economic power and with the most advanced technology, the country of central heating and the best dentists, of incandescent lamps, the telephone, the moving pictures and, of course, aircraft. The fact that America also emerged in the 1870s as the world's leading agricultural producer, and subsequently as the strongest industrial power, did not fail to impress Europeans. But economic power did not translate into political influence as far as European leaders were concerned: America's business was business, not world politics; American imperial conquests came as an afterthought, were small and did not last long.

The great change came with the First World War, and in 1919 there was no world statesman more popular in Europe than President Wilson. But Congress did not ratify U.S. entry into the Leaque of Nations, and for all one knows the League would have failed even if America had joined. There were still some major American initiatives in Europe in the interwar years such as the Kellogg-Briand pact (1928) to outlaw war, and the Dawes (1924) and Young plans to reduce the amount of reparations to be paid by Germany. These were not successes. The Kellogg-Briand pact was signed by the major powers (except Japan and the Soviet Union) but helped in no way to stem the tide of war in the 1930s. It is now of interest mainly because many of its provisions became part of the United Nations Charter. The Dawes and Young plans were not of decisive importance either. Germany prospered in the middle twenties despite the reparations and if, like the rest of the world, it underwent a major crisis after 1929, this was not caused by the reparations. The political damage had been done at the Versailles Peace conference and the German nationalists did the most to make capital of it.

President Roosevelt's attempts to prevent the outbreak of the war in Europe, and later on to limit it, were ineffectual and it was only after Pearl Harbor and America's entry into the war that the last chapter of America's involvement in European affairs began continuing to this day. During the war all sorts of declarations were passed by the leaders of the United Nations, but they referred to a new world order rather than European unity. After the war the tendency in America was to demobilize the armed forces as quickly as possible and to withdraw from Europe as in 1919. But it was not to be; the threat of economic ruin in Western Europe and the danger of a Soviet invasion or at least of the imposition of a Soviet zone of influence in Europe led to the Truman Doctrine and the Marshall Plan. The idea of close European cooperation began to figure prominently in American strategy. The Marshall Plan led of necessity to steps towards integration—the liberalization of trade, a European Payments Union, the Organization for European Economic Cooperation (EEC), and eventually the idea of a common market. American thinking at the time was that Europe would be able to overcome its difficulties only through close cooperation; this was a radical new departure that not everyone in Europe liked. It is interesting in retrospect, that these American initiatives, even if not quite specific, predated the European initiatives for greater unity such as the Coal and Steel community, the Monnet Plan and eventually the Treaty of Rome.

Moves towards common defense followed a similar pattern, even though resistance in this respect was even stronger. American policymakers had no wish to deploy forces in Europe without a commensurate European effort. Washington was looking not for a dozen partners but one partner; after the French parliament had defeated the initiative to bring about a European Defense Community (and after WEU—the West European Union—remained stillborn) NATO was the only realistic alternative.

The makers of American foreign policy in the early postwar period all believed in a united Europe, if only because such collaboration was bound to reduce the burden on America. This was true up to President Kennedy who said in 1962 that a strong and united Europe, which he regarded as a partner not a rival, was part of the American grand design, the main task of U.S. foreign policy. In the years that followed, American enthusiasm diminished. France had virtually withdrawn from NATO; de Gaulle and some of his successors such as Jobert did their best to reduce European cooperation with America (and to prevent the extension of the European Community). America complained that the European countries did not pull their weight in NATO, and felt let down by her European allies in critical situations. As they saw it, the alliance had become a one-sided affair, or, to be precise, had never moved beyond this stage. The situation was further complicated by economic conflicts that persist to this day. Once the main problem in U.S.-European relations had been the "dollar gap" and the (technological) *défi Americain*. But then the various economic miracles took place in Europe, while the value of the dollar declined. Europeans became more and more reluctant to support a world financial system (Bretton Woods) that had been designed by the Americans in their own best interest and that after 1970 seemed outdated. This attitude strengthened those in America who had argued all along that Europe was not so much an ally as a competitor and a rival, and if America was treated as an adversary, why not retaliate in kind? It ought to be recalled that certain initiatives in Congress to reduce U.S. forces in Europe were defeated only by the narrowest of margins (the Mansfield Amendment). If Europeans were arguing that America was a spent force, a growing number of Americans maintained that the Far East was much more important economically for America, and in the long run also politically.

But this orientation towards the Pacific replacing the Atlantic Alliance never became U.S. foreign policy. Nixon and Kissinger had their misgivings about European steadfastness but all the same they declared 1973 the "Year of Europe." It was not a great success but since expectations had not been unduly high from the beginning, disappointment was not that acute. Early in his presidency, Nixon had declared that a united Europe had to be built by the Europeans—by no one else. He thought that if earlier on America had been an eager advocate of European unity, this might have done more harm than good. America would have to follow the process from the sidelines as a sympathetic spectator. In the meantime, the emphasis would have to be on bilateral relations with the various states of Europe.[5]

IV

The recent history of European unity has a certain resemblance to the case history of a manic-depressive. After the dejection of the early 1980s about the lack of progress, a new initiative came under way and by 1989–90 real unity seemed just around the corner and gave way to overconfidence. Prematurely, 1992 was declared to be a historical milestone. America was virtually written off by some European statesmen such as Mitterrand; looking a few years ahead these prophets did not see a major role for the U.S. to play—economically weak and declining as it was, its commitments extending far beyond its real power. (Only five years earlier Mitterrand had compared Europe with a deserted building site.) The future clearly belonged to a united Europe, the greatest common market in the world. Such optimism was greatly enhanced by the collapse of communism and the disintegration of the Soviet empire. The attitude towards America in influential circles in France, Germany, and other European countries became one not so much of antagonism but of pity: poor America, its shrinking political and economic power was a reason for commiseration rather than jubilation.

But 1992 came and went and unkind critics were reminded of the famous verse in Horace's *Ars Poetica*—mountains being in labor and a ridiculous mouse being born. Denmark voted against Maastricht,[6] France approved it with a microscopic majority, and if there would have been a plebiscite in Britain, it would probably have been defeated. As Mrs. Thatcher told her listeners, the people of the Magna Carta would never surrender their liberties to the malevolent and faceless bureaucrats in Brussels.

By the summer of 1993 there was near despair with regard to the stalled momentum of European unity, and even more with regard to the economic and political crises afflicting virtually all countries of the continent. Mitterrand's party suffered a crushing defeat in the French elections of 1993, the German economy faced its severest crisis since the Second World War, Italy and Britain were in deep political trouble, and even such models of prosperity and stability as Sweden and Finland were facing unprecedented economic difficulties. Industrial output declined all over Europe (by almost 10 percent in the case of Germany), the unemployment rate exceeded 10 percent in most European countries. Ironically, the only Western economy to show modest progress was America's. The British economic indicators were also slightly better than those of the European neighbors, but its economic performance had been so dismal in other respects that this hardly mattered.

Seen against this background, European fears about the future, following years of overconfidence, were not entirely groundless. And it was also true that the American condition gave rise to apprehension, domestically as well as in foreign affairs: Bush's foreign policy with all its shortcomings seemed in retrospect a model of vision and competence in comparison with the amateurishness displayed by the Clinton administration in its early phase.

Europe did, of course, face serious problems, economic as well as political. The resistance against European unity had been underrated. What had seemed reasonable to a political elite was taken as self-evident truth, and no serious attempt had been made to explain to the public at large that many of the fears connected with the reduction of sovereignty were unfounded. Norwegians would not have to converse in Sicilian dialect, nor would they become a German colony. It should have been frankly conceded that unification did involve risks and threats, but that none of these were fatal. Shortcomings could be put right as a new Europe was built, the advantages outweighed the losses, and that in the final analysis a united Europe would be in everyone's overall interest.

But the original political impetus seemed to have faded. In the beginning, and for many years after, the two main raisons d'être of a united

Europe were the conviction that another war in Europe (most likely between France and Germany) had to be prevented at any cost, and that a counterweight was needed against the Russian colossus.

By 1992 the danger of another European war had disappeared and so had the danger from the East. In the circumstances the urgency for making some major steps towards unity had vanished. The European nation states had existed for centuries, why make radical new departures, if the old system worked reasonably well? No one in Europe opposed economic cooperation, but in the absence of a clear and present danger, a considerable number of Europeans were reluctant to give up time-honored traditions and customs, and remained fearful of challenges from within and outside that will confront Europe in the years to come and that individual countries will not be able to solve in isolation. The Euroskeptics will have to learn the hard way; the learning process could be protracted and costly. But it is pointless to exert pressure from the outside; the recognition that a united Europe is needed must come from inside to be lasting. Whenever the nations of Europe were forced to unite, the endeavor ended in disaster. All indications show that a free and reasonably prosperous Europe will survive only in unity, but it seems equally obvious that the long road to Europe is not over yet, that the nation states will fight tooth and nail against any surrender of their sovereignty. In all probability, some further shocks are needed to provide fresh impetus to the movement towards unity. Jean Monnet once said that crises are the great federators; Europe is in a state of crisis, but it might not be severe enough to generate the new momentum that is needed.

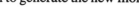

V

But what is Europe, where are its frontiers? It was easy enough to answer this question while the cold war lasted; Europe was the countries this side of the Iron Curtain. With the disappearance of the Iron Curtain there are no such certainties anymore. The "return to Europe" was an essential part of the vision of the Eastern European and Baltic nations. The situation in Russia was more complicated; Slavophilism may be in a state of agony, but the "Eurasians" have had a field day among the Russian right. The term refers to the school of thought that first appeared among Russian emigres in the 1920s according to which Russia's future was in Asia. It had never truly belonged to Europe, and the Europeans had always treated it (according to this doctrine) with contempt as an alien body. It is certainly true that Russia's history points to a *Sonderweg* from the Middle Ages on; what has been said about Germany is *a fortiori* true with regard to Russia, whose traditions differ in important respects from those of Europe. But there is no future for Russia in the East, the Asia the Eurasians invoke exists only in their imagination,not in reality. They have no wish to convert to Islamic fundamentalism and Chinese and Indian culture are infinitely more remote than that of Europe.

The Westernization of Russia is by no means over, it could well be a long process and there will be disappointments and setbacks in the years and decades ahead. The hopes concerning Western assistance will certainly not be fulfilled, and in Eastern Europe as well as in Russia there is the growing realization that certain aspects of the European way of life cannot be copied in conditions that greatly differ from those prevailing in the Western part of the continent.

The disappearance of the Iron Curtain has removed a threat and made an opening to the East possible. This is a great chance that no one could have envisaged even a few years ago. But it is a chance for the distant not the immediate future. Eastern Europe and Russia should, of course, eventually be part of a United Europe. But in view of the enormous economic and social disparities between West and East a common market cannot possibly soon become a reality; all kind of special arrangements will be needed to prepare the way for a gradual rapprochement. And it is not even certain that in its present sorry state Western Europe has the necessary political will to make use of a chance that, if neglected, may not occur again in the near future. A leading European statesman once said that Europe half finished was like a house that the building workers had failed to complete; exposed to the elements it will deteriorate and eventually collapse. There is no denying the existence of this danger.

VI

One of these days Americans may lose patience with Europe. The slow uphill struggle for unity has been exasperating, and if many Europeans believe that no closer collaboration is needed than exists at present, it is not up to Americans to act as advisers and advocates. The unending and frustrating talks about the liberalization of world trade have certainly not enhanced prounited European sentiment in America.

A more detached attitude has much to recommend itself. But it should also be accepted that unless America withdraws altogether from world politics, it will need allies; if so, Europe is bound to be its most important ally for the foreseeable future. American trade with the Far East may increase more quickly in the years to come, but as far as commercial relations are concerned there is bound to be as much (if not more) rivalry with the Far East than with Europe.

Apart from the various written agreements with Europe with regard to defense, commerce, and political cooperation, there has been an unwritten understanding underlying the alliance. This understanding has been at times sorely tried, and as alliances are not eternal, the one between North America and Europe may one day come to an end. But this moment has not yet come, even the most inveterate critics of America in Europe know in their innermost hearts that they still need America even more than America needs Europe. The present state of Europe is not conducive to sanguine optimism, but it is useful to remember that this is not the first time that the idea of Europe seemed to have run out of steam. The European mood tends to change every few years. Measured by the dreams of the early architects of a united Europe, the achievements of the last four decades have been disappointing. Again, as in the 1970s and early 1980s Europe seems to be struck by *aboulia*, that strange paralysis of the political will. Measured by less exacting standards,the achievements are quite impressive; many steps towards closer cooperation seem irreversible and for all one knows one of these days a fresh start might be made. In his *magnum opus* Alfred Marshall wrote that progress in the economic world must be slow for *natura not facit saltum*. This is even more true with regard to political progress, except, of course, in time of war.

Notes

1. *Die Christenheit oder Europa* (1789).
2. Quoted in P.M. Lutzeler, *Europa, Analysen und Visionen der Romantik* (1982), p. 24.
3. Aleksander Borisovich Lakier, *Puteshevstrie...*(1859). An abridged version was published in English by the University of Chicago Press in 1979 as *A Russian Looks at America* (A. Schrier and J. Story, eds.).
4. This refers much more to Western than to Eastern Europe where attitudes towards America were traditionally more positive than in Britain, France, and Germany.
5. Richard M. Nixon, *U.S. Foreign Policy for the 1970s* (1970), p. 32.
6. After a revision of the draft treaty, the Danish electorate reversed its vote and came out in favor of Maastricht in 1993—but not by an overwhelming majority.

4

Public Diplomacy—Poor Relation

Public diplomacy has never been the favorite offspring of U.S. foreign policy. More often it is considered a poor relation, faintly disreputable, with no particular merits in the past and of doubtful relevance in the present time—not to be discarded altogether, but to be kept at a safe distance. The decline has continued for a long time; 12,600 people were employed by the United States Information Agency in 1967, the present number is 8,500 and still falling. The number of those stationed abroad has been halved. Expenditure in real terms is less than it was in 1970. During the last year the attitude of influential sections in Congress has turned from indifference to hostility and as Congress returns from its recess further cuts can be expected. Important USIA programs are discontinued, others radically scaled down. The attitude of the Clinton administration has been, on the whole, one of apathy and indifference; one of its first initiatives was to phase out the Munich-based Radio Free Europe and Radio Liberty. A substantial group of freshman senators and congressmen spent many hours of their valuable time on the floor of the House and the Senate attempting to kill the National Endowment for Democracy, a small but very active and effective organization helping democratic forces in formerly unfree countries, the total budget of which (35 million) is less than the cost of a Hornet fighter bomber. What made legislators accustomed to swallowing camels strain at gnats?

There are several explanations but none of them is entirely convincing and to some extent the issue remains shrouded in mystery. America pioneered public relations, it is the home of Madison Avenue. Advertising, in the widest sense, has always been appreciated in the United States and it spends more for this purpose than any other country—selling cigarettes and soft drinks but not selling America. One single company (Philip Morris) spent more in one year on advertising (2 billion in 1990) than all the budgets of all the U.S. agencies, official and semiofficial, engaged in public diplomacy taken together.

Nor can it seriously be argued—as some have done—that these tools of U.S. foreign policy are no longer needed now that the cold war is over and America no longer faces major threats. There was a brief moment of euphoria following the collapse of the Soviet empire. But no specialized expertise is needed to realize that far from being on the verge of a new order the world has entered a period of great disorder under heaven. This refers to all kinds of regional conflicts, to the proliferation of the means of mass destruction which makes nuclear war in the not too distant future a distinct possibility. It also refers to a potential second coming of fascism and communism and anti-Western onslaughts by other forces. Facing these new dangers a reexamination of old priorities is needed as cultural diplomacy—in the widest sense—has increased in importance whereas traditional diplomacy and military power (especially of the high technology variety) are only of limited use in coping with most of these dangers.

Why is it so difficult to accept these unpleasant realities? Isolationism in its extreme outspoken form has now become rare. Even senators or congressmen who wish public diplomacy to disappear introduce their motion with a statement to the effect that they are not in principle averse to such activities. But the popular (and indisputable) saying that America "cannot solve all the world's problems" sometimes serves as an excuse for arguing that it cannot solve any—or hardly any. The undoubted fact that long-neglected domestic problems ought to be given high priority is used to suggest that in its present condition America has little time, resource, and energy to deal with foreign problems—as if a great power was incapable of dealing with more than one problem at a time.

Underlying the reluctance to accept the increasing importance of public diplomacy is the tacit belief that such activities are in the final analysis a luxury, that they are not really in America's self-interest and that "we are doing them a favor." Seen in this perspective, the bells may be tolling, but they are not tolling for America. This betrays a profound misjudgment concerning the relevance of events outside America, for the security and the well being of this country.

Some of those who disparage public diplomacy seem to believe that the advantages of the American way of life, of its values and institutions are so self-evident that they do not need special promotion. They also appear to think that the future of democratic institutions worldwide is so secure that no particular effort is needed to bolster them.

Some critics consider public diplomacy a typical American aberration that other, more sensible, countries do not share. In this respect, there is admittedly a great deal of ignorance. Travellers in foreign parts know that the BBC World Service is more widely listened to and given greater attention than American sponsored radio stations; even Mrs. Thatcher never suggested that the private sector should take over the BBC. It is less widely known that on a per capita basis France (and many other countries including of late Spain) spend infinitely more on public diplomacy than the U.S., that there is no U.S. equivalent for the foreign presence and activities of the German political party foundations (Adenauer, Ebert, Naumann, et al.), that Iran has more powerful radio stations than the Voice of America—to chose at random a few examples. These facts may still fail to impress those who believe that America's standing in the world is not a matter of high priority. But it is clearly wrong to assert that their indifference is shared by other nations.

Other arguments against public diplomacy vented in Congress include assertions of widespread corruption, of waste and duplication. While human beings are fallible wherever they are stationed and while such transgressions should be investigated and if need be punished, this is clearly another case of straining at gnats. Given the small size of the budget, (less than 1.4 billion of which, furthermore, almost everything is earmarked down to the last million) there could not be much corruption and waste, even if public diplomacy had somehow been taken over by the criminal underworld, using the most fiendishly clever devices to defraud the American tax payer. How little pork, how minute a barrel! It is, of course, annoying that keeping a lowly second secretary at the Tokyo embassy costs the U.S. more than the salary of a U.S. senator. This however, is not the fault of the second secretary but of the high cost of living in Japan—(and in many other countries). And since no country can afford to let its representatives sleep in the streets or starve, such outlay has to be made however grudgingly. In the final analysis, the second secretary with all his allowances will probably be still worse off than he would be in a job of comparable standing at home.

Overlapping is also an argument that does not withstand serious examination. Those complaining would hardly suggest that the American customer's choice should be limited to one sort of car, toothpaste, perfume or painkiller. Foreign customers too, have a variety of tastes and ought to be approached on various levels of sophistication. U.S. radio stations or foundations have a variety of purposes—some are mouth-pieces of the U.S. government, others need more freedom of maneuver to be effective. Some of the U.S. effort should be directed to those left of center— some to those right of center, some should reach unions, some churches, others yet the academic world or chambers of commerce.

For all this a variety of instruments is needed, and if there is a little overlapping, it should be welcomed because it is conducive to competition and the improvement of performance.

It is difficult to find any merit in the arguments mentioned so far and there is reason to doubt whether these are in fact the real, deeper motives of the opposition against public diplomacy. The most basic weakness of public diplomacy is the fact that it has no powerful domestic constituency. Even the most militant antidefense legislators will fight like lions if threatened with the closure of military installations in their congressional district. Public diplomacy has no such base; during the cold war there was a consensus among enlightened officials, elected and appointed, that some expenditure on these lines was inevitable. But for a variety of reasons this consensus did not survive the cold war, even though the objective need is now greater than before.

Furthermore, there has always been resentment on the extremes of the political spectrum that more money was not allocated for their ideological allies abroad. The right has complained that it was no business of the U.S. to support in some countries free trade unions (or even Social Democrats!) against their foes, even if the sums involved were risible by any standard. On the extreme left there were parallel complaints: why assist those who do not qualify according to the canons of political correctness? Yet others have been dissatisfied because their friends abroad were neglected. And since there are each year thousands of applications for grants and only hundreds can be supported, the army of the discontented greatly outstrips those who did get help. Thus, there is a common bond between the disgruntled for personal or ideological reasons and populists opposed to the whole enterprise by sentiment and conviction.

Still more arguments are adduced by skeptics considering public diplomacy a double-edged sword likely to cause more harm than good. If America has no foreign political strategy or if its leaders are waffling or make egregious mistakes, why broadcast (and thus magnify) the fact?

But this is taking a very narrow view of the purpose of public diplomacy which is not merely concerned with daily affairs and putting the best gloss on current U.S. policies.

Its main purpose is, of course, to project an image of American life and values quite irrespective of the events of the day. Its perspective is not measured in weeks or months, to be effective it has to think in much wider time frames. The usual bureaucratic queries about tangible achievement that can be measured and shown at the end of the budgetary year, are simply not applicable.

But there is another, more weighty objection, that concerns the quality of U.S. public diplomacy. It is unfortunately true that its performance has not always been outstanding and the selfcongratulatory statements in the annual reports are sometimes out of place. Several committees have looked into the question of performance, but they have concentrated, on the whole, on technology and the choice of vehicles rather than on substance. The quality of American television and radio in general is not, to put it cautiously, very good compared with many other countries. This is true not just with regard to high- and middlebrow programs, even on the level of soap operas America has been losing out in the former Soviet Union to Mexico and Brazil which have produced and sold more attractive products. America did have two excellent and very effective radio stations in Munich, broadcasting to Eastern Europe and Russia, which as attested by those in the know, including the present heads of governments in Eastern Europe, played an important part bringing the cold war to an end. But it was precisely their success that made them many enemies. Some of these services have been discontinued, others will cease operating in three or four years. The number of employees is reduced from 1600 to 400. The research department, the best source of information in the whole world on events in Eastern Europe and the former Soviet Union has been liquidated. All this on the assumption that the battle for democracy in the former Soviet Union and Eastern Europe has been won...

Opponents of public diplomacy frequently argue that the private sector should shoulder the responsibility, which is about as sensible or practical as suggesting that it should be responsible for U.S. defense, health, education, and the cleaning of the streets. Even if private foundations had the funds to engage in these activities, their interest in operations abroad—with one or two notable exceptions—is now much less than it was in the 1950s and 60s. Some corporations may be willing to invest in regions of special interest to them. But no help will be forthcoming precisely in areas where the greatest needs are.

Fifty years ago or even thirty, radio broadcasts, especially short wave, were one of the main vehicles of public diplomacy. It is still important even though the importance of television is growing. There has been great excitement about the multitude of channels that will be accessible, at least in theory, to a global audience. But closer examination shows that such excitement is misplaced or at least premature. While short wave radio broadcasts are phased out, they have not been replaced by a worldwide television network. Instead we have Worldnet (Voice of America) which is best at satellite teleconferencing, a worthy activity, a kind of international press conference or seminar that usually reaches a handful of people only. This is not the stuff likely to be rebroadcast at peak time by foreign television stations, least of all in countries opposed to the U.S. and its policies.

Neither U.S. commercial channels nor public television produce sufficient programs suitable for showing abroad. In the circumstances, U.S. foreign television would have to produce its own programs; the talent to do so exists and with a little luck sufficient editorial freedom may be given. But the funds for such a venture are nonexistent; outlays for television are approximately five percent of a shrinking USIA budget. Many USIA services have been discontinued, including exhibitions, global and regional magazines, book fairs, book exchange funds. And the fee for a lecture in some distant country is still (I believe) $100—sufficient for gentlemen and ladies of leisure and independent means, but hardly enough to attract those best equipped to appear. As of now USIA is not even represented on the National Security Council.

These facts give a rough idea of the importance attributed to public diplomacy by Congress and the administration. It is pointless to raise the issue of quality, crucial as it is, as long as a minimal budget does not exist. Everyone agrees on the importance of television, everyone discusses various new satellite and digital technologies and the information highway. But in the competition for a global audience the U.S. is not even a starter. The BBC, the French, and the Germans have been more active and have allocated more money. Even countries such as Turkey, Egypt, and Saudi Arabia have more astutely realized the importance of television channels beaming to neighboring countries. In Washington such activities are not even envisaged. As of now, all U.S. public diplomacy aspires to is the production of programs that will be transmitted by satellite to foreign stations in friendly countries, which may or may not use them.

To remedy the present dismal state of affairs, the budget of the various agencies engaging in public diplomacy should be, roughly speaking, three or four times higher than now. They should be given greater freedom of action and be able to attract the best talent available. Given the present mood in Congress and the budgetary cuts, such suggestions are, of course, entirely illusory.

There is always the possibility that a major international crisis will have a salutary effect doing away with delusions about the real state of the world, generating greater awareness of the dangers facing America, and generally speaking, putting an end to lethargy and indifference. But such a crisis might be years off and in the meantime some words of warning are called for. The international agenda tends to ignore the concerns of Washington legislators, just as they, in turn, tend to ignore events outside their own bailiwick. Various clocks are ticking away irrespective of whether people want to listen to them. The proliferation clock is an obvious example, and its consequences are predictable. In a similar way, it is only a question of time until it will be accepted that the U.S. got its priorities wrong in the conduct of its foreign policies and the choice of its instruments. There will always be room for diplomacy but in its present form it is largely an eighteenth-century relic which badly needs rethinking and refashioning. The limits of military and economic power have become all too obvious off late. To dismantle the remaining instruments of U.S. foreign policy at this time seems more than a little foolish. Those who failed to accept the importance of public diplomacy will think of various excuses to justify their misjudgment. But this will be of little help, for in this field there is no room for rush programs to make good the neglect of many years. A price will have to be paid: Races that were run, will not be rerun, just because at the time too many people in Washington overslept.

5

Preparing for the Next Century

With the approach of the end of a century, (and *a fortiori* a millenium) apocalyptic thought has been the historical fashion, manifesting itself in theology, philosophy, literature and the arts. During the 1890s books that were (or could have been) entitled "The End of..."(or "The Decline of...") were frequent. There may be no particular reason why these round figures have such an effect. Perhaps it resulted from a too literal interpretation of certain passages in Revelations: *Post mille annos solvetur Satanas*. In all probability it has been quite accidental, but once a certain pattern has been established, it seems to perpetuate itself. The two books reviewed* are mild cases of this fin-de-siècle literature.

Professor Paul Kennedy had been known in the historical profession mainly for his fine work on the period before World War I. In late 1987 the bestselling *Rise and Fall of the Great Powers*, was published. Written in measured, moderate terms this book nevertheless generated a great deal of passion: the declinists embraced it with great enthusiasm as their most learned manifesto, the opposite camp produced a whole literature to refute Kennedy. That empires have risen and declined throughout history can hardly be denied; if it were different we would still live under the sway of the Mongols or Assyrians or all speak Portuguese or Dutch ("Rome fell, Babylon fell, Scarsdale's turn will come"). It is a different question to what extent imperial overstretch had to do with it and excessive military spending, except perhaps in such cases as Napoleon and Hitler; but these were hardly classical empires. These issues should certainly be explored: If the U.S. had spent, say, 3 percent of its GNP in the period after World War II instead of 5 to 7 percent would it be essentially

*Review of Paul Kennedy, *Preparing for the Twenty-First Century* and John Lukacs, *The End of the Twentieth Century and the End of the Modern Age.*

better off today? I doubt it; even in the case of the Soviet Union (which spent four times or more on a per capita basis) it is far from certain that excessive military spending was the single most important factor for the disintegration of its empire.

In *Rise and Fall* Kennedy ranged widely over many countries and historical periods. In his new book he casts his net even wider, dealing with the demographic explosion, global warming, biotech agriculture, air and water pollution, robotics, the globalization of finance, the impact of multinational corporations on developing countries and other such topics. It is in many ways a laudable, perhaps heroic, enterprise to deal with such broad topics in an age of growing specialization among historians and political scientists. But it is also a high-risk venture. No one can be possibly at home equally in all the disciplines covered by Kennedy; ideally it should be written by a committee in which case it would probably be unreadable.

Furthermore, there is no certainty that its conclusions would be any more reliable. For predictions on demographic and technological development are as risky as those on economic and political trends. Yesteryears' comments on America's relative economic decline make curious reading as the German and Japanese economies are in recession, and U.S. industrial production alone among the developed countries shows an annual increase of more than 4 percent. The U.S. unemployment rate is 7.1 percent and falling slightly, those of Germany and Sweden are higher, let alone the other European countries. Perhaps everyone entered a phase of relative decline. Kennedy could have not foreseen this as he did not foresee the impending demise of the Soviet empire in 1988. Perhaps the present trends are as misleading as those of yesteryear, but the question arises—if the immediate future is inscrutable, how reliable are the forecasts concerning the more distant one? How certain can one be as to who will be winning and losing in the years to come?

The issues raised by Kennedy and the dangers invoked are all very real. In fact, there is perhaps an excess of caution in this book, for instance, in describing the woes of U.S. education and health care. But all this has been said many times before. In fact, there is little in this book that attentive readers of the weekly *Economist*, fortified by *World Resources* 1990–91, *World, Population Prospects, Development Report*, and other such statistical handbooks will not have read before, and not just once. Towards the end of this book Kennedy reaches the unstartling conclusion that "as the Cold War fades away we face not a new world order, but a troubled and fractured planet, whose problems deserve the serious attention of politicians and public alike." Is it hopeless? Not quite, it may still be possible for intelligent men and women to lead their societies through the complex task of preparing for the century ahead. But how could they do this if according to Kennedy nothing is certain except that we face innumerable uncertainties: "Interventions could produce their own unforeseen and unintended changes."

Do we know how many developing nations will be able to follow East Asia's growth? No, says Kennedy, it is impossible to tell. Can we be certain that Europe will be better off in the next century? Yes—if it manages to solve its problems. But if it does not resolve the cluster of challenges confronting it, "it will suffer the consequences." Kennedy does go as far as saying that conditions in Africa are likely to stay bad and that the prospects of the former Soviet Union are not rosy either: "The Western democracies might be unwise to assume that the collapse of the 'evil empire' is going to be an unqualified advantage to themselves." Whoever made such assumptions? Or elsewhere: "In the light of the broad global trends discussed in the preceding chapters, we should not be surprised if further internal and regional conflicts break out." And "simply because we do not know the future, it is impossible to say with certainty, whether global trends will lead to terrible disaster or be diverted by astonishing advances in human adaptation." If awards were given for popularizing the uncertainty principle in history, this book would rank high among the contenders.

Professor Kennedy can certainly not be accused of sensationalism: His book has been ridiculed by reviewers for the frequent "on one hand— on the other" and "it remains to be seen" approach and, generally speaking the constant hedging of bets. This is a little unfair, for the only prudent way of writing a book like this is to point to various scenarios. Kennedy was not well served by his publishers who announced that he would tell us who would be the winners and losers in the decades to come. He is a very circumspect man: if the present growth rate in China will continue as in recent years, progress will be assured. But then he reminds us that economic gains might be swallowed up by population growth—which means that all the bets are off.

In the case of India and China the author does make a policy recommendation—the only logical solution (to assist China and India in their race against time) is for the developing nations to help them with capital, technology, and brain power. But this is not a very realistic or helpful suggestion. Even if the issue would figure much higher on the Western and Japanese agendas, the needs greatly exceed the means of the developed countries—especially at a time of recession. Did the author not know this when he made his logical proposal.

Altogether, this book gives the impression as if the original idea came from a publisher rather than an author, and that the latter gradually realized that he faced an impossible mission. The public likes to read books in which either the coming apocalypse or a brilliant future for mankind are outlined with utter conviction. If Toynbee or Spengler or their imitators had sounded their trumpet less certainly, who would have listened to them? Mr. Kennedy's book is sensible on the whole but there are too many platitudes, nor does he know the answers to the questions he poses better than the next man. It may still be of some use in view of stating some cardinal problems and also because of the rich statistical material. But I doubt whether he will be eager to engage once again on a venture of this kind.

John Lukacs, also a history professor, cannot be accused of excessive caution. He is a man of aggressive certainties based on a firmly conservative and religious *Weltanschauung*. A native of Budapest (on which he wrote a very informative book) he is the author of works covering various aspects of twentieth-century history.

In his history of the cold war, a previous book, Lukacs made it clear that he did not like communism, but he disliked the anticommunists even more, and most of all (if I understood him correctly) the Social Democrats, to whom he then thought, the future belonged: Russia like America was moving towards a welfare state. Some fifteen years later this unfortunate thesis was picked up for a while by some misguided Sovietologists. Now he seems to have put his money on nationalism (or national socialism) even though he does not particularly like it. He may be closer to reality this time, at least in the short run.

He writes well and is refreshingly free of academic jargon. His references are not his Hungarian namesake or Marcuse or sundry social scientists, but to Jacques de Rivarol, Jacob Burckhardt, Tocqueville, and Belloc/Chesterton. The eccentricities are sometimes engaging; it would be tedious to have a uniform intellectual spectrum in our historical and political literature. There is, furthermore the occasional insight not found in mainstream academic writing. But too often the idiosyncrasies get out of hand and there is a tendency to make sweeping statements on the basis of flimsy or nonexistent evidence. Thus, in the present book (to give but one example) he builds a whole new theory on the difference between the meaning of *grazhdanin* (in Russian) and citizen (or *citoyen*). *Grazhdanin* (Lukacs claims) means the inhabitants of a state, not a city (as in the West). In the West all civic freedoms had come from the city, in Russia they had not; in any case Russian cities had no walls, there was no border. But the word *grazhdanin* is etymologically derived from *gorod* or *grad* (which means city) and this word, in turn comes of *ograda* (fence). Thus much about the theory; freedom in Russia did not grow in the cities, but nor did it come from the state. Elsewhere he comments on an "excellent conservative journal named *Vekhy*" (which never existed), calls General Vlasov a "Dostoevskyan figure" (which he was no more than, say Molotov or Gromyko), sees the roots of Russian duality (between East and West) to this very day in the history of the Russian Church.

At the Brandenburg Gate Mr. Lukacs meets officers and soldiers of the Russian army selling dark fur caps, army coats and all kind of military medals. The vendors, alas, are gypsies from Romania and Yugoslavia; one would imagine that a native of Budapest would know the difference between a Russian soldier and a gypsy, but perhaps Mr. Lukacs had been away for too long from these parts. From the Berlin gypsies to Johann Strauss's *Gypsy Baron*; the author presents a perfectly accurate description of the operetta, and then—a mighty jump—he argues that Eastern Europe may become the central theater of world history. Vienna and Budapest (he predicts) are on the way to becoming twin cities, like Buda and Pest, divided by the Danube. Assertions of this kind are stretching imagination and credulity beyond permissible limits.

Mr. Lukacs writes with greater authority on France and England than on Russia and Germany. Unfortunately there is not that much to be said at present about France and Britain in the context of world history. "Something new and probably unexpected will emerge in Western Europe during the next few decades. What this will be I do not know." Even the Delphic oracle was less cryptic.

Looking further ahead Lukacs sees the end of the modern age, that is to say, the expansion of Europe, liberalism, humanism, privacy, the age of the book, and so on. He sees many threats to civilization, not least an oppressive democracy, that is to say the tyranny of the majority—"the rule of popularity, often dependent on the lowest of common denominators." He is not entirely pessimistic—apace with the passing of the modern age the respect for its culture and civilization among thinking men and women will continue to grow. And he recalls La Rochefoucauld who has taught us things are never as bad, or as good as they seem, a maxim of which Lukacs' compatriot Theodor Herzl was very fond. Or as Micawber said, perhaps something will turn up.

What is one to make of this curious book? It is a mixture of *aperçus* on world history and politics, and a travelogue (impressions of Budapest restaurants, Berlin department stores, the White House), at times amusing at others boring, sometimes original and interesting, at others absurd and insensitive. Sometime it seems that Evelyn Waugh was the intellectual godfather of this book, an English eccentric (partly phony), funny and exasperating. There is the Waughian rudeness; Lukacs relates how he said in a Budapest restaurant in a loud voice and in the presence of the physicist, that Edward Teller is the Zsa Zsa Gabor of American physics. He must have thought this a witty or profound remark, otherwise he would not have preserved it for posterity. He could be right, but since he is neither movie critic nor nuclear scientist, how would he know? Evelyn Waugh did not write history; for a book entitled *Budapest Revisited* he might have been the right mentor, for the *End of the Twentieth Century and the End of the Modern Age* he was not.

6

The End of the Cold War

The Cold War finally ended as the Soviet Empire collapsed. The Soviet Empire collapsed because of a breakdown in self-confidence on the part of its rulers and the mistaken belief that the Soviet system could be reformed. The crisis of confidence arose for a variety of reasons. The economic system worked badly. The rate of growth from the 1970s on was smaller than in most European countries, let alone the Far East. The supply of goods and services to the population was qualitatively bad and quantitatively insufficient, especially in such vital sectors as housing. The planned economy showed little or no capacity to adjust itself to new trends in technology. Instead, it concentrated on the old and outdated heavy industries, and lagged behind in electronics, chemical products, and information, to give but a few examples. The crisis was aggravated by long-term economic factors such as the degradation of the human condition, the enormous population losses from World War I onwards, including the destruction of the most prosperous peasants and large parts of the intelligentsia. The cost of military spending and of empire also figured in the Soviet decline, the former admittedly far more than the latter. (According to most Western experts, Soviet military spending had been between 8 to 15 percent of the GNP; in fact, as it subsequently appeared, it had been considerably higher.)

The quality of life deteriorated rapidly all over the Soviet Union, alcoholism and crime increased substantially, as did child mortality, and the health of the population and life expectancy palpably declined.

However, there was no economic inevitability about the downfall of the Soviet Union. The system was still workable, people had become accustomed to it, and the national income continued to rise slightly, even under Andropov. The system might have muddled through for another ten years, perhaps even a little longer, and it is just possible that in that period a "Chinese approach" would have attempted economic reform without corresponding political liberalization. However, even if successful, such "controlled reform" under strict supervision from above would probably also have resulted in the breakdown of the empire.

The main causes of the fall are impossible to quantify; they are also rooted in the fact that from the early 1970s onward the mood of the country changed from (relative) optimism to pessimism. This was caused by the ever-growing discrepancy between the official propaganda, which claimed that the country was growing richer and happier all the time, and Soviet reality. The leadership was not only corrupt (which might have been tolerated) but also perceived as inefficient—the gerontocrats became the butt of jokes. The poor (including old-age pensioners) grew poorer, the lot of the rich (the *nomenklatura*) improved in relative as well as absolute terms. The war in Afghanistan became highly unpopular, as it was not quickly brought to a successful conclusion. The Soviet atlas, including Eastern Europe and the countries of "socialist orientation" were considered parasites by many Russians. Moscow's Eastern European empire was a shambles. Romania and Yugoslavia did what they wanted, Hungary pursued a course of reform, followed with distrust in Moscow. The Polish situation was highly unstable and there was the fear that Moscow might have to interfere militarily, as it had done elsewhere in Eastern Europe on past occasions. At the same time nationalist tensions grew inside the Soviet Union. Under Brezhnev a policy of live-pand-let-live had been pursued, but a high price had to be paid. The satraps in Central Asia and the Caucasus were permitted to do what they wanted, provided they paid lip service to the system and its ideology. The exodus from Central Asia of Russians who felt unwelcome began well before Gorbachev. The trend was not towards cultural assimilation but, on the contrary, towards nationalist self-assertion.

Nevertheless, all these and some other negative trends were not necessarily fatal. Setbacks in the foreign political field were bothersome, but there was no acute danger. Eastern Europe was not in a state of open revolt, there still was the fear there that the Soviet army would put down any serious challenge without much difficulty. The quality of life was deteriorating, but there was no political outcry against conditions perceived as intolerable. The dissidents were few and isolated; their message did not reach the masses. Nationalist ferment was growing but it was not yet massive. The security organs were still firmly in control and could have put down local separatist agitation and activities quickly and effectively had they been given orders. An attempt at coordinated action against the center by non-Russian nationalities was unlikely as long as an effective dictatorship was firmly in the saddle.

The general mood was bad and virtually no one, except a few Stalinist veterans, believed any longer in the canons of Marxism-Leninism. But it is a long way from such dissillusionment to the conviction that the apocalypse is at hand—and to concerted political action.

If so, why did the Soviet Union collapse in 1991? Partly, because there was not just one crisis but several, the interaction between various negative trends. To paraphrase a fashionable term, it was a negatively synergistic crisis; each individual trend was feeding on another, augmenting the general crisis. More important yet, some of the rulers, notably those who came to power in 1986–87, believed their own propaganda, namely that their system was deeply rooted, that the levers of power were firmly in their hands (the KGB, the armed forces and the various sections of the party, and the state bureaucracy). Hence their conviction that economic and political reform, needed to cope with the various negative trends, could be controlled. But this was a mistaken belief, and thus it came to pass that the huge edifice collapsed without even having been seriously challenged. The Tsarist, the Ottoman and the Austro-Hungarian empires fell after years of war and major defeats, the Soviet Empire, to the disbelief of the rest of the world, disintegrated without apparently any immediate reason.

The role of accident was very great at the beginning and the end of Soviet history. Without Lenin there would not have been, in all probability, a revolution in 1917, and in this case there might not have been a second chance for the Bolsheviks. While the Soviet system was doomed in the long run, without Gorbachev it would not have collapsed at the time it did.

Attempts to defuse, if not to end altogether, the cold war had been made well before Gorbachev: the Nixon-Kissinger detente was the most spectacular but by no means the first or last such initiative. But it brought no decisive change; in fact, tension between the two superpowers rose precisely before the turning point was reached in 1986–87. There was gloom and doom among critics of American foreign policy in the United States as well as in Europe. Some historians invoked 1914 and the outbreak of the First World War, theologians were talking in apocalyptic terms at mass demonstrations scheduled to save world peace at the very last moment. However, the missiles were deployed in Europe, SDI came under way in the United States, but the horrible consequences predicted by some did not take place. On the contrary, beginning with the Reykjavik Conference (1986) relations between Moscow and the West dramatically improved.

The reasons for the change in the attitude of the new Soviet leadership (Gorbachev and Shevardnadze, his foreign minister) were threefold. They had reached the conclusion that the West had no aggressive designs vis à vis the Soviet Union. They believed that the Soviet Union could not afford yet another ruinous bout in the armament race. (There was no certainty that SRI would work, but in any case it would have involved the Soviet Union in yet another substantial defense outlay.) Lastly, the new Soviet leadership believed that their system could exist without the state-of-siege mentality that had prevailed since Lenin's days. This specific part of Communist doctrine was used to justify the dictatorship, the deprivations and the maintenance of a huge apparatus of terror and propaganda. The first two assumptions were undoubtedly correct, the third was highly dubious. It underrated the centrifugal tendencies in the Soviet empire: once the image of the omnipresent and all powerful enemy disappeared, it became impossible to justify the enormous defense spending and the maintenance of big armed forces and huge defense industries. The leaders also underrated the difficulties involved in the transition to civilian uses of the military-industrial complex, a problem that will face Russia for a long time to come.

In the event, the East European empire collapsed in 1989 as the Brezhnev doctrine was dropped. During the years that followed (1989–93), there was a near-total preoccupation with domestic affairs in Moscow that made an aggressive foreign policy impossible. Foreign policy at the time meant primarily relations with the successor states of the Soviet Union. Moscow agreed to withdraw its troops from Germany and the Baltic and reached various agreements with the West. This meant, to all intents and purposes, the end of the cold war. Russian interests would still be pursued in the neighbouring countries, and this was a potential source of tension and conflict with the West. But such tensions have existed all throughout history.

The end of the cold war came as a great surprise to politicians in the West and the experts alike. "Hawks" in the West were surprised because they had believed that the Soviet threat was immense and that the end of Soviet power was nowhere near. The "doves" were doubly wrong because they had shared the appraisal of enormous Soviet strength and had drawn from it the conclusion that in view of the fact that the Communist powers had reached parity with the West, or even overtaken it, the Soviet Union had to be appeased by farreaching concessions.

How to explain this misjudgement? It was based on the assumption that the breakdown of the wartime alliance in 1945–47 and the outbreak of the cold war were partly or wholly the fault of the West, above all the United States. It was believed that diplomacy had not been given a fair chance to settle the dispute with the Soviet Union. Soviet demands were not unreasonable: following its experience in World War II it was only natural that Moscow regarded East Europe and the Balkans as its *cordon sanitaire*. If in the course of establishing its sphere of influence it imposed its political system on Eastern Europe, this was regrettable but had to be accepted in the interest of world peace. The Soviet system was basically conservative, it had no interest in the export of revolution. Thus Soviet policy was essentially peaceful or at least not aggressive. Stalin's crudity and mistakes had played into the hands of American hawks who were out to have a confrontation, aggressively promoting a policy of the open door. This and the hysterical fear of Communism, utterly divorced from reality, were the mainsprings of U.S. strategy, not the alleged battle between freedom and enslavement. Seen in this light, the history of the postwar era, particularly after Stalin's death, but even earlier on (Stalin's offer on Germany in 1952), was a chain of opportunities missed by the cold warriors in Washington and the other Western capitals. Eventually the military-industrial complex had developed a vested interest in the perpetuation of the cold war.

This appraisal was wrong in all essential points. It was true that Soviet policy was essentially conservative and the export of revolution was not actively pursued if there was a major risk involved. There were exceptions, such as the unleashing of the Korean War and the war in Afghanistan. But the expansion of the Soviet sphere of influence was still pursued and it is by no means certain that the Soviet leadership would have shown restraint but for the presence of major Western military deterrents. It is possible that the cold war could have ended earlier, but only if the West had made far-reaching concessions that would have helped to consolidate the hold of Soviet power. However, in the final analysis, the whole system was based on the need of an outside threat to justify its very existence. But for the existence of this threat, there was no justification for the dictatorship. While Soviet policy was not bent on relentless expansion, it would have been foolish on the part of the West to lead it into temptation by showing weakness or by confusing signals (which had, *inter alia*, caused the war in Korea). After the disintegration of the Soviet Union and East Germany, documents were uncovered according to which detailed blueprints existed for offensives into Central and Western Europe and the occupation of these areas. It could be argued that military action against NATO was quite unlikely, but it cannot be claimed that the idea never crossed the minds of Communist strategic planners.

It is difficult to generalize about revisionist thought on the cold war in the West, because there were at least three major varieties of this school, and, while all of them were wrong, some of them were more wrong than others. Furthermore, revisionist attitudes changed with time. Since the 1970s, it has been the fashion to emphasize Soviet strength—the Soviet camp was a military giant (Richard Barnet), Washington had no alternative but to compromise. Frightening scenarios abounded—with Soviet submarines and surface ships armed with cruise missiles off the American coast. Seen in this perspective, the world was moving away from capitalist democracy, communism was growing stronger not only in the third world but also in Europe (the rise of Eurocommunism). In these circumstances, it seemed almost suicidal to make the promotion of democratic institutions and human rights the cornerstone of U.S. foreign policy. It was ridiculous to assume that the Soviet system faced a crisis—the Soviet people and those of other Communist countries were reasonably happy with their lot and supported their governments. This, by and large, was the revisionist credo up to about 1980. As doubts appeared in the West with regard to Soviet strength in the following decade, a growing number of voices claimed that the Communist leaders felt besieged and that for this reason it was wrong to drive them into a corner. As the cold war ended, there was yet another sharp turn in the argumentation of the revisionists. It was now claimed that the Soviet "threat" had been mythical all along. Western hawks had misled public opinion, magnifying a nonexisting danger. The Soviet Union had not only been peaceful but very weak; in brief, hundreds of billions had been spent without any need.

Some Western critics were extreme, others more moderate in their approach. The former opposed Western (especially) American foreign policy *tout court*, because of its rapacious, aggressive, pathologically anticommunist character. Such views could be found not only among staunch antiAmericanists in Europe, but also inside the United States, particularly at the time of and after the Vietnam War. If America had been wrong in Vietnam, it must have been wrong elsewhere too. However, such views were not widely held among experts, and they had little support outside the universities and some churches.

More frequent and more influential were the moderate revisionists, who put less stress on American villainy and more on misunderstandings: Western leaders and their advisers tended to misunderstand Soviet motives. Consequently, there was a constant spiral of escalation, hardline Western politicians were providing indirect maintenance to the hawks in the Kremlin—and vice-versa. As Soviet foreign policy became more aggressive in Afghanistan and elsewhere in the late 1970s, it became the fashion among the moderate revisionists to apportion blame more or less evenly. Neither side could bear sole responsibility for the outbreak of the cold war, both sides had committed grievous mistakes. A postrevisionist school appeared on the Western scene; one of their leading representatives, John Gaddis, wrote that the idea of freedom proved more durable than the practice of authoritarianism, and as a consequence the cold war ended. The same author also noted that "many of us had become too sophisticated to see...that the cold war really was about the imposition of autocracy and the denial of freedom." "Sophistication" is probably not the most fitting term: far more important was the fact that many of the Western cold war critics were diplomatic historians specializing in American foreign policy without much knowledge of things Soviet. They were at sea when dealing with the mainsprings of Soviet domestic policy, communist doctrine and its impact on foreign policy. They saw the Soviet Union more or less in the same light as the United States or other Western democracies; such parochialism ("mirror imaging") was bound to lead to mistaken assessments concerning the character and the aims of non-Western regimes. With the break-up of the Soviet Union and the end of the cold war, this school of thought acknowledged that its earlier appraisal had been mistaken. Arthur Schlesinger, to give but one example, who once believed that there had been an "international conspiracy of hardliners...in a weird lockstep marching the rest of us down the road to extinction", concluded a few years later, that the proponents of liberal society had been right: "After seventy years of trial, Communism turned out (by the confession of its own leaders) to be an economic, political and moral disaster."

Such admissions could not be expected from those revisionists who had opposed Western policy in the cold war era for ideological reasons. They regarded the Soviet collapse as a disaster, they felt as if a horse on which they had gambled for a long time had stumbled and not finished the course. They claimed that America had lost the cold war as much as Russia, because it had been economically ruined and suffered political and moral exhaustion as the result of the armaments race. The real winners had been Germany and Japan. Others, on the contrary, claimed that America had won the cold war but that this was a major calamity, because as a result America (and the West in general) had become too strong and could dictate to others, whereas in the past the Soviet Union had always acted as a counterweight and restraining influence. These arguments can hardly be taken very seriously—neither had the West lost the cold war nor had it become overwhelmingly strong. It is no surprise that some critics of Western policy during the cold war era should be reluctant to admit their errors of judgment as the Soviet Union collapsed and the cold war ended. Such admission of error is painful and much against the human grain. Hence the emergence of a new literature trying to prove that their arguments (or at least some of them) had been right—perhaps the West was in decline after all, perhaps there would be a second coming of Soviet power (or something resembling it) at some future date? But this is, at best, *Zukunftsmusik*. It is quite likely that Russia and some other former Soviet republics and Eastern bloc countries will not copy Western examples in their economic development and internal politics. It is equally likely that there will be future conflicts between a new Russia, still a great power, and the West. But all this belongs to a post-cold war era, different in most essential respects from the historical period under discussion.

Following the break-up of the Soviet Union and the end of the cold war, a great many new sources have come to light, especially in the Eastern capitals, and there has been a rethinking of this whole period on the part of Russian public figures and historians. Such rethinking does not, of course, extend to neocommunists and those of the extreme right, who continue to view the West as Russia's eternal enemy. As they see it, the cold war was a mere episode in the age-old campaign of the Russophobes to do as much harm as possible to Russian interests. And the cold war ended, not because of Russian weakness, but because traitors and fifth columnists, agents of the West in the Kremlin, conspired to surrender needlessly all the conquests made in the Second World War—and even accept the disintegration of the Union.

Soviet historians could not make a significant contribution to the cold war debate before *glasnost*, firstly because of the official party line, which made no provisions for deviations whatsoever, secondly because they had no access to their own archives. This changed after 1988–89, and while few Russian historians have reached the conclusion that the West was always right, and Moscow always the guilty party, they have changed their positions on the beginnings as well as on the end of the cold war, on the origins of the Korean War, on Cuba and Berlin, on Angola and Afghanistan. In all these cases, the Soviet leadership was ready to risk (local) war because it thought that there were few risks of determined Western resistance. Former leading Soviet foreign policymakers such as Falin, Bessmertnykh, and Chernayev, have concluded that a Western policy of concession would not have brought the end of the cold war, whereas the "position of strength" strategy, much maligned at the time, contributed to changing Soviet arms policy and ending the cold war. All other considerations apart, the Soviet Union could no longer afford to compete in the armament race.

Such views, needless to say, were totally at variance with the opinions of Western revisionists in earlier years. The details of cold war history and its end are bound to be studied and reassessed for many years to come in West and East. But as far as the broad outlines are concerned, a new consensus is in the making in view of the facts that have come to light in recent years.

Part II

The Dawn of a New Era

7

Post-Fascism, Post-Communism

As the age of fascism and communism appears to recede to the past, it should be possible to look back with greater detachment and reach a deeper level of understanding. But for the time being this is little more than a noble dream. The new dawn of freedom, to begin with seems as yet uncertain; political movements have arisen in various parts of the world, which in some essential respects share basic features with fascism. The inspiration may be religious-radical in some cases, ultranationalist in others. Fifty years ago it was generally accepted that fascism was an exclusively European affair and this was by and large true. Being a modern phenomenon, fascism was unthinkable in premodern societies, it was possible only on a certain level of economic, social, and technological development. Fascism beyond Europe was called "false fascism," which was true at the time but is no longer correct with regard to the more advanced parts of the third world. The demise of communism, has also been less than total, the *nomenklatura* in most of these countries had a soft landing. The new rulers are no longer communists but neither are they social democrats or liberals or conservatives. If the general situation deteriorates all kinds of extremist regimes might emerge.

Whether to call the new extremists of the right neofascists or postfascists is a moot point. Other terms have been suggested including "right-wing radicalism," "nationalist populism," "radical or right-wing populism," right wing extremes," "revolutionary nationalism," but these are no more satisfactory. The debate about labels will go on for a long time, it is of interest mainly to perfectionist taxonomists. Fascism resembles pornography, it is difficult, frequently impossible to define in an operational, legally valid sense. Those with a little experience know it when they see it.

These developments on the political scene should not necessarily affect our assessment of the past, and it is sometimes argued that historians
and political scientists have made huge progress over the last decades
analyzing fascism and communism. On the factual level and concerning
the study of specific aspects this is certainly true, but does it apply to
interpretation?[1] There is the legacy of the past: It is unthinkable that
German nationalists (such as, say Ernst Nolte and Rainer Zittelmann)
will ever reach agreement with Jewish historians (such as Saul Friedländer
and D. Diner) about the place of the Holocaust in history. Those who
believe that historical truth is easier to attain from a point of view of
equidistant from the "extremes" have put themselves in a safer position,
whether they are closer to historical truth is by no means certain.

Among the literature on Nazism in recent years there is the influential
thesis of a leading German historian that everything considered, Hitler
was a weak dictator and that much of the time chaos prevailed under the
surface of the Third Reich. (The same thesis, was put forward some
years ago with regard to Stalin). A group of younger German historians
including Susanne Heim and Goetz Aly attribute the final solution to the
ambitious planning of the technocrats to establish a new order in Eastern
Europe. The Jews in other words were killed not because of anti-semitism
but because of the desire of the planners to rationalize industrial production, to remove the premodern sectors, and to reduce overpopulation. In
a more recent work (*Endloesung*, 1995) widely hailed in Germany, Aly
slightly modifies his views inasmuch as he considers the dynamic of the
Nazi resettlement policy merely one of several factors which led to the
mass murder. But he still believes that Himmler, Heydrich, Eichmann, et
al. somehow manoeuvred themselves into a cul de sac, that there had
never been an order by Hitler to exterminate the Jews (even though in a
famous speech in 1943 Himmler said that there had been such an order),
and that the Jews were killed if not as the result of a series of accidents,
in consequence of some imperfect blueprints made by not very farsighted
planners. This view of the final solution as a genuinely rational concern,
social and economic, is shared by Zygmunt Bauman, a British professor
of Polish origin. Arno Mayer a Princeton professor has put forward a
different theory according to which Hitler had the Jews killed mainly
because he hated the communists so much. A whole legion of social
historians of the left and the right has focused its research on Nazism as
a modernizing factor. The state of affairs is further confounded because

the arguments of the revisionists of the left are picked up by the revision-ists of the extreme right, so that in the end it is exceedingly difficult to establish with any certainty who claims what and from what ideological vantage point. Broadly speaking, the right wants to "historicize" the Holocaust, that is to say to put it into a wider historical perspective.

This means equating the mass murder of World War II with the civil war in Bosnia or perhaps in Somalia, and to demand an end to "the Auschwitz propaganda" which in the words of a recent writer "has no purpose other than inculcate a bad conscience among the Germans." According to this school of thought, bringing up Auschwitz except in a footnote is tantamount to the suppression of freedom of thought. And the prison doctor treating Knut Hamsun, though a democrat, behaved, in principle, not differently from the way the Auschwitz doctors did. (Hamsun, the great Norwegian writer, was also a collaborator with the German occupants and therefore arrested.[2] An interesting argument though it omits the fact that Hamsun was released from prison after a short while whereas the patients of the Nazi doctors were less fortu-nate. It may be true on the level of abstraction that as, Harvard histo-rian Charles Maier has written, historicization need not necessarily lead to apology, but in actual fact it usually does.

The revisionists of the left, on the other hand, want to "sociologize" the mass murder. They pay little attention to ideological (and even politi-cal) considerations and concentrate on socioeconomic factors. The net result of these approaches, while not identical, is very similar.

These are by no means fringe views, and very often they are given a sympathetic hearing by mainstream historians. They are welcome as novel interpretations that should be given serious attention and further explored, even though it may appear in the end that the original claims were some-what exaggerated. A majority of historians in Germany and elsewhere now probably belongs to the "historicizers": there are notable exceptions such as German liberals of the older generation such as Karl Dietrich Bracher and Eberhard Jaeckel.

About three-quarters of the population of Germany wants a line to be drawn below the Nazi past and German historians do not live in a politi-cal vacuum. The figures for Britain and America may be less dramatic, but there too other historical concerns are taking over and academic fash-ion calls for new historical and sociological perspectives on Nazism. Historians are more and more interested in social history, and the history of everyday life for the great majority was perfectly normal, except that the whole enterprise ended in disaster. The great majority were not Jewish, nor anti-Nazi and they enjoyed themselves. Seen in this light "historicization" and "sociologization" are indeed inevitable. Only Jewish historians, overtaken by these developments find it difficult to draw a line under the extinction of one-third of their people and they will be criticized for being unforgiving and unyielding.

There was, of course, more to Nazism than Auschwitz, and it is certainly true that at the bottom of some of the revisionist arguments there is usually some rational kernel. The argument about chaos in the Third Reich and Hitler's weakness is an obvious example. It is perfectly true that Hitler (and Stalin) did not personally take every decision, which was physically impossible. On issues that were not central to his beliefs Hitler would prevaricate or change his opinions from one day to the next. He was not omnipotent, on some issues he left the initiative to others especially after the outbreak of the war. In the meantime his aides were scheming against each other, quarrelling and fighting for influence. At times Hitler acted as a reluctant arbiter, at others he did not want to be bothered at all. But it is ridiculous to imagine that he presided over a bureaucratic chaos, leaving initiatives to his underlings, playing them out against each other.

Whether an individual is strong or weak, tall or short, clever or stupid, is a relative statement, it depends on the yardstick used. Compared with Orwell's *1984*, Nazi Germany (and, *a fortiori* fascist Italy) were in a permanent state of anarchy. Compared with other systems known in history they were effective dictstorships. It is astonishing all things considered, how much Hitler interfered and to what extent he was in control. A random look at the instructions emanating from his chancery shows that he gave orders that Wilhelm Furtwängler, the famous conductor should not participate in the Salzburg festival of 1938, that residents of Munich should be permitted to drink "strong beer," opposing a planned reduction in the alcohol content. He ordered that a public statue on the Rhine should be illuminated at night; that the iron bars on the windows of a museum in Munich should not be painted black but bronze-gold; that his aides should wear rubber soles; that Gerhardinger, an obscure painter should not be mentioned in the media; that prominent foreign visitors should not be fed tinned mushrooms because of the danger of poisoning—this in May 1942!; that foreigners should be given no angling permits; that the monthly maximum for renting a garage should be seven marks all over Germany. He wanted to know how many violins the Vienna Philharmonic had in 1942 and how much artificial honey was produced in Germany; he ordered that Schiller's *Wilhelm Tell* should no longer be performed (June 1941) and that male personnel should no longer serve in restaurants. He decided, among many other things that the physicist Heinrich Hertz, a half Jew, should not become an unperson and that the term *Kilohertz* should also be used in future.

It could well be that Hitler's instructions concerning angling permits for foreigners were occasionally disregarded on the local level, and that in some places a rent higher than seven marks was taken for garage rentals. And it is, of course, also true that on many subjects there were no instructions at all. However, there is overwhelming evidence that on the issues close to his heart, for instance the destruction of his political enemies at home, the murder of the Jews, rearmament, foreign policy and the conduct of the war, power was concentrated in his hands and no one could possibly deviate for any length of time from the guidelines set by him. And if Hitler did not take certain important decisions, all that matters is that he could have taken them and would have been obeyed.

The breakdown of the Soviet Union had a certain impact on the field of Soviet studies. It led (within modest limits) to a spring cleaning, causing a rethinking of earlier approaches on the communist regime that were clearly wrong. Students of fascism, on the other hand, have suffered no such trauma. If the disappearance of the DDR had any impact, it was that of reinforcing the nationalist arguments.

Neither right nor left see any urgent need to reconsider their theses about subjects such as Nazi rationalization and modernization and it would be unrealistic to expect a quick change in this respect.

* * *

Of the postmortems on communism, François Furet's *Le passé d'une illusion* (1994) an essay (of more than 500 pages) on the communist idea in the twentieth century is the most noteworthy so far and has attracted much attention well beyond France. Furet one of the great historians of our time teaches both at the Sorbonne and in Chicago; he is known for his pioneering work on the French revolution which has greatly contributed to a reassessment of that event (or series of events) in our age. Together with Denis Richet, Pierre Nora, and others he frontally assaulted (and defeated) the Jacobinian orthodoxy that dominated French historiography for almost a century. He also showed how this treatment of the French Revolution (including the terror) influenced the reception of the Russian Revolution (including the purges and the terror.) His new book contains much of great interest about communism and fellow travellers in France between the two world wars and after. Furet writes in part from the vantage point of an insider; he was a member of the Communist party from 1949–1956. He says that he now looks at his blindness "*sans indulgence mais sans acrimonie.*" Much of the book seems to me eminently sensible, some is brilliant. I shall concentrate in the following on my disagreements.

The central part of the book is devoted to the relationship between communism, fascism, and antifascism, and it is in this context that questions and doubts arise. Is it really true that the European left (as Furet writes) was antifascist but not antitotalitarian? (p. 502). This was almost correct with regard to France after the Second World War, what with the predominance of Sartre, Merleau-Ponty, and their like. But France is not quite Europe, even though French intellectuals sometimes tend to think so. But even in France in the 1930s when fascism was the central political issue few people on the left outside the Communist party had any sympathy for Stalinism. The most determined resistance and the most systematic intellectual confrontation with totalitarianism came precisely from the democratic left. Virtually all theoretical thinking about totalitarianism came from the German and also the Russian democratic emigration. The former prominently figures in Furet's book, but not the latter. The fault is not Furet's; the importance of Russian emigre thinking with regard to the origins of the "totalitarianism" concept has been generally ignored so far, even though *Sovremennye Zapiski* (the Paris published main literary-political journal) offers much of interest, as do the journals of the Mensheviks, the S.R.s and the essays of G. Fedotov.

There is a tendency in Furet's book to equate communism and fascism; having devoted years of my life to pointing out common origins and features between these two movements and systems, I find myself in the unaccustomed role of disagreeing with what seems to me simplification. It is fully understandable if a Soviet writer such as Vasilli Grossman (1905–1964) the author of *Life and Fate* whom Furet quotes at length, was struck by the common features between Stalinism and Hitlerism. Grossman was a writer of powerful novels, he lived under a totalitarian regime in which knowledge about the Nazi and fascist systems was systematically suppressed. When confronting Nazism, the shock of recognition in his case, and that of some contemporaries, was almost blinding. Furet is not a novelist but he still argues that Mussolini and Hitler were deeply influenced by Lenin and Stalin, and that as Waldemar Gurian (on whom more below) did put it, Hitler accomplished better than Stalin Lenin's totalitarian promise, that in Nazi Germany the most perfect Bolshevik state was established.

Furet's star witness is Hermann Rauschning, his three most important conceptualizers and interpreters are Hannah Arendt, Ernst Nolte and again Waldemar Gurian. Rauschning figures even more prominently in Richard Pipes recent *Russia Under the Bolshevik Regime* in a similar capacity. He was a German conservative from Poland who joined the Nazi party and at one time became head of the (Nazi-dominated) Danzig (Gdansk) local parliament. When he discovered that Hitler was not a conservative at heart he defected (in 1936) and emigrated. His book, *The Revolution of Nihilism* (1938), made him known, and his next book, *Conversations with Hitler* (1939), became an international bestseller. It consists of alleged Hitler quotations such as "National Socialism is what Marxism might have been if it could have broken its absurd and artificial ties with a democratic order," and "I have learned a great deal from Marxism."

Rauschning's second book is well written, interesting and at times prophetic. But it is not a primary source; it has been known for a long time that these were not conversations with Hitler, (the French title was even more emphatic *Hitler ma dit...*) whom Rauschning seldom saw, and with whom he did not talk alone (for all we know) for more than a few minutes. Rauschning was neither Boswell nor Eckermann, this was an essay in anti-Hitlerian propaganda, and as such perfectly legitimate, and apparently also an endeavor to improve Rauschning's finances. He later emigrated to America and with his earnings he bought a farm. Rauschning's books are still of considerable interest as the views of a contemporary observer. However, they are no more a primary source for Hitler's *obiter dicta* or innermost thoughts than Mr. Furet's book or my article.

Next Hannah Arendt's *Origins of Totalitarianism*, in Furet's words the most important intellectual contribution to the analysis of communism. Hannah Arendt's work, published in 1951, was certainly the most influential book at the time on this subject, linking the Nazi and communist phenomenon as "essentially identical." But Hannah Arendt does not deal with communism except in passing, the book has much to say about Captain Dreyfus and Cecil Rhodes but hardly anything about Lenin. She was aware that the Marxist-Soviet dimension of the book was missing and intended to write this part in 1952–53 but somehow (as her biographer reports) never did. What she has to say about the Soviet Union was exaggerated—she glosses over the differences between Nazi Germany and the Soviet Union. She argues, for instance, that Hitler never intended to defend the "West" against Bolshevism—which is perfectly correct. But she then continues that he always remained ready to join "the Reds" for the destruction of the West, even in the middle of the struggle against Soviet Russia which is not true. Her convictions in this respect were emphatic but not apparently very deep. In subsequent editions of the book she retreated from her earlier exaggeration to new opposite ones. By 1957–58 she had reached the conclusion that ever since Stalin's death the Soviet Union had engaged in "detotalitarianization" which was only partly correct. ("The clearest sign that the Soviet Union can no longer be called totalitarianism in the strict sense of the term is, of course, the amazingly swift and rich recovery of the arts in the last decade—1965"). This is a breathtaking reversal of her earlier views with which neither Mr. Furet nor other serious students would agree. And what does all this leave of Mrs. Arendt's original thesis about the fundamentally new phenomenon ("the horrible originality of totalitarianism") based on depersonalization, the "mob," loneliness, the emergence of mass society, of remaking reality and changing man? Seen in this light Stalinism was merely the old-fashioned tyranny of one man; with the death of the dictator, totalitarianism seems to have evaporated.

Seen in retrospect, the value of Arendt's book was not in startling new insights on the Soviet Union (or indeed on Nazi Germany) but in having started the discussion of totalitarianism which has not ended to this day.

* * *

The reception of Hannah Arendt's book and its impact is covered in detail in a recent, wide-ranging study on the totalitarian debate, Abbot Gleason's *Totalitarianism* (1995, chapter 6). A professor at Brown University, he belongs to the generation that rebelled against the "Manichean world view" of his father, a well-known historian and (temporarily) senior official in the CIA. Over the years the younger Gleason came to realize that the cold warriors were not all wrong; in retrospect he is glad "that Stalin's enemies on our side were ideologically well armed" and he notes in retrospect that "most people on the Left have been highly resistant until recently to any suggestion that the classification of the Soviet Union as totalitarian is more than a conservative canard."

Yet with all the good will to be fair to all sides, old prejudices die hard and as a result the "cold warriors" of yesterday are often described as shrill, self-serving, fanatical, and laughable, whereas their opponents, even if wrong, seem to have behaved in a measured, sober, and statesmanlike way.

There is, for instance, a reference to the brilliant Peter Ludz, a leading West German student of East German affairs. The unsuspecting reader cannot possibly know that it was more owing to his influence than to any other that the study of East Germany took a wrong turn some twenty-five years ago. The achievements and the rootedness of the East German regime were grossly exaggerated, and as a result the downfall of the DDR came as a total surprise to this school of students of East Germany.

Does Gleason's book then bear out Furet's strictures about the lack of antitotalitarian enthusiasm on the Left? Only up to a point, for of the "cold warriors" mentioned in Gleason's book many were neither conservative nor neoconservative; this is simply the old conditioned reflex, to classify as such the more outspoken critics of Soviet policies. But George Orwell was not conservative nor was the AFL-CIO nor was Norman Thomas, even though he wrote in 1948 that "Communism, whatever it was originally is today Red fascism." One could add easily many more names to this list.

* * *

Hannah Arendt's guru on Communism and the Soviet Union in the early days was Waldemar Gurian, a Notre Dame professor, born in St. Petersburg of Jewish parents, educated in Germany, and converted to Catholicism. He died in 1954 and Hannah Arendt wrote a moving memoir, reprinted in *Men in Dark Times*. Reviewing Gurian's *Bolshevism* in the *Partisan Review* in 1953, Hannah Arendt called it the "best analytical history of Bolshevism." Gurian was very knowledgeable on Russian literature and history, he followed Soviet and emigre publications and wrote about Russian affairs throughout his life. A deeply conservative thinker, a pupil of Max Scheler and Carl Schmitt, he was among the pioneers of the comparative study of "Red" and "Brown" Bolshevism. But he would not quite equate them. He conceded the "divergent contents" of National Socialist and Bolshevik doctrines, but maintained that these were less important than the totalitarian structures the regimes had in common.

These arguments involved Gurian in certain difficulties. Was it really possible to "take over and imitate Bolshevik methods without accepting the contents of Marxism-Leninism?" Could one maintain at one and the same time that Nazism and Bolshevism were nihilist—and that they were secular religions and that, at least, in the case of Bolshevism, ideology was of great importance? How great is the attraction of a nihilist religion?

At the distance of four decades, and with benefit of hindsight it is easy to point to the weaknesses of such interpretations; Hitlerism and Stalinism were unprecedented phenomena, it was difficult to generalize. Events were changing rapidly and it would have been a near miracle if contemporaries had presented instant explanations that were correct in all essential points.

Hannah Arendt, for instance, wrote in 1948 that without concentration camps, without the undefined fear they inspire and the very well-defined training they offer in totalitarian domination, a totalitarian state could neither inspire fanaticism nor maintain a whole people in complete apathy. (*Partisan Review*, 7, 1948). But there were no such camps in China, in Eastern Europe, or in Italy, and the number of inmates in the German concentration camps in the winter of 1936–37 was less than 10,000. But the German regime was still totalitarian.

Lastly, Ernst Nolte. The German philosopher of international fame has always been primarily interested in fascist ideology rather than the reality of Nazism. He has given vent over thirty years to a great many ideas about the war guilt of the Allies, about the Jews and Zionism, about "transcendence," about the fascist epoch being over. He has surveyed the interpretations of fascism over the ages and has written on fascist parties that did not come to power. But he acquired fame not for these valuable studies but for the treatises in which he tried to demonstrate that neither fascism nor genocide were unique. This, to a large extent, caused the famous *Historikerstreit* in the 1980s and generated many attacks from outside Germany. More recently Nolte has received substantial support in his own country from a younger generation of writers who accepted his nationalist writings as a liberating act.

Furet thinks highly of Nolte's work ("one of the most profound of the last half century") though he regrets Nolte's "exaggeration" on Jewish subjects. We shall leave aside Nolte's Jewish *obiter dicta* they are not relevant in the present context. What remains are Nolte's theses on the relationship between Bolshevism and Nazism (and fascism in general). They can be summarized as follows: Nazism was a reply, a justified reaction to Bolshevism. Asiatic barbarism was imported to Germany from the East: the party discipline, the Gulag, the purges, the terror. Nazi violence was almost always preventive, the Nazi policy of extermination in the East was a copy of the Bolshevik extermination of the kulaks and other class enemies, Gestapo methods were a copy of the GPU, the Russian political police. There was a real threat of a Communist takeover in Germany in 1932–33, and later in Europe, of which Hitler was mortally afraid. Hence Hitler's defensive policy of forestalling the Bolsheviks in 1941. Seen in this light Hitler and also Mussolini appear as (reluctant) pupils or at least imitators of Lenin and Stalin. Given the realities of world affairs, did they have any alternative but to combat Asian barbarism by the same atrocious means?

It is intelligible that views of this kind should be voiced by a German nationalist eager to reduce Nazi and German responsibility for the crimes committed in peace and war. It is less obvious why anyone not belonging to this category should accept such versions (or perversions) of history.[3]

What is the evidence for the Nazis' (and the fascists') mortal fear of Soviet communism and their apprenticeship at the knees of Lenin and Stalin? There was a limited Russian impact in the very early days on the Nazi leaders when refugees from Russia brought the *Protocols of the Elders of Zion* to Germany; these gurus were not however communists but belonged to the extreme right. Readers will look in vain for any mentioning of Lenin in Hitler's *Mein Kampf*. Marxism does appear a few times, but Hitler makes it clear that he refers to the Social Democrats, not the communists.

There is no evidence that Hitler and the other Nazi leaders spent sleepless nights because of fear of communism and the ease with which they destroyed the KPD in 1933 justified their appraisal. In a few weeks nothing was left of the strongest and most faithful Communist party outside the Soviet Union. As for Mussolini he repeatedly ridiculed the idea that there had been a danger of a communist takeover at the time of the "March on Rome." Up to the outbreak of the Second World War, the Italian radio magazines featured the programs of Radio Moscow, which also tends to show that the fascists cannot have been very concerned about Soviet propaganda.

There were, of course, anticommunist speeches by Hitler and Goebbels, much anti-Soviet literature was published, but this has never been in doubt. The decisive issue is that Hitler went to war in 1939 not against the alleged *Weltfeind* (global enemy) but against Britain and France and he declared war in 1941 against the U.S. without any good reason from his point of view instead of concentrating all efforts against the Soviet Union.

Nolte's sources are curious, his star witness is Zinoviev, the Bolshevik leader who allegedly wrote on September 17, 1918 that "we must attract to our ranks 90 million Russians out of 100 million citizens, the rest should be destroyed." Zinoviev was a hysterical loudmouth; as a politician he was never taken very seriously. The statement, which allegedly appeared in a provincial newspaper (*Severnaya Kommuna*), has been quoted endlessly for many years by the Russian extreme right. I never met anyone who actually saw the original. But if one assumes for argument's sake that it does exist, what would it prove? Outrageous and bloodthirsty statements have been made at all times by individuals.

Another favorite Nolte source is Alexandra (Alia) Rachmanova, a Russian emigre of 1917 vintage. As a boy in Germany, I used to read her enormously popular documentary novels, published in installments in illustrated weeklies with titles such as *Als Milchfrau in Ottakring* (A Milkmaid in Working-Class Vienna) and *Tragödie einer Liebe*. There is nothing essentially wrong with *Trivial Literatur* as historical source material. But neither should one regard doubtful Zinoviev quotations and the likes of Mrs. Rachmanova as sufficient factual bases for sweeping generalizations. In brief, Hitler and Mussolini were not the disciples of Lenin and Stalin. They showed not the slightest interest in either Communist ideology or Soviet practice. They realized much earlier than Stalin did the uses of nationalism to mobilize the masses. They did not need Stalin to understand that all political parties but their own should be dissolved. The Gestapo and OVRA owe nothing to GPU inspiration or methods. Information about the Russian labor camps on a large scale was received in Germany well after the Nazi concentration camps were established. Goebbels was impressed by Eisenstein's *Battleship Potemkin*, but there never was a Nazi film on similar lines. German academic research on the Soviet Union led in the world before 1933; when the Nazis came to power they closed down much of it and dismissed leading specialists—they simply had no interest in the subject. The picture drawn about Nazi fear and trembling before Soviet bestialities and communist fanaticism is grossly exaggerated. The Nazis thought they would defeat the Soviet Union as easily as they had the German Communist party in 1933. Hitler and Goebbels did use the "Bolshevik danger" to frighten the German capitalists, and they regarded the Soviet Union as their enemy, but all this is not exactly a sensational revelation.

* * *

Bolshevism was not "better" than fascism but in certain important respects it was different. In the Soviet Union as in Nazi Germany and Fascist Italy terror and propaganda played a central role, there was a monopolistic state party in all three countries, there were many similarities which were far from skin deep. All three, to different degrees, belonged to the modern, totalitarian species of tyranny. The differences between them were conditioned by history, ideology, social and cultural traditions.

Furet is absolutely right in pointing to the common features of the totalitarian regimes, and those who dismissed them (and still continue to do so) were and are mistaken. In the circumstances, is it not pedantic to quibble about the extent of the communalities; a little more or a little less, does it really matter? It is a discussion that has been going on for sixty years and may go on at least for another sixty. It would matter little if we could take it for granted that fascism and communism are a thing of the past.

But neither fascism nor communism are quite dead; they may come back in unfamiliar guise. Rauschning says that Hitler told him in 1934 that while Nazism would never become communist, the Bolsheviks would gradually turn national socialist. Whatever the origin of this comment, Rauschning or the *Führer* himself, it was a remarkably astute observation. As we approach the end of the century a convergence of fascism and communism seems quite probable. What was (erroneously) stated in the past about "Red" and "Brown" Bolshevism or (or Red and Brown fascism) may, paradoxically come true in the future.

There is reason to assume that we shall be spared a second coming of Stalinism and Hitlerism. But the impulses that gave rise to fascism and communism have by no means disappeared and the so called "objective conditions" are auspicious for the rise of a new synthesis of populism and nationalism. The weaknesses of Western societies are known and need not be reiterated in detail—the lack of cohesion in society, social changes making for ferment and uncertainty. With the weakening of the center, ethnic separatism flourishes, individuals and group interests become stronger than the common bonds. For reasons unknown, apocalyptic fears tend to grow towards the end of a century, and *a fortiori* a millenium.[4] Having shown their inefficiency there is the call to replace political parties by citizens' initiatives, perhaps with an occasional plebiscite—"direct" rather than representative democracy. Slogans stressing law and order and strong leadership become popular.

The populists advocate a "third way" between capitalism and communism, the inspiration could be either nationalist or religious-fundamentalist or a mixture of the two. Old fashioned racialism is out as much as the cult of the *Führer*, but so is proletarian internationalism and Marxist doctrine. Communists and fascists are aware that they have to shed some of their cherished beliefs if they want to make a comeback anywhere in this world. And they also realize that they have to join forces. Not everyone on the extreme left (and right) will agree to collaborate with their erstwhile enemies. But the majority seems to be ready for such an alliance against the common enemy—the democrats, the liberals, the "West." Those on the left and the right unwilling to make such sacrifice will be reduced to sectarian insignificance.

Despite the Italian MSI, despite Le Pen and Haider a fascist revival in democratic Europe seems less likely than in Eastern Europe and the Middle East and South Asia. The ultra-nationalist passions in Europe are spent, what kind of fascism is this without fanaticism, without violence in the streets, torchlight parades, remilitarization and wars of conquest? A second coming cannot be ruled out but it would be a tame "defensive" fascism and the old labels would no longer fit. Today's European fascists or parafascists no longer wish to spend their money on big armies but want to keep out immigrants. Nor do they want empires, at most a "fortress Europe."

Chances are better in Eastern Europe and the former Soviet Union where a "red-brown" alliance of ultrapatriots and communists has in fact come into existence. Prospects are best in the Middle East and North Africa, and also elsewhere in what was once called the third world.

There fanatics can still be mobilized with much greater ease; 30,000 were killed in ideological battle in Algeria, compared with a few hundred in Italy and Germany prior to 1923 and 1933. The demographic weapon is formidable; at the end of the Second World War Algeria had 7 million inhabitants and Algiers, the capital 200,000. Today's figures are 31 million and two million respectively. True, the demographic weapon, the resulting poverty and unemployment, makes it certain that every political system, however radical and aggressive, is bound to fail unless it manages to reverse this trend. But in the age of the means of mass destruction it may fail only after a major disaster.

All this is not foreordained, and it seems to lead far beyond historical fascism and Bolshevism, beyond stormtroopers and blackshirts and the moustaches of Hitler and Stalin. And yet, Furet noted in his book that "Bolshevism and National Socialism shared a veritable religion of power, overtly professed. In order to conquer the old and to maintain their power, all means are justified." World conquest is not now on the agenda but the belief, the religion of power has not disappeared. The model of old-fashioned dictatorship no longer works to be effective in the modern world, tyranny has to be in the fascist tradition.

Notes

1. There are excellent new works even on interpretation—above all Stanley Payne's magisterial *Fascism, History and Interpretation* (1995)—but these are the achievements of individual writers, there is nothing even remotely resembling a consensus.

2. R. Maurer, in H. Schwilk and V. Schacht (eds.), *Die selbstbewusste Nation* (1994), p. 73.

3. Hannah Arendt argued the opposite case: If towards the end of his life Stalin was about to engage in a major anti-Semitic campaign, this showed the extent to which he had been influenced by Hitler (preface to part 3, "The Origins of Totalitarianism," p. xxxix, 1973 edition). In fact there is no evidence that Stalin needed Nazi inspiration or vice versa; their crimes came to them quite naturally, they were home grown, and no foreign importations were needed.

4. The connection between fascism and fin de siècle remains to be investigated in detail; on the one hand fascism as a reaction against "decadencence," on the other, the inspiration provided by it with d'Annunzio as an obvious example. There are many other examples such as Maurice Barrès (from Decadence to the Action Française) and Julius Evola (from Dadaism to ultrafascism). But fin de siècle is not what it used to be; before it was Oscar Wilde, the *Yellow Book, A rebours,* and Viennese impressionism. Now it is New Age and postmodernism as a philosophy and cultural epoch. Perhaps the twentieth century did not deserve any better; the fin de siècle first appeared in a comedy, now it has become a tragicomedy.

8

The Empire Strikes Out

How great a matter a little fire kindleth! When Gennadi Yanayev informed the world on August 19 of Mikhail Gorbachev's sudden illness, he and his fellow plotters could not possibly have foreseen the consequences of their action: the burial of communism in Russia and the disintegration of the Soviet Union as we have known it in our time.

Rumors about an impending coup had been rampant for a long time. Even dates had been hazarded in September and October last year, and again in December. Eduard Shevardnadze had warned in his resignation speech of a coup. Aleksandr Yakovlev, once Gorbachev's closest ally, had mentioned this threat on August 1, and again a few days before the tanks began to roll, when he resigned. On July 22 an open letter had been published in *Sovetskaya Rossiya,* the mouthpiece of both the communist diehards and the nationalist party: "How could it have come to pass that we left in power people who do not love this country, who behave like lackeys vis-à-vis their well-wishers from overseas?" The appeal stated that there were more patriotic leaders to be found in Russia, and that the armed forces would support them in accordance with their sacred obligations. The manifesto was signed not only by several leading publicists of the right, but by the commander of the Soviet army, General Valentin Varennikov, and the deputy minister of the interior, General Boris Gromov (of Afghanistan fame). They, too, had been appointed by Gorbachev, who left soon afterward for a well-deserved holiday in the Crimea.

After the coup Yakovlev related a conversation with Gorbachev in which the president had dismissed the warnings: "They are cowards, they won't dare...." In fact, the eight members of the "Emergency Committee" were neither adventurists nor right-wing extremists. They were cautious, middle-of-the-road apparatchiks who made the decision, without apparent enthusiasm, to depose the man who had appointed them.

They assumed that a stand had to be made in defense of their power and the privileges of their caste. Marx once noted that ruling classes seldom if ever surrender their positions voluntarily, and Russia was no exception.

The plotters were also convinced, not without reason, that the policies pursued by Gorbachev had failed, that Gorbachev was utterly discredited, that order had to be reestablished ("no more experiments") to prevent general chaos and economic ruin. As far as they were concerned, their own interests and those of their country coincided. They also thought that a mere show of force would be sufficient to defeat the liberals and the separatists.

Hence the curious halfheartedness in the execution of the coup. It goes without saying that if it had been executed by the obvious candidates (the black colonels of the nationalist Soyuz faction), or if the leading figures of the old regime had been assassinated or merely arrested, or if the Russian Parliament had been stormed by a fews tanks and communications had been cut, the insurgents would have stayed in power for the next five or ten years. Of course, they would have failed in the end; but the years between would have been exceedingly uncomfortable ones for the Soviet Union and the rest of the world.

Myths spread fast, and it is now widely believed that the coup, carried out by a group of adventurers of the extreme right, was defeated by the people's power. But the gang of eight was not defeated by the people of Moscow. The Soviet capital is a city of some 10 million inhabitants. (Nobody knows the exact figure, because there are many hundreds of thousands of *limitchiki*, illegal residents over and above the official limit imposed.) Of these, according to a poll carried out on the second day of the coup, some 73 percent were opposed to it. But these 73 percenters did not take to the street. They were anxious, they were grumbling, but they thought it was no good to argue with tanks. Most of them also went to work. It was owing to Boris Yeltsin and his supporters—several thousand determined men and women defending the Russian Parliament during the critical hours of Monday and Tuesday—that Russia's honor was saved.

There was more opposition in Leningrad than in Moscow, and there was resistance in the Kuzbas region of Siberia and even in the Far East. But the first reaction from the republics was either favorable to the coup, or very cautious (the Ukraine, Kazakhstan). Not a single republican leader outside the Baltic countries condemned the coup. Islam Karimov of Uzbekistan welcomed it as "vital for the restoration of discipline."

Nursultan Nazarbayev of Kazakhstan, the cleverest and most progressive of the Central Asian leaders, carefully refrained from denouncing the coup until it became clear that it had failed. By Wednesday Karimov and Nazarbayev announced that they had left the Communist party in protest and that they had banned Party cells in government. Sviad Gamsakhurdia of Georgia, living up to his reputation as an eccentric, did not condemn the plotters either, albeit for different reasons. As he saw it, Gorbachev himself had engineered the coup, and he stuck to this version even after the coup had failed.

The Orthodox Church leaders did not respond for many hours to Yeltsin's appeal to condemn the coup. Aleksandr Bessmertnykh, the foreign minister, announced that he was running a temperature, and went fishing: an old Russian anti-pyretic. The Soviet envoy to Japan declared that the coup was absolutely necessary, and forty-eight hours later said that he was truly relieved that Gorbachev was back as the stabilizer. Guerman Gventsadze, the Soviet chargé in Dublin, called the coup constitutional, and observed that the emergency committee had wide popular support. (Two days later he made it known that his original statement had been misinterpreted.) There were countless such cases, and even more cases of fence-sitting. Mass support for Yeltsin materialized only on Tuesday night. By Thursday, however, hundreds of thousands demonstrated, and on Saturday a million people paid their last respects to the victims of the coup.

Why did the committee fail, if there was so little resistance? The answer is that there may not have been much active opposition to the plot, but there was not much public support for it either. The conspirators did not seem to have a majority of votes for convoking the Central Committee, which would have given their action at least an aura of legality. Worse, there was no unanimity in the army and the KGB. Some key commanders, such as the head of the air force, but also some naval, KGB, and parachute commanders, refused to cooperate. These were not great liberal reformers; they simply did not want to become involved in party politics. Among the army commanders, there was apparently a majority in favor of a military show of strength—but not in favor of bloodshed.

The plotters could still have proceeded with their plans, using some reliable elite units to storm the Russian Parliament and to arrest the main oppositionists. They could have called for mass demonstrations against Gorbachev; and it is quite likely that they would have had a big crowd in the streets of Moscow, for Gorbachev's unpopularity is legendary. But this went against their grain. The conspirators were not populist rabble-rousers, and their hands were trembling. At this stage, in the late hours of Tuesday afternoon and into the early hours on Wednesday, their resolve faltered. There was no obvious leader among them to stiffen their backbone, and the first defections took place: Valentin Pavlov suddenly developed high blood pressure, and Anatoly Lukyanov simply kept in the background. The old Bolsheviks had known the golden rule of insurgency: to press ahead relentlessly once the decision to act had been taken. But the plotters of 1991 were not of the caliber of Lenin and Trotsky. They were bureaucrats, not professional revolutionaries. They ignored a rule that any self-respecting nineteenth-century insurgent would have regarded as rudimentary.

The coup was in considerable part the result of Gorbachev's long-standing failure to act decisively. In the early years he had been a major liberating force. Perhaps he even knew, back then, what he wanted to achieve. But he never had a clear, consistent course of action. He veered left and swerved right. He pushed through all kinds of half-baked projects. He did not defend his democratic allies, and he made many disastrous appointments. He postponed for too long action on the status of the non-Russian republics. And thus, in the end, he found himself virtually isolated. Yeltsin, on the other hand, showed not only courage but a faultless sense of timing. His choice of advisers and assistants, moreover, was infinitely superior to Gorbachev's. He deserved to emerge as the hero and the victor of the August revolution.

And yet, in the final analysis, is it fair to put all the blame on Gorbachev for the failure of reforms? He had no power base other than the Party, the KGB, and the army, and they did not want radical change. He inherited an economy and a social system that no longer functioned. He faced political apathy among the masses, a lack of initiative and creativity, an absence of a civic spirit and a democratic tradition. Thus he lost, within two years, all political credit. But even a political genius might not have succeeded in these conditions. Surely it was unrealistic to hope that the consequences of seventy-four years of Soviet rule could be overcome within a few years. And a well-meaning compromiser was certainly not the right candidate for the demolition job.

Then, almost miraculously, the movement for radical reform was given a second chance as the result of a bungled coup carried out by the wrong plotters at the wrong time. The opportunity was seized by Yeltsin, not by Gorbachev. He, Gorbachev, failed to understand that within three days a revolution had taken place. The results of that revolution are known: the breakdown of the Union and the passing of the Communist party as the ruling force in the country. It is the most important political change in the Soviet Union since 1917. But it is also a giant step into the unknown. The components of the Soviet Union are now as close to chaos and to ruin as they were before the gang of eight made its move.

The breakdown of the Union was probably inevitable under the circumstances, but it is still a disaster. For it is a retrograde development. At a time when all over Europe the general trend is toward unification, the tendency among these newly independent states is toward separatism. Much worse, since none of the new independent republics is ethnically homogeneous, and since the new rulers will not be primarily concerned with the rights of minorities, all the preconditions will now exist for national strife on a massive scale. Some of the minorities may leave: it is unlikely, for instance, that many Russians will stay in Central Asia. But their return to Russia, embittered and without means, will only add to the social and political ferment.

In the Caucasus, a civil war has been raging for the last two years, and it is impossible to see what force will now prevent open warfare between Armenia and Azerbaijan and between Georgia and the Ossetians. The predominantly Russian inhabitants of the eastern Ukraine have not much in common with the Ukrainian-speaking (and Uniate Catholic) western Ukrainians, and the willingness on both sides to make compromises cannot be taken for granted. Westerners often talk about Muslim Central Asia as if it were an entity, but the only common feature among its inhabitants is their hatred of the Russians. National tensions there are running deep, and once the Russians are gone, the situation may well turn into a brutal free-for-all. Even inside the Russian republic there are strong separatist movements: the Tatars in the Kazan region have insisted on autonomy for a long time, Siberians want their own republic, and there is trouble in the Crimea and elsewhere.

Although Yeltsin has been generous vis à vis the other republics, he certainly has no wish to liquidate the RSFSR. In the short run, the Russian federation, Azerbaijan, as well as the five Central Asian republics might sign a new Union treaty, and White Russia and the Ukraine can perhaps be persuaded to enter into a close relationship with the new confederation. From the Russian point of view, close cooperation with the Ukraine is infinitely more important (for historical and political reasons as well as economic ones) than the link with the Central Asian republics and Azerbaijan, the most backward and the most corrupt parts of the former Soviet empire. Their interest in *perestroika* and *glasnost* is strictly limited; they wish to maintain the link with Moscow because they vitally need Russian economic support. But sooner or later they will break away, and Russia will be considerably better off without them.

The new political map of the former Soviet Union will not be firmly established for years to come. Perhaps there will be greater willingness to cooperate once the euphoria of independence-at-any-price gives way to a sober confrontation with economic realities. Most of the newly independent republics will lose their traditional markets and will be saddled with industries (more often than not geared to work for the defense sector) for whose output there is no demand. Once the Ukraine was a major food exporter, but Western Europe produces much more food now than it can consume, and the last thing it needs is the import of steel and similar commodities. Illusions about speedy integration into a common European market are bound to fade very soon in Eastern Europe and the Soviet Union.

The Russian republic is the only force that counts in terms of world politics. Yeltsin's position seems unassailable at this moment; he boldly seized the initiative, and the old communists are on the run. But there is a mass of discontented people, and as the domestic situation deteriorates they will gain new courage. The bungled coup makes a repeat performance in the very near future unlikely, but in a year or two there could well be another attempt to turn back the clock, carried out by men whose hands may not tremble. Indeed, since the present honeymoon will not last many months, even a legal constitutional challenge to the reformers cannot be excluded.

Although communism is widely detested, the democratic movement in the Soviet Union has not yet put down deep roots. Outside Moscow, Leningrad, Sverdlovsk (Yeltsin's erstwhile power base), and a few other major cities, old-style Communists are still in power and the majority of the population has been apathetic. White Russia is still known as the Soviet Vendée (a reference to the most counterrevolutionary region in France at the time of the revolution), even if its head of government had to resign. As Christ stopped at Eboli, *glasnost* and *perestroika* never really transformed Odessa and Rostov; Baku and Saratov, Perm and

Gorki, Novorossisk and Chabarossk. Whoever has visited the cities of Central Russia not that far from Moscow, places such as Vologda and Yaroslavl, Tula and Tambo, Tver and Kaluga, knows that virtually all the key positions of power, in politics as in the economy, are in communist hands.

It is comparatively easy to make changes in Moscow and Leningrad. Who will replace the local bureaucrats, the police chiefs, and factory managers elsewhere? After 1917 it took the Bolsheviks four years to prevail outside Moscow and Leningrad. Today the communists are more deeply entrenched in these places than the tsarist bureaucracy was (and there are many more of them), and it is doubtful whether Yeltsin has four years at his disposal. Lenin and Trotsky sent the Red Army to suppress local uprisings: Yeltsin will probably not be able to do the same.

Many millions of party and state bureaucrats will now lose their jobs, not to mention the army and state security officers. Unlike after 1917, however, there will not be a mass exodus of the losers. The Russian nationalists were caught off balance by the coup of the gang of eight, and by Yeltsin's decisive action. Still, sooner or later they will rally again to their cause. There are millions of them. They are firmly convinced that the loss of empire was brought about by an act of high treason. They are anti-Western, anti-Semitic, populist opponents of the liberalization of the economy. They believe in a united, indivisible Greater Russia. Some elements of the old Communist party will transform themselves into Social Democrats, but others, will join forces with the extreme nationalists, and this may pave the way for a second coming of National Bolshevism. This will be abetted by the existence of a considerable *Lumpenproletariat*; in the recent RSFSR elections, Vladimir Zhirinovsky, a rabble-rouser who was almost certainly sponsored by either the Party apparatus or the KGB, polled some 8 million votes on a platform whose most prominent plank was the lowering of the price of vodka.

The new Russian federation, in sum, will be a giant cave of Adulam in which the great mass of the discontented will gather. If they find a charismatic leader, and if the shortages should become even more acute, a new bid for power is almost a foregone conclusion.

Hows long will Yeltsin and his supporters be able to maintain the momentum of their campaign, and what can we do to help?

After a recent visit to Germany, I returned with the clear impression that East Germany is about to turn the corner. There is still much discontent, and it will probably take another two years until significant sections of the population will enjoy the fruits of the recovery. To achieve this, West Germany had to invest sums much greater than originally planned: up to the end of next year, the total may well amount to about $150 billion. And East Germany was a country of less than 17 million. The Soviet Union, by contrast, counts some 295 million inhabitants. The sums needed for the rebuilding of the Soviet economy ought to be measured in trillions. The fact that the East German work force was of a higher caliber, and that the old Soviet Union (with its division of labor of sorts) is now dissolved, does not help either.

The United States' capacity to help is limited by its enormous domestic problems. The Japanese are reluctant, Germany has given more than the rest, and the other Europeans talk of hundreds of millions when hundreds of billions are needed. It has been argued by some misguided spirits in the West that Gorbachev fell because the West refused to give him the economic help he needed. But no amount of Western loans and credits would have made the difference, because under Gorbachev the preconditions for improvement, that is to say, structural change, did not exist. They do exist, however, under Yeltsin.

Help, urgently and on a massive scale, is now needed—not so much in money, but in kind (for example, food to alleviate critical shortages). Above all, it is necessary to modernize the Soviet communications system, which is, at the present time, the essential precondition for economic progress. Such first aid cannot come from the private sector; Soviet foreign reserves are down to between $6 billion and $7 billion. Its debt repayment bill will be more than twice that much toward the end of the year. The prospect of these enormous quantities of assistance may not be a very tempting proposition for the West, but the alternative is even less inviting. It will certainly be more expensive to contain Yeltsin's successors.

The shock waves of the Russian earthquake will continue, and the ultimate outcome of the present struggle for power in Moscow will not be certain for a long time. Yeltsin and his opponents might be challenged in the capital. Almost certainly there will be open and passive resistance on the local level. It is not at all clear that the cause of freedom and radical reform will prevail in the near future. And it will be a near miracle if it triumphs peacefully, without the application of force. With some luck, Russia might escape another ruinous civil war. But there are no certainties, except that the country has now entered, at long last, the postcommunist stage of its history.

9

The Fall of the Soviet Empire

The Soviet empire has fallen, the suddenness and magnitude of the collapse has befuddled Western observers as well as many Russians. The new Russian history textbooks are dealing in great length and detail with the enormous price in human life of seventy years of communism. But the latest issue of the *American Historical Review* publishes an article claiming that reliable archival sources show that the number of victims was not remotely as high as argued by Western and Eastern alarmists such as Robert Conquest, let alone by Russian dissidents such as Solzhenitsyn and Roy Medvedev.

Speeches made and papers submitted at recent academic conferences in Moscow maintain that far from enjoying mass support in 1917, the Bolsheviks had engaged in a military coup supported by army deserters, elements of the *lumpenproletariat* and some misguided utopian intellectuals. Recent American books and articles, on the other hand, express the firm conviction (again on the basis of much material from the Russian archives) that the Bolsheviks did have mass support, above all from the politically conscious workers. Many American academics strongly oppose the term "totalitarian" with regard to the Soviet Union; they consider it a loaded, unscholarly term belonging to the realm of cold war thinking which should be discarded. But in Russia "totalitarian" has become in recent years one of the most frequently used terms in the political dictionary.

More books have been published in America of late arguing that America was mainly to blame for the cold war and that the Soviet danger was a figment of imagination, that U.S. arms spending was not only unnecessary and harmful but delayed real detente.

Leading Russian scholars (and diplomats such as Falin and Bessmertnykh and also generals) have gone on record arguing that blueprints for a military invasion did exist, that Soviet military spending (and the nuclear arsenal) were considerably higher than even the CIA suspected and that but for Reagan's SDI and the earlier decision to deploy the Euromissiles the Iron Curtain would not have come down.

One could adduce more examples for this strange and growing asymmetry in the views of mainstream American Sovietology and what the Russians now say and write. If these Western experts are right something is seriously amiss with the Russians; they either do not know the recent history of their own country or deliberately falsify it or suffer from an advanced case of compulsive masochism, putting the worst possible gloss on their own past. Perhaps Russian history should be rewritten not by the Russians who cannot be trusted in their present distraught state of mind but by the more objective and detached American Sovietologists.

But how far can our Sovietologists be trusted? Almost a quarter of a century ago a new breed came to the fore in American universities stressing views very much opposed to those of a previous generation of Soviet experts. These revisionists (as they came to be called) maintained that most earlier writers had been politically biased, staunch cold warriors unwilling to accept that the Soviet Union had many substantial achievements to its credit. The revisionists on the other hand were open-minded, had no axes to grind.

Not everyone agreed with these claims but, as a recent writer in the *Slavic Review* noted, the insights of the new thinkers were now so widely accepted that time had come to drop the term "revisionism," which had become, in fact, the new orthodoxy.

If such thinking prevailed in the universities, things went less well in the real world. There had been some rumblings even before 1987, but it was only with the coming of *glasnost* that revisionism faced a real crisis. The revisionists could claim that no one had anticipated the sudden fall of the Soviet system and that it was wrong to single them out for blame. True enough, but the revisionists (in contrast to the "traditionalists") had also painted a picture of the Soviet system and its achievements that was, to put it mildly, not quite correct. As far as they were concerned *perestroika* had already been carried out under Brezhnev.

Thus the revisionists were not overjoyed by the revelations emanating from Russia under *glasnost.* They disliked the whole atmosphere in Moscow which they described as emotional, unscholarly, sensationalist, and thus quite untrustworthy. As they saw it these were mainly the outpourings of novelists and poets, there were no footnotes, merely hearsay and folk-lore. And what could a professional historian do without footnotes?

It was impossible to ignore the new information altogether. Yes, the situation in Russia had been worse than assumed in certain respects. The social science methods had been a little disappointing. Stalin's role had perhaps been a little underrated, and perhaps there had been, after all, for a while a totalitarian dictatorship. Few Sovietologists would claim any longer even jestingly that "we are all Leninists now."

The Moscow revelations brought about certain changes even in the titles of new books. A study entitled *The Anti-Bureaucratic Purge* would now be called *Stalinist Terrorism*. This would have been unthinkable seven or eight years ago, first because Stalin was considered relatively unimportant and second because terrorism was a loaded, unscholarly term that was to be shunned. But by and large, the revisionists continue to believe that they were essentially correct, or at least more correct than their opponents. Not surprisingly a counteroffensive came under way in reply to the denigration of the record of Sovietology, for instance in a special issue of the quarterly *National Interest*. Too many people had invested too much intellectual capital, the reputation of too many Sovietologists was at stake and thus new conferences were convened and new articles and books began to appear proving that from their assess-ment of the revolution of 1917 to their view of the cold war the revision-ist case still had much to recommend itself.

Not all the news from Moscow was bad. On one point the revelations seemed to confirm revisionist earlier claims; this concerns the number of the victims of the system. True, these revelations came from the KGB, the ministry of the interior (which controls both the police and many archives) and the army high command. But they provided many foot-notes for our scholars.

What new light has been shed on the victims of the terror, and is it at all reasonable to expect accurate figures? It has been known throughout history that the greater the crime, the fewer (and the less reliable) the documentation: the number of victims in the Armenian massacres vary between 100,000 and two million, the number of victims killed by Croat fascists in World War II between nil and 600,000; there are no exact figures for Pol Pot's massacres, and it was recently argued that fewer people might have been killed in Auschwitz than originally assumed, closer to 2.5 million than to 4 million. But this does not necessarily mean that the total number of Holocaust victims was less. Estimates concerning the Holocaust vary between five and six million, except among the Holocaust deniers who claim that no one was killed in the first place. We do not know, even approximately, what Russian losses were in World War Two, not even in the war with Finland in 1939–40. The fate of 80,000 Americans in World War Two has not been accounted for to this day and only 10 to 20 percent of the documents relating to the Kennedy assassination have been released so far in the country of the Freedom of Information Act.

There is a striking similarity between revisionism in the field of Nazi and Soviet studies. In Germany some of it comes from the extreme right, ultranationalist camp and one need not elaborate on the reasons. But to a considerable extent such thinking came from academic circles whose inspiration was anything but right wing. They argue that Hitler (like Stalin) was a weak dictator, a bumbler and stumbler, the German terror was largely unplanned and fortuitous, carried out by an overzealous bureaucracy. The main reason for the killing was economic, or alternatively, Hitler had the Jews exterminated because he hated the Communists so much.

Some of the estimates of the number of victims of the Soviet purges (Solzhenitsyn's 15 to 25 million between the years 1928–53) have always struck me as excessive—and there were even higher ones. For the country would have come to a standstill if such a high percentage of the male population of working age had been killed or incarcerated. But what is one to make of the official Soviet figures put out by the spokesmen of the Russian security services and now picked up by the *American Historical Review*? According to these statistics less than 700,000 men and women were executed and the total number of Gulag inmates was never higher than three million, of which the great majority were not political prisoners. These discoveries were made in certain archives where the documents should not have been in the first place, they were publicized (with rare exceptions) in journals of the neocommunists and/or the extreme right. Furthermore, the structure and the composition of the Russian archives has little changed since the olden days (except for the top leadership which consists of Gorbachev and Yeltsin nominees). There is no control whatsoever of what kind of material has been preserved, whether it has been doctored, and how much of it has been put at the disposal of outside researchers.

That full lists of victims were not found, that no master list ever existed, is admitted by Russian officials and their American customers. One example for the problematical character of the new figures should suffice. The Russian figure for those executed in 1939–40 is very small, a few thousand. But 10 to 15,000 Polish officers were killed that year in Katyn forest. There are no exact figures to this day; apparently the number of those murdered was even greater than the Poles had thought. But Katyn was an exceptional case, some will argue. True enough, but it took place ten miles outside a major Russian city (Smolensk) and if so, how many exceptional cases could there have been in the vast unpopulated areas of North Russia, Siberia and Kazakhstan? Speaking of Kazakhstan, something like 1.5 to 2 million Kazakhs somehow disappeared in the 1930s. According to the official statistics they escaped abroad—to China?—to the moon? According to independent writers some 1.5 to 1.75 million perished. So the Kazakh case was also unique.

German statistics are more reliable than the Russian, and access to them has been unfettered after 1945. But as the Auschwitz case shows, in the final analysis the historians have to rely on rough guesses. In the Russian case there can be no certainties at all, and it is therefore not surprising that there are great differences in the estimates of victims between an enlightened revisionist such as Alec Nove (of Glasgow) and a firmly committed one like the Australian Geoffrey Wheatcroft, the former mentions 10 to 11 million, the latter 4 to 5 million.

Another scholar (R. Reese) has recently investigated the purge of the Red Army in 1937–38. According to earlier estimates 25 to 50 percent of the officer corps had been affected; a revisionist author claims that the figure was much lower—a mere 7 percent. His findings are based entirely on figures published by press organs of the Central Committee of the defunct Communist party and the army general staff. (The latter organ never believed in *glasnost,* until fairly recently it was edited by a committed Stalinist with strong fascist inclinations.) The author reports that some 38,000 officers were affected—not a small figure, more than the total officer corps of the U.S. armed forces in 1939. This is more or less what earlier Western authors had claimed. But Reese notes that the Red Army was apparently much bigger than earlier assumed, hence the smaller percentage.

What if the new figure is correct? Does it follow that the impact was much smaller as Reese maintains? Hardly, because junior officers were little affected, whereas among the higher echelons (marshalls, generals, admirals), the rate of attrition was 50 to 80 percent. The disappearance of these men could not be kept secret and had a tremendous impact. It created the impression that the Red Army was leaderless, it made it easier for Hitler to make his decision to attack, it induced the democracies to consider the Soviet Union an unreliable and ineffective ally. A figure of 7 percent means precisely nothing in this context, it is like a coroner's report to the effect that the extremities of the corpse were in good shape, too bad that it was decapitated. Or it is like arguing that Russian literature did not suffer since only a few individuals such as Mandelstam and Babel were killed and Tsvetaeva driven to suicide, whereas hundreds of Stalinist hacks prospered.

The debate in years past was not primarily about figures but about origins and consequences. How can anyone now doubt the consequences of the terror? The epitaph on that period should be the one appearing on St. Paul's Cathedral in London written by Wren's son: *Si monumentum requiris, circumspice.* Freely translated it means: If you want to know the true outcome—look around you, consider the present state of Russia and the former Soviet Union.

These days a great many fascinating questions face the student of Russia: Why did the empire collapse, why did most experts misjudge the situation and what are the future portents? Why should anyone decide that the top priority is the immersion in the KGB and MVD documents? Because he (or she) is eager to discover what they hoped to find in the first place. Among very primitive people and young children there is the frequent belief that whatever is written (or printed on white) must be authentic. The idea that even something written or printed could be forged or correct but misleading in a thousand different ways, involves a certain amount of sophistication.

It is difficult to accept simplicity of mind as the root cause of the recent publications. One could think at least of several other, more important reasons. One is the rejection of inconvenient evidence, a syndrome well known to psychologists. This is no monopoly of Sovietology but a common human feature. To admit error is always a painful experience, tantamount to losing face. Secondly, there is the general crisis in recent years in political science, political sociology, sociology, and social history. Expectations were very high, the results meager. Experts in related case studies, such as for instance China, Cuba or the DDR were no less mistaken than the Sovietologists, and some of their aberrations are even less explicable. It is far easier to be mistaken about the Soviet Union, a mysterious and distant country that was largely closed to foreigners, than about East Germany, a much smaller place, visited each year by millions of West Germans speaking the same language. And yet, the assessment of the situation in the DDR among the West Germans was totally mistaken, and while everyone was wrong, the political scientists were those most mistaken.

Some senior members of the fraternity have now conceded this; Soviet studies simply could not learn that much from political science theory with its commitment to quantification and its abstract, overarching models (Alfred G. Meyer). But others, on the contrary, have redoubled their efforts to hunt for new theoretical concepts like medieval alchemists in search of the philosophers' stone. Some like F. Flaron and F. Hoffman have suggested Clifford Geertz classic "Deep Play: Notes on the Balinese Cockfight" as a model ("your view of *perestroika* and post-Communism may never be the same again"). Another, (Mark Saroyan) has pointed to Althusser and Foucault as guides to Soviet nationality problems. Whoever believes that Althusser and Foucault can shed light on the fighting in Tadzhikistan or Nagorno Karabakh must be as unbalanced as Althusser was. While some of the revisionists believe in the sanctity of KGB texts and statistics as if they were Holy Writ, another writer has managed the not inconsiderable feat of not mentioning a single Russian source in a book on the Cold War. The author seems familiar with the writings of Charles Krauthammer and George Will but appears not to have heard of Molotov. He seems to believe that the cold war was a struggle between the *Nation* and *The National Review*.

No one can possibly know how many people perished in the various Russian purges. But we do know what their effect has been. Perhaps the KGB figures are correct, though this seems unlikely, perhaps twice or three times as many people were killed. Those who claim to have found confirmation for their "lower figures" tell us that according to the KGB files 681,000 men and women were executed in 1937–38 and millions perished in the early 1930s. This compares with about twenty people executed for political reasons in Fascist Italy during twenty years and 10,000 inmates of Nazi concentration camps in 1937. Never in modern history were that many people killed in time of peace. If so, why the compulsive search for lower figures, why the spurious claims ("we can now document the scale of the repression"), why the search for absurd theories explaining mass murder as a "radical reaction to bureaucracy," or a "chaotic wave of voluntarism and revolutionary puritanism"?

There are answers to these questions, but psychologists are probably better qualified to deal with them than historians.

10

Splendor and Misery of Sovietology I

The cherished dream of Communist ideologists has come true: Sovietology has passed away. But, there is no one to rejoice at this.

I do not know who first coined the term "Sovietology" and when; it was probably only after the Second World War. In many dozen books and hundreds of articles Soviet readers have been told that Sovietologists were not only wrong in their facts and comments, but deliberately lying and distorting, haters of communism and the Soviet Union, in brief, evil people.

Western Embellishers

It was, alas, a caricature of reality. While there were few Stalinists among Western experts, there were even fewer Russophobes. True, many of them committed mistakes—but these were usually not the mistakes about which Soviet propaganda complained. In fact, the picture painted by the Sovietologists was often too rosy and recently a post-mortem has come under way in the West: How to explain why so many of them overrated for so many years the achievements—political, economic, social, and cultural of the Soviet regime?

I have to declare a personal involvement. My interest in Russia and the Soviet Union goes back many years; I still remember, for instance, the first issue of *Voina i rabochii klass*. I was the editor from 1955 to 1965 of *Survey,* a leading academic journal devoted to Soviet affairs. I have also written a history of Sovietology—the only one in existence (1967, republished 1988), I believe. But I have never been a fully fledged member of the fraternity of Sovietologists because my interest also went into other directions. From 1965 to 1987 I was director of an institute devoted to the study of the contemporary history of Europe in general. A famous poem asks:

What should they know of England
Who only England know?

and the same is true with regard to Russia.

To assess the achievements and failures of Sovietology, to gain the right perspective, it is useful to know about the problems of the study of other countries and political movements. I was only marginally involved in the quarrels and polemics among the Sovietologists. For such detachment a price has to be paid but it also has its advantages.

Thanks to Lenin and Stalin for Great Russia

The first generation of what we now call Sovietologists was dominated by a few major academics who had known tsarist Russia well—for instance, the Englishman Sir Bernard Pares (1867–1949) who had taught at Moscow University in 1899–1900 and the American Samuel Harper (1874–1950).

For them the revolution was an unmitigated disaster. They loathed Lenin and Trotsky, but as the years passed they came to like Stalin. In the case of Pares this meant the justification of the Moscow trials and purges of the 1930s, whereas Harper took the Stalinist Constitution of 1935 seriously and applauded it.

Stalinism reminded them of the old Russia—at least in some respects. In any case under Stalin the revolution had been buried and Russia became an almost normal country—cause enough for satisfaction, if not jubilation. German Sovietology—leading in the world before 1933— was more realistic. It was, however, mainly preoccupied with facts and there was not much attempt at theoretical interpretation.

The second generation of Sovietologists arrived on the scene during the Second World War. Only a few of them had a strictly academic background—such as Merle Fainsod of Harvard (1915–1972) who wrote the classic textbook *How Russia is Ruled* and Hugh Seton Watson (1915– 1986), professor in London and son of a famous father, also a historian.

But many other leading figures came from a different background— Leonard Schapiro (1908–1983), the author of the best history of the

CPSU so far, was a lawyer by training, Edward Hallett Carr (1892–1982) had worked for the British Foreign Office and the *Times* and later wrote a ten-volume history of the Soviet Union, covering the period 1917–1935. The American Bertram Wolfe (1896–1977) and Isaac Deutscher (1907–1967), biographers of Lenin, Stalin, and Trotsky, had been members of the Communist parties of the USA and Poland, respectively. One could easily give other such examples.

No Russian names have been mentioned so far, and it is interesting, in retrospect, that the emigrants had a very small impact. True, there were some excellent historians among them such as Mikhail Karpovich (1888–1959) and Georgi Vernadsky (1887–1973). But as far as the history of the Soviet Union was concerned, they were not much in appearance with a few exceptions such as Boris Nikolayevsky, a former Menshevik, brother-in-law of Alexei Rykov, and a walking encyclopedia on all things Russian.

Outside Onlookers

Partly this was the fault of Western experts who were put off by the claims of the émigrés that only they could understand their native land. But it is also true that even some of the major figures of the emigration, such as Berdyayev and Timasheff, whatever their other merits, were a little suspect as guides to current events in the Soviet Union. They were swerving from the rejection not just of socialism but of parliamentary democracy (1923–28) to genuflections to Stalin and Stalinism (1944–47).

More reliable were the Mensheviks; their journal *Sotsialisticheskii Vestnik* was probably the best, most informative current interpretation of Soviet affairs. Perhaps the most impressive commentator on the Soviet Union was a theologian, Georgi Fedotov. But very few people had ever heard of *Novy Grad,* the journal in which he published his articles, and so he was ignored and, unfortunately, has not been rediscovered in Russia to this day, while many lesser men have been celebrated as great thinkers.

If one reads today, forty years after the event, the main works of the leading representatives of the second generation of Western Sovietologists, one finds that they have stood well the test of time. They assized correctly the Stalinist system and its successors, perhaps some of them overrated the importance of Communist ideology, and underrated the vested interests of the *nomenklatura* (the very term was not then known). Perhaps they underrated somewhat the role of accident in history. But most present-day Soviet readers, experts or not, will find very little to quarrel with them.

There were two notable exceptions among these masters—Isaac Deutscher and Edward Hallett Carr, whose judgment, in retrospect, was quite wrong.

Although a Murderer, He was a Good Man

They had a considerable impact at the time partly for ideological reasons, partly because of the sheer size of the work; no one would lightly dismiss a history of ten massive volumes—full of details, facts, and figures. Deutscher was an excellent writer, his style was vivid, perhaps he should have written novels rather than about politics.

But he was a passionate Leninist who fervently believed that while Stalin was a cruel dictator, Stalinism was historically inevitable, and after the death of the *vozhd* (boss), history would "clean" his life's work from all ugly stains. He expected in 1953 that Russia would return to pristine Leninism, greater freedom, greater prosperity, less barbarism.

Unlike communist propaganda writers, Deutscher was often wrong but never boring, he presented his views, often successfully though not always truthfully, as objective and dispassionate. To this day his Trotsky biography (in three volumes) and his Stalin biography (first published in 1949) are reprinted, many years after the death of the author—despite the fact that it is now common knowledge that Deutscher's basic thesis was quite wrong—that Stalin was a great man who made some mistakes but whose overall role was positive because he made his country strong and prosperous.

Edward Hallett Carr was not a Leninist, not even a socialist but a Hegelian, who believed that all historical realities are reasonable, and he had a predilection for strong rulers. While Hitler was alive, Carr was very much in favor of doing business with him. For the same reason he had a weakness for Stalin—yet another strong ruler. He also believed that Lenin's and Stalin's policies were inevitable and, by and large, successful—in foreign policy, the economy, social changes, and so on.

Of course, he was not a party member and did not have to justify every twist and turn in the party line. But, by and large, he supported Stalin, and believed that the West could learn a great deal from Stalinism and that, in any case, the future of mankind belonged to Soviet communism.

True, during the last two years of his life he voiced some doubts—he died close to 90 a few years ago. But there is no trace of such reservation in his huge *History of the Soviet Union*—a monument of industry, rich in detail, but almost totally without value because of its basic misjudgments.

Yet another person ought to be mentioned in this context. Hannah Arendt's (1906–1975) name has been known until recently only to a few specialists in Russia. A philosopher of German-Jewish origin she published in 1951 a book *Burden of Our Time* (*Origins of Totalitarianism*) that proved to be quite influential.

She was a very learned woman, a star pupil of two of the greatest twentieth-century philosophers, Heidegger and Jaspers. But she lacked political instinct and knew next to nothing about Russia and communism—not the language, history, nor had she ever been to Russia. It is interesting to compare her with the French political philosopher Raymond Aron (1905–1983) who was also no Soviet expert, but who was a political thinker of the highest order, whose ideas have remained of great interest to this day.

Arendt had the disdain of the philosopher for facts and her ignorance did not prevent her from erecting a great ideological edifice. She was preoccupied with totalitarianism. This was not her discovery, students of Nazi Germany and Fascist Italy had widely used the concept well before the Second World War.

She rightly pointed out that there was a fundamental difference between an old fashioned dictatorship and a totalitarian regime based on terror and propaganda. But then she went on making Stalinist Russia even more totalitarian than it really was, claiming that such a regime could never change, and that there was virtually no difference between Nazi Germany and Stalin's Russia, which again was no more than a half truth.

Hannah Arendt's views found more admirers among literary figures and feminists than among Sovietologists. But they did influence directly or indirectly the general public, until a few years later, after the Hungarian rebellion, she radically changed her opinion. All the claims about totalitarianism were dropped; and she transferred her interests to other topics such as American political philosophy.

However, among the Western experts the debate about totalitarianism in Russia continued; we shall show in the next chapter how in the late 1960s a younger generation of Sovietologists—"revisionists" came to reject it—not because of any dramatic new events inside the Soviet Union but because of the student revolt of 1968, because of Vietnam and other such developments that radialized many of the younger Western experts and turned them against their own country.

11

Splendor and Misery of Sovietology II

The 1950s and 1960s were the golden age of Sovietology in the West. Funds were made available, places like St. Anthony's College in Oxford and the Harvard Russian Research Center prospered, some excellent young people were drawn into the field, first-rate studies appeared covering various aspects of the Soviet experience—political, social, economic, and cultural. True, Sovietology never had a party line, there were always differences of opinion, sometimes profound, in assessing things Soviet. But by and large this was a period of great productivity and high quality, and if opinions were voiced that were clearly wrong or stupid, these represented a small minority.

Towards the later 1960s the situation began to change. There were a number of reasons, but the most important issue was generational change. The late 1960s witnessed a radicalization in the universities, partly as the result of the Vietnam war, partly because of the students' revolt affecting both America and Western Europe.

The West is in Decline, So the East is Palatable

The general *Zeitgeist* was pro-left, anti-American, pro-Third World, and it was probably inevitable that the attitude towards the Soviet system should become more positive. The younger generation of Soviet experts wanted to distance itself from their predecessors. They rejected the "totalitarian model" which they regarded as cold war propaganda; true, the Soviet system was a dictatorship, but the West was not perfect either. And in the circumstances the proper position for a scholar was one of equidistance, perhaps even moving a little closer to the Soviet position. Because, as they saw it, the Soviet system was a "development dictatorship of social justice" aiming to make the Soviet people freer and more prosperous, whereas the Western systems were both reactionary and in decline.

Books began to appear claiming that Stalinism had positive consequences because it had carried out, for instance, a cultural revolution. Others claimed that the importance of the Gulag and the purges had been greatly exaggerated, only few people had lived in fear in Russia, only some tens of thousands had been affected. Altogether, the Soviet system was far more democratic (and less aggressive) than a former generation of Sovietologists had assumed. It was a different kind of democracy, and it was still somewhat behind the West in living standards and economic performance. The Soviet regime was very popular, it was rapidly catching up with the West, it had made many achievements in various directions and in the meantime the West had a great deal to learn from the Soviet experience. Critical assessment of Soviet politics was dismissed as a remnant of "cold war mentality," not scholarly but propagandistic.

Communism Should be Known from the Inside

This was the ideological dimension of the "revisionist revolution" but it was by no means the only one. It has been noted that the earlier generation of Soviet experts had spent at least part of their working lives outside the universities; they had been in politics, many of them knew Marxism-Leninism and the Communist parties from the inside. They had developed an experience and instinctive knowledge that most of the revisionists almost entirely lacked. Their whole lives had been in college campuses, they failed not only to understand communism, but politics in general—except perhaps university politics. They suffered from what psychologists call "mirror imaging," that is to say, they interpreted events in the Soviet Union more or less in terms of what they were accustomed to at home. Thus, to give but one example, the Soviet government was thought to operate in a way not very different from the American, the Communist party of the Soviet Union, while perhaps a little peculiar, resembled in many respects political parties in the West.

What they lacked in instinctive understanding and experience, the "revisionists" tried to compensate for by way of "social science methods." The late 1960s and the 1970s witnessed the triumphant entrance of all kinds of social science techniques, paradigms and models that were then fashionable in the West, into the field of Soviet studies—

with devastating results. They had to do with "developmental bureau-cracy," with "upward mobility," with a special Soviet approach to "modernization," and other such concepts. These were grandiose ideas and they had little in common with Soviet realities. Historians were writing books in which they demonstrated that the Bolshevik coup of 1917 had not been a coup but an inevitable and ultimately beneficial social development, the same was true with regard to the collectiviza-tion of agriculture. The Soviet system was not (and probably had never been) totalitarian, but authoritarian. It was never made quite clear what "authoritarian" meant, for de Gaulle was also authoritarian, so was, say, Morocco or Jordan. Did it mean that the Soviet system was like that of France or Morocco?

Hitler and Stalin are Hamletian Figures

This kind of "revisionism" led to horrible and often grotesque distor-tions of reality, but it is only fair to add that Soviet studies were not the only field affected by this disease. Very similar developments could be observed, for instance, among the students of Nazi Germany in the 1970s.

Suddenly books appeared claiming that Hitler had not been very pow-erful and important, that Nazism had also been a "developmental dicta-torship," that it had never really been a totalitarian regime and so on.

This revisionism did not come from the right (from among the pro-Nazis), but on the contrary, from among the left, the believers in modern methods of social sciences—with an admixture of Marxism. As in the case of Sovietology, there was a revolt against the previous generation of experts and their theories—and the consequences were surprisingly simi-lar. The result of these studies was ridiculous: A Hitler (and a Stalin) who were Hamletian figures, prisoners of the bureaucracy; half the time they did not even know what went on around them. Such an interpreta-tion had nothing in common with the real state of affairs but it was quite fashionable in academic circles. Thus, for instance, the books of Robert Conquest on the Stalinist purges were dismissed as nonobjective, and nonacademic, just as in Germany scholars drew attention to the fact that they had never found a document in the archives concerning a written order by Hitler to kill all Jews. The idea that the greater the crime, the less likely that there had been a written order in Moscow or Berlin in the first place, did not occur to these scholars.

But there was yet another reason (or reasons) for the failure of many Sovietologists and this is the most difficult to explain. The field of Soviet economic studies in the West included many excellent experts—perhaps the general level was higher in this field than in any other. Nor were there any Marxist-Leninists among them. Many first-rate books were published over a long period. But on basic issues, such as the size of the Soviet GNP, the quantity and quality of Soviet industrial output, the percentage of military spending, on all these and some other issues, leading experts were consistently wrong—and not only the academics but also the CIA and other government departments.

They consistently overrated Soviet economic performance mainly, no doubt, because they took the official Soviet figures too seriously. Of course, they did not quite believe them, but they thought that there must be some relationship between these figures and the truth.

They refused to accept that many of these figures were rooted in fantasy and that, for all one knows, the Soviet leaders (certainly under Brezhnev) were as ignorant as the Sovietologists about the real state of the economy, because they were misled by their underlings, who, in turn, were misinformed by the local informants. Paradoxically, these propagandistic lies did the Soviet Union much harm. For once Western governments reached the conclusion that the Soviet economy was much stronger than it really was, this meant (they believed) that the Russians could spend much more for military purposes than they really did. Hence the need for the West to increase its defence spending. In other words, as the result of the Soviet misinformation an arms race came under way which the Soviet Union could not win, and which, in fact, weakened its economy inasmuch as civilian spending decreased.

However, it is also true that there never was unanimity among the Western Sovietologists. If it was fashionable in the 1970s and early 1980s in many Western circles to take a view of the Soviet system and the leadership that was much too favourable; there were many dissenters, not only among the older generation. Gradually even some of the revisionists came to doubt their own wisdom. Thus, it was realized in the West even before Gorbachev that at some time in the 1970s there had been a basic change of mood—from optimism to pessimism—in wide sections of Soviet society. This in turn led to searching questions what were the reasons of this change—the realization that the economic situation was getting worse, or a deterioration in the general quality of life, or the feeling that the old leadership had run out of ideas, or that the country was adrift? These were, of course, crucial questions, and when the great crisis came in 1989–90 it did by no means come as a total surprise to many leading Western experts.

Thus, in retrospect, the failure of Sovietology was essentially the failure of a generation—not all, but many of them, those who had entered the field in the late 1960s and early 1970s, who had basic socialist sympathies (and thought that the Soviet Union was a socialist society!). Events in the Soviet Union in recent years have come as a great shock to them, they feel betrayed when Russians write and talk about "totalitarianism"— something that Western Sovietologists had argued for so many years, did not exist. To admit profound mistakes is always difficult and people will think of a hundred excuses not to concede that they have been wrong. For this reason it is not surprising that so far "revisionism" has not admitted its bankruptcy. But it does perhaps not greatly matter, for a new generation of Sovietologists has meanwhile appeared on the scene, with a more realistic approach, quite different in outlook from the revisionists.

Part III
Russia, Right and Left

12

Russian Nationalism

A Time of Troubles Fuels the Right

Once again Russia is entering a *smuta,* a time of troubles, the out-come of which cannot be predicted. Only one thing is certain: the reap-pearance of a nationalist movement, one firmly believing that Russia's rightful role as a great power can only be saved by a strong authoritarian government. For many years students of Russia focused on the left; hav-ing been decisively defeated in 1917, the right no longer counted politi-cally, and ideologically it had nothing of interest to offer. Yet today the whole spectrum of Russian politics has moved to the right and become more nationalist.

This trend is a reaction to the breakup of the Soviet Union and is bound to continue. Much nationalist sentiment could be contained or assuaged if moderation and common sense prevailed. But those attributes are always in short supply in times of crisis. Millions of Russians still reside in the former republics of the empire, and separatist groups inside Russia itself insist on autonomy and even full independence. Allowed free rein such pressures threaten the survival of the Russia republic.

Given the strongly nationalist moods that also prevail among the non-Russian republics and ethnic groups, the stage is set for collision. The age of aggressive nationalism and nationalist conflict that ended in west-ern Europe, by and large, in 1945 has returned with a vengeance in East-ern Europe and the former Soviet Union. Thus present conditions in Russia are not conducive to consolidating democratic ideas and institutions. Nationalist forces, some of the extreme right, others moderate, have a reasonable chance in the struggle for Russia's soul and political future, at least in the short run.

Competing Ideas of Nationalism

For all its nuances and tendencies the supreme moral authority of Russian nationalism is academician Dmitri Likhachev, the grand old man of Russian historiography and letters. Neither a politician nor head of any party, he stands to many Russians, except those of the extreme right, as the conscience of the nation. With emphasis and eloquence he has argued that true patriotism spiritually enriches the individual, as it does the nation, and that patriotism is the noblest of feelings.

Members of the educated Russian public who constitute the national liberal camp share many of Likhachev's views. As moderate nationalists they are perhaps comparable to European conservatives, with an emphasis on patriotism and in many, but not all cases, a shared religious faith. They want a free Russia (not necessarily patterned on Western democracy) and are deeply saddened by the loss of large territories populated predominantly by Russians. Among the national liberals are, for example, Sergei Averintsev, a distinguished historian of medieval culture and theology; Alexander Tsypko, one of the political scientists who acquired fame in the *glasnost* era; some editors of the literary magazine *Novy Mir* as well as literary critics such as Igor Vinogradov and Alla Latynina. Above all there is Aleksandr Solzhenitsyn and his circle.[1] Finally there are political leaders from Boris Yeltsin to Anatoly Sobchak and Sergei Stankevich who, following the downfall of the Soviet Union, insisted with increasing frequency and intensity on Russian concerns and interests.

It is probably easiest to define the national liberals if they are compared with the radical democrats, who exist by and large in the Sakharov tradition and are comparable to the West's liberal democrats. For radical democrats the creation of democratic institutions is paramount; the absence of such institutions was the main cause of Russia's misfortunes, and they fear that individual freedom will not be secure until democratic institutions are firmly entrenched. The radical democrats have no wish slavishly to imitate the West, but nor do they feel any urge to follow a decidedly Russian social and economic policy. They see no specific Russian tradition that could now serve as a guide for the perplexed.

Most radical democrats are not religious. They regard the loss of traditional Russian territories as a misfortune but see no way to undo it, at least not in the foreseeable future. They have no agreed upon program for Russia's economic system. Some support a classical liberal philosophy along the lines of Hayek and Friedman, others are Social Democrats. They strongly insist on a multiparty system and regard the extreme right (as opposed to the more moderate national liberals) as the main danger that, if in power, would lead Russia back to tyranny, war, and total disaster. They love the culture of their native land; in fact they are often more Russian—in the tradition of the nineteenth-century intelligentsia—than they know. But they are pitiless in their criticism of the dark side of Russia's past. They are open to Western influences, and their feeling of nostalgia for old Russia is not as intense as that of the national liberals.

Given Russia's past and the enormous difficulties ahead, national liberals think that an (enlightened) authoritarian regime is more or less foreordained.

They hope that religion will play a crucial role in the future. They tend to idealize pre-1917 Russia and envisage a political and social regime not altogether unlike the one prevailing then—of course cleansed of its negative features but in line with old Russian traditions. Most believe that the price that had to be paid of late for freedom was probably too high. What future is there for a Russia deprived of the Ukraine, White Russia, the Crimea and predominantly Russian northern Kazakhstan?

This is the strongest point in their thinking, and it is shared to some extent by the radical democrats. The Balkanization of the former Soviet Union is a tragedy; it will certainly make democratization infinitely more difficult. It is paradoxical that at a time when borders are disappearing in Western and Central Europe, the trend in the east is toward secession and separatism. While on a level of abstraction every nationality, even the smallest, has the right on sovereignty, objective factors—not least the intermingling of races and people in the modern world—make this often impossible. There is no moral commandment that they should exert their abstract right.

Soviet rule was in some cultural respects less repressive than tsarist rule toward the nationalities. But Soviet experiments at coalescence (*slyanie*) were unsuccessful, since they were imposed from above. Resentment against Moscow grew and, once political controls were removed, there was no holding back the nationalities from seceding, whatever the cost. In the Soviet Union and tsarist Russia membership in a multinational state had certain advantages, like being part of a prestigious club. But once the reputation of that club declined sharply, this specific motive disappeared.

If Russia had tried to accommodate Ukrainian nationalism, the split might never have occurred. But a serious attempt based on true federation involving home rule was never made and, once the majority of Ukrainians had voted for full independence, there was little the new Russian leadership could do to maintain the union. A closer relationship may emerge in the distant future, once the dreams attached to sovereignty fade. In the meantime, however, Russian patriots will only feel impotent frustration at having to exist without Kiev, the cradle of Russian culture and statehood. The only alternative from a Russian "patriotic" point of view is to invade Ukraine, hardly a practical proposition.

Trauma of Soviet Breakup

The breakup of the Soviet Union is the central event bound to shape the course of Russian nationalism and Russian politics as far ahead as one can see. It could be compared with the impact of the 1919 Versailles Treaty on postwar Germany and with the loss of North Africa for France in the 1950s and 1960s. Versailles, with the concomitant feeling of national humiliation, was one of the main factors in the rise of National Socialism; the retreat from North Africa brought France to the brink of civil war.

Seen in retrospect the losses suffered by Germany and France were far from fatal. Germany lost its unimportant colonies and a few provinces such as Alsace Lorraine, Poznan, and parts of Upper Silesia, inhabited largely by reluctant Germans. The loss of the Maghreb resulted in the exodus of several hundred thousand French citizens. The new Russia, on the other hand, has no more than half the population of the old Soviet Union, and many millions of ethnic Russians now live outside Russia; they have become ethnic minorities at the mercy of new not-so-tolerant masters.

Ten years after the loss of the Maghreb, France was better off and at greater peace with itself than ever before. Seventy years after Versailles, forty years after another lost war, Germany is the strongest country in Europe.

The Russian shock, however, is more severe. True, the loss of empire had not come as the result of military defeat. True, some Russian nationalists had argued for a long time that their country would be better off without the Central Asian republics and perhaps also the Caucasus. Russia, they claimed, had been exploited and in some ways subverted by the non-Russian republics. Russian nationalists such as writer Valentin Rasputin had suggested well before August 1991 that Russia should take the initiative and leave the union. But imperial ambitions and feelings of historical mission were still very much present and, in any case, no one had assumed that the Slavic republics would secede.

The full extent of the trauma is realized only as time goes by. As in Germany after 1918 there was much readiness to accept all kinds of "stab in the back" theories—the disaster had been caused by Russia's sworn enemies abroad and at home. There was growing resentment particularly against the ingrates in the Baltic countries, Ukraine, Moldova but also the Caucasus, who had after all benefited to no small extent from Russian help and protection. There is growing anger about the treatment of the Russians outside Russia. Is it not the duty of the Russian government to protect Russian interests outside the borders of the old Russian Federation? Had not all self-respecting countries throughout history been ready to protect the lives and interests of fellow citizens if these had been in jeopardy?

This mood is widespread and would have been suicidal if the radical democrats and national liberals had left patriotism and the defense of national interests to the extreme right. As in Germany after Versailles it would have been tantamount to surrendering the country to extremists. The great danger is that the republics that seceded might prove increasingly recalcitrant in their nationalist intoxication, unwilling to accommodate legitimate Russian interests. This in turn would make the Russians even more resentful and hostile, prompting conflicts even less amenable to solution. Appeals to reason in such circumstances are bound to fall on deaf ears, and the stage is set for an outburst of the worst instincts. This was the lesson of the new order established after Versailles.

Russia, it is sometimes said, has been condemned by history and geography to be a great power. But what if the forces of cohesion should be weaker than generally believed? What if the disintegration of the Soviet Union should be followed by the disintegration of Russia and the emergence of several smaller independent or semi-independent units, such as Tatarstan, Siberia Yakutia, and others? This possibility had been discussed even before the Soviet Union ceased to exist, and it certainly cannot be ruled out at the present time.

The argument runs approximately as follows: it is easy to imagine Russia as a great power or as a multitude of small units. Anything in between would be unstable and unlikely to last. True, there are forces opposing further disintegration, the Russian nationalists and the old communists on the one hand, and the West on the other. But how strong are they? The West wants a new world order in which peace and quiet prevail, so as to be able to cultivate its own garden. A united Russia, provided it is not too strong, would serve Western interests better than a chaotic state of affairs, which would create new political and economic problems, possibly a stream of refugees and, generally speaking, an enormous zone of insecurity extending from St. Petersburg to Vladivostok.

The assumption that political conditions in Russia will become normal as the result of successful economic reform cannot be taken for granted. Quick improvement in the economic situation is unlikely and, in any case, man does not live by bread alone. People need spiritual beliefs, myths and symbols, and some countries such as Russia need them more than others. Human existence is not a financial balance sheet, a series of profits, losses, allocations, and budgets.

In this respect postcommunist Russia is a desert. Both communism and nationalism are adrift; this is why they may find it easy to get together on some common ground. The churches seem to have neither the message nor the apostles that could generate the energy, enthusiasm and willingness for sacrifice that will be needed in the years to come. Such a vacuum opens the door to all kinds of madness.

After the Second World War Germany and Japan succeeded in rebuilding prosperous and civilized societies without the benefit of a specific German or Japanese idea or faith. True, their defeat had been total, which made it easier to make a new start and shed outdated beliefs. It would have been suicidal for Germans, Italians, or Japanese to refuse to accept their fate; they had to accept it to survive. The Russians, on the other hand, were not defeated in war. On the contrary, successive generations were educated in the belief of their invincibility, military and otherwise. In these circumstances a truly new beginning is psychologically much more difficult.

Who Belongs to the Nation?

In a time of deep crisis the negative ugly aspects of Russia's past—tyranny, darkness and servitude—tend to overpower Russia's beautiful and harmonious features. But there always was a Russia that was a source of pride to its sons and daughters, a Russian people described by J. C. Kohl in an 1842 guidebook as showing "great cheerfulness in the midst of desperation, very tolerably agreeable and gay." Other foreign visitors, while writing scathingly of the psychological effects of despotism, also noted Russian hospitality and kindness toward perfect strangers, the sense of charity and *shirokayn natura*—the generous nature of the Russian people. They had much to say about Russia's many great talents and cultural achievements, a literature that went further back in time than English, French, and German, a folklore as rich as the Russian language and folk songs, sentimental, sad or gay, as moving and beautiful as any in the world. Russia's openness to new influences, they also remarked, was perhaps greater than any other country.

Nature played a crucial role in the development of a specific character of the Russian people—the infinite, open spaces, the Russian forest and majestic streams. No people has been closer to nature than the Russian, and no authors have more lovingly written about it. True, much of this belongs to a rural Russia that is gone forever. But neither the golden nor the silver age of Russian culture emanated from rural communities. If, as Likhachev and others believe, there will be yet another cultural renaissance, it will again come from the cities.

The greatness of Russia has never been in dispute, and the greater the achievements, the greater the pain felt at the end of seventy years of ruin and destruction. Where the national liberals (and *a fortiori* the extreme rightists) have gone wrong is in believing that only they have been feeling the pain, whereas the radical democrats are "cultural nihilists," ignoring or despising everything Russian. This is not even correct with regard to the old Soviet regime; if under Lenin, Stalin and their successors irreplaceable monuments were destroyed and other horrible damage done, it is also true that many more copies of the Russian classics were printed (and performed and exhibited) than in the seventy years before the revolution. A wholly negative attitude toward traditional Russian culture prevailed only for a few years under Soviet rule and only in a few disciplines.

The accusations against radical democrats of harboring a nihilistic attitude toward Russian history and culture are untrue, unless of course one implies that a true patriot has to admire and cherish everything that happened or was produced before 1917, however evil, ugly or stupid— for "our country, right or wrong." The charges of cultural nihilism and "cosmopolitanism" on the part of the extreme right are red herrings—with some exceptions, such as the role of the Orthodox Church in a future Russian society. Not all those on the right are religious believers, and not every one on the left is an atheist. But it is true that the democrats, by and large, stand for a secular society, whereas the right, including the national liberals, is willing to give the Orthodox Church a central role in the political life of the country.

Russian nationalists of the extreme right claim that patriotism, nationalism, and chauvinism are synonyms.[2] In their hearts and politics they differentiate little between patriotism and nationalism. As they see it, nationalism is the most sacred inspiration in life; only through belonging to a nation (or a folk) does the life of the individual gain spiritual meaning; differences between nations are fundamental and commitment to one's nation transcends all other obligations.

Who belongs to the nation? Only ethnic Russians who also belong to the Orthodox Church. Catholics, Muslims, Protestants, or Jews can be Russian subjects, they can be tolerated and given freedom of religious practice, they even can be given certain civic rights. But since "Holy Russia" is meaningless for them, they cannot be true Russians.[3] Some enlightened souls on the right are willing to make concessions; certain individuals of non-Russian blood can become true Russian patriots and identify themselves thoroughly through a great effort and their willingness to sacrifice for the motherland. But these will always be a very few. Others, more extreme, will not make exceptions whatsoever: a Jew baptized is a thief pardoned, as a Russian proverb says.

This kind of argument involves the extreme right in many problems and inconsistencies for which there might be no answers. The religious test for membership in the Russian nation is senseless in the postcommunist era. According to the most favorable polls less than half the Russian population are religious believers, let alone practicing members of the Orthodox church.[4] To replace the religious with a racial test for belonging is not feasible, partly because as a result of Nazism this kind of doctrine has become impossible to accept by all but a few sectarians. Even if it were different, racial doctrine would not be applicable in a country with so much intermingling of peoples and races.

Russia's national liberals (moderate conservatives) hope for peaceful cooperation, a joining of forces in the reconstruction and healing process in a country that has seen so much strife. But there can be collaboration only if there is common ground. With the extreme right's crucial emphasis on Russian exclusivity, fear of anti-Russian intrigues, its deep enmity against cosmopolitans and cultural nihilists, its psychological need for enemies, can the Russian right envisage the removal of barricades, which it may need as much as Erich Honecker needed the Berlin Wall?

The basic differences between liberal Western and authoritarian Eastern nationalism have been noted for a long time.[5] Nationalism in the West emerged in countries that were ethnically more or less homogenous or whose borders were at least well defined; they were economically and culturally highly developed. Nationalism in Eastern Europe (and in the Third World) arose—or was invented—in conditions that were altogether different; hence its antiliberal character, the suppression of minorities, the frequent conflicts and wars with neighbors, and generally destructive character. True, not all Western nationalism always behaved according to these high standards. But since the bitter lessons of two world wars, Western nationalism has, by and large, lost its aggressive character.

In recent years nationalist politicians and groups have mushroomed all over Eastern Europe and the successor states of the Soviet Union. Since their trend is predominantly toward separatism or aggrandizement (or both), their potential for conflict and destabilization is immense. The prospect that moderate nationalism will prevail over its more nasty alternative is uncertain.

There was a time when European rightists rejected freedom, their conversion to modern democracy came only gradually. In the ninety years since it first appeared, the Russian right has not made any significant progress. It has neither advanced toward acceptance of democracy nor has it made the transition to full-fledged fascism. There have been certain changes; nineteenth-century pan-Slavism no longer makes sense in the contemporary world, and it has been replaced by Russophilia.

It is true that as communism is bankrupt and the Soviet Union has fallen apart, a political vacuum has come into being. But it seems unlikely that it will be filled by a native Russian fascism. Soviet leaders, on the whole, shielded their people from a surfeit of information about Nazism and Italian fascism; for over half a century only a handful of books were published on the subject, none of them very illuminating, and many aspects of fascism were altogether taboo. But even the least informed Russian knows that Hitler was not a good man, that the Nazis treated the Russians (not just the communists) as subhumans, that they killed millions of Russians and caused immense destruction. All this is too deep in popular memory to permit a reanimation of Nazism at the present time. The most that can be attempted (and it is tried) is to introduce national socialism through the back door, without any reference to Hitler, Mussolini, and historical fascism.

There may be yet another reason that makes it difficult to preach unalloyed fascism in present-day Russia and this is, paradoxically, its resemblance to Stalinism. The Russian extreme right stands for authoritarian government. But the "cult of personality" such as it existed under Hitler and Stalin cannot be propagated in Russia now except perhaps among the most backward sections of society. The same, mutatis mutandis, applies with regard to the central role of the state party, an essential fixture of fascism. Russians have been immunized, at least for some time to come, against the leading role of a party of this kind under whatever guise.

There are certain features specific to Russia's extreme right, at least with regard to emphasis. This refers above all to Satanism, the Judeo-Masonic plot, and xenophobia. All fascist, para- and prefascist movements believed to some extent in conspiracies; none liked Jews, freemasons, and detractors of their respective history and culture. But in no other country were the ultraright patriots so hypnotized by the intrigues and other hostile actions of enemies that were almost entirely imaginary—and in any case of no great consequence. What could have been the reason—atavistic fear, a feeling of inadequacy and inferiority vis-à-vis the diabolical enemy or perhaps a specific Russian fanaticism? But if such fanaticism had existed, it would have shown itself in other ways, which it did not: there have elsewhere been cases of cultural ultra-nationalism comparable to present-day Russia. But nowhere has the belief in conspiracies been so pronounced.

Perhaps it is unfair to charge the Russian extreme right with a lack of originality. For the number of doctrinal varieties is as limited on the right as it is on the left. In one form or another all the ingredients of a movement of the extreme right—conservative, fascist or parafascist—have been used somewhere in the past. As far as fascism is concerned, there is truly nothing new under the sun, except perhaps the fact that in Russia it is postcommunist in character. Only the future will show what this could mean in practice—that, despite all its opposition to communism, it may inherit certain of the same essential features.

Authoritarianism Probable

Much thought has been given by students of twentieth-century history to the determinants of the growth and success of fascism. It is by now common knowledge that, as in the case of communism, "objective conditions" are not sufficient by way of explanation. Objective conditions— economic crisis and breakdown or absence of democratic institutions—have frequently existed. But unless there was a fuehrer, a duce, who together with likeminded followers created a dynamic mass movement, such opportunities have passed unused.

Experience does not bear out the assumption that once the objective conditions exist, the leader is bound to appear sooner or later. His presence is a historical accident, and for this reason predictions about the likelihood of the seizure of power by a fascist movement are risky. While it is possible in the case of contemporary Russia, it still seems unlikely, be it only because of the divisive character of the Russian extreme right—not by accident (as Marx would have said) but as a result of the wide variety of interests and inspirations represented in these circles.

It is easy to think of reasons that seem to favor the growth of some extreme nationalist movement—the feeling of humiliation following the breakup of the Soviet Union; the need to pursue an assertive policy vis-à-vis the former republics in defense of Russian interests and the presence of many millions of Russians abroad; the bad economic situation and the need to engage in unpopular reforms; the frequent impotence of the authorities in face of a breakdown of law and order; the fact that democratic institutions are not deeply rooted in Russia; the traditional psychological need for a strong hand; the old Weimar dilemma of how to run a democracy in the absence of a sufficient number of democrats; the deep divisions on the left.

All these and other circumstances seem to bear out those on Russia's extreme right who have claimed all along that time works for them. Indeed some observers have argued that the prospects of Nazism in Germany in 1932 were less good than in present-day Russia—if only because when the German crisis came democratic forces had been in power for more than a decade. And is it not also true that postcommunist Russia is repeating the mistake committed by Weimar—giving absolute freedom to the enemies of democracy?

While full-fledged fascism still seems unlikely in Russia an authoritarian system based on nationalist populism appears probable. The blueprints for a Russian version of national socialism have existed for a considerable time. They envisage "union between labor and capital," a broad political movement or, in its absence, the security forces assuming the necessary functions of control in society. Such a regime would be a regrettable step backward in Russia's political development but it would be wrong to classify it as fascist.

To be a good Russian, it is said, one has to cast one's eyes back to the glorious deeds of the virtuous ancestors. This is how patriotic inspiration has been provided everywhere, especially at a time of spiritual as well as political crisis. Totalitarian revolution and liberal reform have failed. Neither the international proletariat nor the fellow Slavs, and certainly not the other nations of the former Soviet Union, have shown enthusiasm to link their fate with Russia's. In these circumstances a retreat to the nation seems the logical and indeed only possible response. Other nations have reacted in a similar way in times of crisis. The Russian slogan *nashe* (ours) is an equivalent of the Irish *sinn féin* (we alone); no phrase has been dearer to the hearts of French nationalists than *la France seule.*

The reference to the glorious deeds of virtuous ancestors, of a golden age, a paradise lost and to be regained, are of course mere myths, for there was no golden age. But myths still have their use and, if all other bonds have broken down, why disparage the appeal to nationalism in order to mobilize a people to undertake the giant efforts that will be needed to extract it from the morass and to build a new base for its existence? The temptation is great, but the doubts whether such an appeal will achieve its aim are even greater. Nietzsche once wrote that to be a good German means to de-Germanize oneself.[6] The same may well apply to Russia in its present predicament. What Nietzsche had in mind was of course not to accept slavishly some foreign model, not to shed old traditions just for the sake of making a break with the past—this had been tried from Peter the Great onwards and did not work too well. What Nietzsche did have in mind was that "if a nation advances and grows, it has to burst the girdle given to it by its nationalist outlook."

What Russia now needs, the glorious past and the virtuous ancestors cannot provide—namely, to build a new economy and a new society. Nationalism has great power to mobilize the resources of a people against foreign enemies. But the threat facing Russia does not come from the outside. To the rebuilding of the country nationalism per se cannot make a decisive contribution. It can appeal to the historical and cultural cohesion of the people, to common values, to idealism. But it has no specific ideas to offer derived from Russia's past.

All this refers to moderate nationalism; the ideas of the extreme right are not only mad but evil. By creating foes where none exist they deflect the energies of the nation from where they are most needed—coping with the real dangers, the immense work of reconstruction. If their views were to prevail, the extreme right could well achieve what neither Hitler nor Stalin or his successors succeeded in achieving: the total ruin of the country. At present this seems to be a farfetched proposition, for the Russian people is no longer an ignorant herd.

Who then will help Russia in its predicament? The reply, paradoxically, is contained in Eugen Pottier's song that was for decades the official anthem of the Soviet Union: help will not come from outside/neither God nor a master will bring salvation (*Ni dieu, ni maitre*). It can come only through the Russian people's own efforts, its good sense and its fortitude in the face of adversity.

Notes

1. There has been, not surprisingly, constant ideological fluidity. While Solzhenitsyn has been defended against the democrats by liberals, such as G. Pomerants and A. Nemtser, some of the erstwhile Christian Democrats (A. Gulyga, Y. Kublanovsky, V. Aksiuchits) have moved toward the right.
2. "Spravochnik patriota chernosotensa," *Russkii Traktir,* no. 1, 1992.
3. This has been the prevailing view since the later Slavophiles. Quoted from Ivan Aksakov, "Myslima li Russkaya narodnost vne Pravoslaviya?" An article originally published in *Den,* 1 August 1864; republished in *Russkii Rubezh,* no. 4, 1992.
4. According to a September 1991 *Vox populi* poll, 51 percent of men surveyed considered themselves religious believers, not necessarily of the Orthodox Church.
5. John Plamenatz, "Two Types of Nationalism," in E. Kamenka (ed.), *Nationalism, the Nature and Evolution of an Idea* (1973). The author, a student of Marxism and nationalism, was a native of Montenegro.
6. *Menschliches-Allzmenschliches,* 11 vol. IV, p 159.

13

Rightwing Extremism I

One of the most interesting features of the present intellectual ferment in the Soviet Union is the emergence of a new Russian (as distinct from Soviet) ideology. Unlike the disreputable and internally divided Pamyat, the members of the new Russian right are respectable and highly placed members of the establishment, government officials, writers, scientists, painters. They have their well-wishers in key positions from the Politburo downward, their own literary magazines, *Nash Sovremennik* (Our Contemporary, founded by Gorky), *Molodaia Gvardia* (Young Guard), *Moskva.* Patriotic clubs are proliferating to which people of different persuasion or ethnic origin have no access. This movement resembles an influential Masonic lodge, though the comparison would be strongly resented. Still, the similarity is uncanny: to a young man from the provinces arriving in the capital to gain fame and fortune in the media, in literature, music, or the visual arts, this cabal can bring publicity, open doors, and provide good notices, assuming that our hero subscribes to their doctrine.

In the beginning there was only Pamyat, a group of uniformed thugs that first appeared on the scene in the early 1980s. In order to camouflage their activities, these thugs portrayed themselves as an association for the restoration of churches, graveyards, and other such monuments. The authorities turned a blind eye, but when they realized that Pamyat was not just fanatically anti-Jewish, but also that it would dearly love to hang the communists and a great many other "anti-patriotic elements," the official attitude became less benevolent. Pamyat and its supporters did not do well in the 1989 elections to the new Soviet parliament, however, and the authorities seem to have decided that instead of banning Pamyat they would encourage a variety of competing groups. Thus, during the past year a great number of local, regional, and nationwide organizations have come into being, with names such as Workers Front, Fatherland, and United Council of Russia, and Rescue (Salvation). All of them preach a return to patriotism, law and order, and other traditional values. and protest against the alleged discrimination of ethnic Russians. The Workers Front is bitterly attacking the (liberal) intelligentsia and demanding that the right to vote should be restricted to the factories—which means, in practice, that the majority of the population would be denied democracy.

This phenomenon of the new Russian right is rooted in the general crisis of Soviet society, in the disappointment with the Party, the unions, and other official organizations. It is a search for new frameworks for action. Although communism has been a bitter disappointment, there is no love for capitalism; there is, on the contrary, resentment against the nouveaux riches (according to some estimates, there are now 175,000 millionaires in the Soviet Union) who made their money not through honest work, enterprise, and inventiveness, but by cheating the Soviet worker, by black market activities, and so on.

Although estimates of the size of the .New Right are unreliable, it is significant that at a time when most periodicals and newspapers are losing readers, the circulation of *Nash Sovremennik* has risen by two-thirds. There are some indications, though, that New Right organizations have not been doing too well among the workers. The striking miners and railway workers have pressed very specific social and economic demands that have little in common with the programs of the patriotic societies. The New Right's influence in the lower ranks of the Party and state bureaucracy, in the ranks of those afraid of losing their jobs in a major reform, and in some circles of the intelligentsia seems to be larger.

It is difficult, moreover, to point to any specific class or social group that displays particular affinities for the New Right. The geographical distribution of these notions is easier to establish. Sympathies for the New Right have certainly been stronger in declining regions (beginning with Leningrad), in badly run cities with outdated industries and major ecological problems, and in regions in which there is political and social pressure against the ethnic Russians by local nationalities. Like fascism, the New Right appeals not to any specific group but to the *spostati,* to the dissatisfied people of all classes—of which there are many in the Soviet Union.

According to a remarkable essay by the Moscow writer Mikhail Leontiev, in the Riga weekly, *Atmoda,* the doctrine of the extreme right is largely based on fear of the "satanic forces" that undermine everything sacred to the heart of Russian patriots, exploit the people, install local mafias to corrupt the population, instigate social and national strife. Leaders such as Mikhail Gorbachev and Alexander Yakovlev are mere puppets, manipulated by international financial corporations and Zionist billionaires. Old-fashioned fascist or Stalinist doctrine, Leontiev says, would have little effect in the present situation, but as the disorientation of the masses is growing, the appeal of fear is great.

Who are the potential saviors of the Russian people in this hour of grave danger? Pyotr Stolypin's name is mentioned with increased frequency. He was the most capable statesman of the late tsarist period, but he has been dead for a long time. Solzhenitsyn's authority is very often invoked. When he was in trouble, the far right attacked him as a traitor, but their attitude has changed over the last year or two (the fact that Solzhenitsyn has written at great length and with much enthusiasm about Stolypin may not be fortuitous). Lastly there is Yegor Ligachev, regarded by many as Gorbachev's main antagonist in the Politburo. We know, from a recent interview, that Ligachev is a great admirer of the writers who are the spokesmen of the right wing, and he shares much of their criticism of the destructive influence of the "liberals" in Soviet political and intellectual life. But Ligachev is also an old communist; he would not find it easy to give full support to a movement in total opposition to Marxism, to the October Revolution, to the Bolshevik policies since the Revolution.

The emergence of the Russian nationalist movement does not come as a total surprise. Its leading advocates have been publishing their essays for twenty years or more. Under Khrushchev and Brezhnev they had to be much more circumspect; open attacks against Marxism and the old Bolsheviks would have been unthinkable. Today they are quite common. The doctrine of the New Right is, essentially, that the Russian people is gradually becoming a stranger in its own home, that it is biologically and culturally threatened by extinction. This notion rests, in turn, on the assumption that an immensely cunning and powerful enemy has decided to destroy the Russian people, its tradition, and its culture. The enemy consists, above all, of Trotskyites, Zionists, and Masons, but also of anti-Stalinist historians, liberal novelists and playwrights, and advocates of economic *perestroika* who dream of reintroducing capitalism in Russia.

All these are, of course, code words. "Trotskyite" no more refers to Lenin's comrade-in-arms, who has been dead for fifty years, than "Zionist" means the followers of Theodor Herzl; and there have been no Masonic activities in Russia for the past seventy years. In fact, a Trotskyite is a communist (perhaps a social democrat, or even a liberal) who happens to subscribe to an internationalist ideology, be it Marxism or liberalism or some other cosmopolitan creed. In this light, Marx too was a Trotskyite, and so were Lenin and Stalin; and Marx was a Zionist *avant la lettre,* because he was a Jew by origin.

The views of the thinkers of the New Right have been a matter of growing concern to the Soviet reformers, but of less concern to the Party hierarchy, which probably considers them a useful antidote to the "liberals." Fascination seems a more appropriate reaction than horror. There are people of the left and people of the right in every country that allows freedom of expression, and there is no reason why the Soviet Union, if it is to become an open society, should be an exception. Certainly the ideology of the New Right is of great interest to a student of twentieth-century European culture; he will be reminded of Maurras and the *Action Française,* of the German *Kulturkritiker* of the right, of Knut Hamsun, and others, not to mention the right-wing thinkers among the Russian émigrés, who now enjoy a great vogue.

Some Russian liberals take a less detached view—Leontiev, for example, in the article quoted above: "The danger of a fascist coup is growing daily in our country, inasmuch as the fascist consensus is not limited to exalted youngsters with swastikas on their leather jackets, but includes representative elements of the creative and technical intelligentsia and strengthens its influence in the political establishment (the Party apparatus, the army, and the security organs)." What if a leading Western intellectual were to express solidarity with the Ku Klux Klan or with Lyndon LaRouche? Would he not be considered beyond the pale?

Members of this "Russian party" have angrily protested against their adversaries' practice of branding them "informers," "fascist," or "parafascist." They would have a stronger case but for their own unsavory record, the appeals to the Party organs (including the KGB) to "take measures" against liberals and cosmopolitans allegedly undermining the moral of the Russian people. They were in the forefront of the campaign in the 1960s against the monthly literary magazine *Novy Mir,* the main bulwark of liberalism at the time; they asked for Solzhenitsyn's head; they now want to close down *Ogonyok,* the most popular weekly.

The Russian intelligentsia has been cut off for many decades from the rest of the world. Right-wing intellectuals may be genuinely unaware that their "facts" and arguments are not new, that they were widely aired by profascist writers in Russia in the 1920s and 1930s. Perhaps they would be embarrassed to advocate these theories if they knew their antecedents and their consequences. One document widely circulated in rightwing samizdat in Moscow is based, in fact, on speeches made at the Nuremberg rally in 1936. When this became known, there was considerable chagrin; Hitler, Alfred Rosenberg, and Julius Streicher are not considered good company in Russia, even at a distance of fifty years.

Why the sudden preoccupation with the crimes committed by the Bolsheviks against the Russian peasantry and other classes in the 1920s? Surely the confrontation with current problems is even more important; and it is not a little strange to make Sverdlov, Trotsky, and Zinoviev responsible for policies carried out many years after their deaths by Stalin, Molotov, Zhdanov, and Voroshilov. It would be convenient if it could be shown that the revolutionaries who caused all the misfortunes to Mother Russia were of alien stock, but this, alas, is not easy to prove. For the Dekabrists (Decembrists) and the Narodovoltsy (radical populists) were no more Jews than Lenin, Khrushchev, and Brezhnev (or Mao and Tito). There must have been some, even many, bad Russians who turned against their own people. Perhaps the whole Russian intelligentsia has been following false prophets.

The "Russian party" is not cut of one cloth. The apocalyptic wing, writers such as Vasili Belov, Yuri Bondarev, and Valentin Rasputin, maintain that the Russian people is on the brink of total disaster, that an attempt to save the nation must be made even at this late hour, though it may already be too late. But other ideologists of the extreme right, such as the writer Vadim Kozhinov, are much less alarmist. True, they say, Russia faces very serious internal problems in agricultural production, in its crime rate, in the spread of drugs, in its rebelling minorities. But seen in international perspective, these difficulties are neither unique nor even particularly severe. America has a much greater drug problem, Britain has to cope with the IRA, and so on.

Historically, the "Russian party" consists of two factions that originally differed on matters of principle. There are the Russian nationalists, whose homes are decorated with icons and pictures of Stolypin. They have no sympathy for Marx, who wrote nasty things about Russian history, and they loathe Lenin, a déraciné Russian who had not the slightest interest in, or feeling for, Russian traditions. And there are the neo-Stalinists, who have little enthusiasm for the icons and for the "old women in old villages." Stolypin ("the hangman") is anathema to them. They would not be caught dead in a cathedral.

Despite these internecine differences, the new "Russian party" is united by three main planks: its populism; its belief that of all the Soviet republics, the Russian has been the victim of the most discrimination; and by its campaign against what it calls "Russophobia."

The Russian nationalists have gradually accepted that, though the Revolution of 1917 was a disaster, it cannot be undone. Since they never advocated capitalism, but rather something akin to a conservative *Ständestaat,* they find it relatively easy to embrace a populist platform, which is opposed to *perestroika,* the market, and private initiative. Their spokesmen, such as Mikhail Antonov and Anatoli Zalutsky (the latter is a Jew by origin), have charged Tatyana Zaslavskaya, one of the founders of Soviet sociology and an early member of Gorbachev's brain trust, with the destruction of the Russian village, and they consider the Gorbachev version of *"enrichessez-vous"* (that is to say, encouraging the cooperatives) exceedingly dangerous.

This is accompanied by anti-intellectualism. These writers rail against the nefarious role of the intelligentsia, the traditional bugbear of the Russian right for the past 150 years, who, they argue, have detached themselves from the people and forgotten their national roofs. The "Russian party" has no sympathy for atonal music, or for Freud, Einstein, or Kafka, or for most of Western culture, mass and elite, of the past 100 years. But the neo-Stalinists have realized that the old Party orthodoxy has had its day. They understand that much of it will have to be jettisoned to attract the masses. This results in a left-wing populism of sorts. This trend, too, is not entirely new; it began in the 1930s under Stalin but it has gathered speed in recent years.

And there is the matter of discrimination against the Russian Soviet Federative Socialist Republic (RSFSR). The neo-Stalinists claim that the standard of living is lower there than almost everywhere else in the Soviet Union except the Central Asian republics, that every other republic has its own television network, academy of sciences, encyclopedia, publishing houses, and so on. The RSFSR does not even have its own KGB. Such a state of affairs obviously must be remedied.

All these complaints have some justification. But Soviet television is, in reality, Russian television; the same is true for the Great Soviet Encyclopedia, and so on. In the state and Party leadership, the Russian element is overrepresented, and the same applies to the army and other key positions in the Party, state, and society. The income level in the RSFSR is lower than in some other republics, but this is owed to a variety of factors such as the poor quality of the soil in northern Russia and its lower productivity compared with, say, the Baltic republics.

To put right such "discrimination," work has now begun on a new Russian Encyclopedia. This raises delicate questions. Some purists have claimed that Jewish writers, such as Isaac Babel, belong to the history of Jewish literature, rather than to the history of Russian literature, and that there should be no room for, say, Chagall, even though he was born in Vitebsk. Should one include Pasternak and Mandelstam, who also do not hail from Vologda or Tambov? The best known and most loved Soviet comic writers were a team named Ilf and Petrov, but Ilf's name at birth was Feinsilberg. Should one include half of their works, and which half? Should the entry "chess" be deleted from the Encyclopedia? Valentin Sorokin, a poet writing in the August issue of *Nash Sovremennik*, favors deletion. He writes: "I do not wish that a Bashkir, Jew, Tartar or Georgian should compose poetry in my native language. I do not want it, I do not trust them. A Bashkir will not give me the music of my tongue but only a Russian."

Such ideas have occurred to people in other countries in previous ages. For the time being, however, Pasternak and Mandelstam (not to mention Vysotsky and Galich) are more widely read and admired in the Soviet Union than Sorokin and even the most famous of his friends. And the neo-Stalinists have a bigger problem. What writers in Russian literature can be trusted? The classic dictionary of the Russian language, on which every Russian writer has depended, was composed by a nineteenth-century savant named Dal, who was Danish by origin. Pushkin had some African blood in his veins. Lermontov's ancestors came from Scotland. Gogol was a Ukrainian by origin, Herzen was half German, and there are even some suspicions about Dostovevsky if one goes back far enough in what the Nazis called *Sippenforschung* (looking for your racial antecedents). The believers in the purity of Russian blood are left with Turgenev and Chekhov, whom they do not like because they were "Westerners." There is also Gorky, but he wrote very bad things about the Russian peasantry, much worse than any of the accursed cosmopolitans.

Finally, the main component, the strangest component, of the thinking of the Russian right is its abhorrence of "Russophobia," a concept that in its modern form dates back to the 1960s, and that has gained more and more prominence of late. It means the hatred and the fear of Russia and the Russian people. It is the title of a long essay by Igor Shafarevich, a well-known Russian mathematician, which was published first in samizdat some years ago, later by a Russian nationalist group in Munich, and eventually by the monthlies *Nash Sovremennik* and *Kaban* in the Soviet Union. According to Shafarevich, there has been a deliberate attempt by Western historians, and also by some Russian writers, to denigrate Russian history as backward, cruel, despotic, hostile to civilizations, a nation of serfs and a danger to all mankind.

Though such sentiments were voiced in hours of anguish by Pushkin and Lermontov, by Cha'adaev and Herzen and Chernyshevsky, these classics of Russian literature are not the villains Shafarevich has in mind. His ire is directed against the late Vasili Grossman, against Richard Pipes, against dissidents and émigrés not remotely as well known to the average Russian as Pushkin and Lermontov but far more convenient as targets. The Russophobes are said to hate Russia with a deep, burning, physiological hatred, because of her forests, fields, and climate, because of her customs, because of her history and culture. These haters include virtually the whole revolutionary movement beginning in the 19th century. Above all, they include the Jews, who are singled out because of their belief in their own mission, notably Heinrich Heine, the Hebrew poet Chaim Nahman Bialik, and George C. Marshall, former chief of staff and secretary of state. (The name Marshall, Shafarevich explains, is Hebrew, and means being a clown in the ghetto.) Shafarevich says that he will not die in peace unless he succeeds in bringing this message to his people.

For Shafarevich's comments on more recent events, one has to turn to his long essay in the centrist-liberal journal *Novy Mir* in July 1989. Its theme is that Russia should not imitate the Western way of life, because the West is in the throes of a deep spiritual crisis, which will lead to a socio-ecological catastrophe. He has some very harsh things to say about the Western belief in progress, and in particular about the United States, which exploits the rest of the world to keep up its artificially high living standard. (Shafarevich is not a believer in Lenin's theory of imperialism.)

His antisocialist convictions are second to none; his anti-Americanism and antiliberalism are of the right, not the left. He concedes that Western liberalism has done much for the spread of humanism. But his humanism was always inwardly directed, for domestic, not foreign, consumption. He refers at length to the refusal of the Western liberal-progressive intelligentsia (Shaw, Wells, Feuchtwanger, Rolland, Einstein, Upton Sinclair) to speak out against the horrors of Stalinist Russia. He reports Solzhenitsyn telling him of his discovery, much to his surprise, that there exists a whole literature in the West about the Soviet concentration camps, but that nobody paid attention until his Gulag trilogy appeared; and in a similar way, Shafarevich continues, even Stalin's campaign against the doctors was virtually hushed up in the West. Only when things began to improve in the Soviet Union after Stalin's death did Western liberals begin to be heard: more proof that their real inspiration was not anti-Stalinist, but anti-Russian.

Strange arguments, stranger conclusion. In a recent interview in *Knizhnoe Obozrenie* (Book Survey), Shafarevich recommended the publication of a Russian émigré author named Ivan Solonevich. The choice is interesting, for Solonevich advocated a "social monarchy" for Russia. Shafarevich forgot to mention that his apostle of social monarchs did not have Sweden, Norway, or Denmark in mind; he was, during the 1930s, one of the most fervent collaborators with Nazi Germany.

Is Shafarevich following in the footsteps of Philipp Lenard and Johannes Stark, the great German scientists, leaders in their fields, winners of the Nobel Prize, who believed that Adolf Hitler was the greatest German who had ever lived? I have read his earlier nonmathematical writings and saw him interviewed on Moscow television a little while ago. He is in his sixties, fast talking, short of breath, not a demagogue, quite sincere, a man of character, not a forceful speaker, an eccentric perhaps, but not a fascist. Maybe he is right to warn against borrowing billions from the West. Perhaps copying Western institutions would merely result, as Shafarevich puts it, in becoming another Latin American country. But what is the religious-patriotic alternative to which he indirectly refers? Iran?

There is a strong element of paranoia in the new Russian ideology. The search for the origins of this ideology takes one back to Dostoyevsky's *Diary of a Writer,* to a chauvinism that claims to be humanistic, that is partly religious in inspiration. But there is also an admixture of the Stalinist mentality. With all the hostility of the nationalists toward Stalin, these people are products of the Stalin era in Soviet history. It was one of the basic tenets of that age that giant conspiracies were afoot, at home and abroad, to bring down the communist regime: that wreckers and spies were lurking behind every corner. A belief in the "hidden hand" may be found in many political cultures, of course, not least our own; but it has been particularly strong in Russia, where it was, for long periods, official state policy. The advocates of the Russophobia concept have never quite rid themselves of the legacy of the days when they marched in the ranks of the Komsomol, the Soviet youth organization, of its enthusiastic self-righteousness, its fanaticism, its absence of skepticism and self-criticism.

Another one of the central features of life under Stalinism was intellectual isolation. This generation has missed almost a century of world intellectual history. Now it discovers all kinds of thinkers, left, right, and center, Arnold Toynbee and Jean-Paul Sartre and Hans Freyer, positivists and metaphysicians, conservatives and radicals. They have no clear notion of how all these thinkers do or do not hang together, who was important and who was not. Shafarevich, for example, genuinely believes that the attitude of the *Nation* and the *New Statesman* toward Stalin and Stalinism was the attitude of all (or most) liberals in the Western world. He and his ilk are ignorant of Western reactions to the Moscow trials and the Stalinist terror (other than Feuchtwanger's book *Moscow 1937*). They prefer to believe that Stalinism was a global intellectual phenomenon "from Madrid to Shanghai" (in Kozhinov's words). This theory has a great many advantages. Why blame the Soviet people if everyone else applauded Stalin, too?

How can anyone with a modicum of common sense believe that Russophobia is the most important and most immediate threat to the existence of the Russian people? Of course, there are those who do not like Russia and the Russians; they can be found among the minorities in Central Asia, the Caucasus and the Baltic region, among Russia's neighbors in Eastern Europe and the Far East. But Shafarevich's preoccupation is with "spiritual Russophobia." He and his companions have persuaded themselves that it is most rampant among the very people who love the Russian language and Russian literature, who dream about their past in Russia, who cannot end their not-so-happy and rather one-sided love affair with Russian culture. And Russian national consciousness is not such a tender plant that it would wilt at once if exposed to the winds of change. How many Englishmen are losing sleep as the result of the resentment against their country in various parts of the world? How many Americans worry about anti-Americanism?

Igor Shafarevich has been much in demand in recent weeks. He has appeared in the journals of the right as well as the left, he has been interviewed on national television with the deference due to a great thinker. He has been quoted in some journals with approval, in others with dismay. He has signed an open letter charging *Oktiabr* (October) with Russophobia because it published Vasili Grossman, and calling for action on the part of the authorities. Only yesterday, of course, he was himself at the receiving end of such "administrative measures."

Such views are taken seriously in the Soviet Union today. It would be wrong to treat the neo-Stalinists as eccentrics. Firm convictions tend to have influence at a time of intellectual confusion. The Soviet Union now faces something akin to an ideological vacuum. Marxism-Leninism still serves as the state ideology, but there is no real conviction behind it. What belief can succeed it? The doctrines advocated by Shafarevich and his colleagues are certainly a serious contender. Some claim (mistakenly, I believe) that they are the only contender.

The opinions expressed by Shafarevich are not those of a voice calling in the wilderness. There have been dozens of similar essays of late; nor are his views particularly extreme. (Compared with other authors in journals such as *Molodaia Gvardia* and *Nash Sovremennik,* our academician is a paragon of sense and moderation.) How much political importance, then, should be accorded to this new-old trend? It certainly reflects the mood of some sections of the population. If the party of reform in the Soviet Union should suffer a major setback, these ideologists will be in greater demand. Liberals in and out of Moscow fear that it is only a question of time until Russia is engulfed by reactionary and obscurantist forces. It is true that the Soviet Union is passing through a serious crisis, spiritual as much as political and economic. But luckily there is no Gresham's law of history.

14

Rightwing Extremism II

Black Hundred—1994

Some words of explanation are needed to accompany the Russian edition of *Black Hundred*. Russian readers ought to be reminded that my study was written for a Western public. In a book written for Russians I would have been shorter on some topics and more detailed on others. It was not my intention to write a book about Russian patriotism in general, or about the Russian right or the conservatives in general. These are important subjects but my focus was on the extreme right, those, broadly speaking, in the tradition of the Black Hundred. I deliberately say "broadly speaking" because the situation in post-Communist Russia in 1994 is, of course, quite dissimilar to that in tsarist Russia in 1905. The fact that the extreme right and the neo-Bolsheviks have moved closer together (not only in Russia but also, for instance, in France) has not been a mere accident. Radical populism can move "left" or "right" with equal ease, the old labels do not make much sense, in any case. In 1905 the Black Hundred and the Bolsheviks killed each other, today their relations are much better.

Some of the reviewers of this book in English and German have expressed surprise about the fact that the author wrote in a detached way about ideas and people with which, quite obviously, he was not in sympathy. But it was not my intention to write a polemical book. As a student of fascism I know that this is not a movement that can be combatted or refuted by rational argument in the same way that an anti-Semite will not come to like Jews even though it might be shown to him that a good number of them got the Nobel prize, play chess and the violin quite well.

Among the more intelligent sayings of Mr. Sergei Baburin when he explained why he did not join the Front of National Salvation was that he finds it difficult to work with people who cannot put two sentences together without cursing the Judeo-Masonic conspiracy. Likewise I thought it pointless to remind the reader on every page of this book that the extreme right is bad medicine and that in a position of power it would lead Russia to total disaster. On these issues readers have to draw their own conclusions.

I have in this book concentrated much more on the ideas of the extreme right than on its organizational structure, and this for more than one reason. Mainly perhaps because the parties and sects constantly change, they unite and split every few months, merge again, change their names—it is difficult to keep track of this constant movement, and impossible to do so in a book. For by the time the book comes out there will be new alignments that no one could have foreseen—and that may not last in any case.

How important is the extreme right? In September 1993, in an American review of this book entitled "False Alarm," Professor Richard Pipes, the well-known historian, wrote that Pamyat was small, that there would be no violence in Moscow, and that the future of Russia would be a political and economic success story like Germany after the Second World War. It is perfectly true that *Pamyat* is small (although many Western experts believe that this is the most important group on the Russian right) but the timing of the article and the title were unfortunate because two weeks later fighting broke out in the Russian capital on a scale unprecedented since 1917.

I am not a dark pessimist as far as Russia's future is concerned, and I find the fashionable despair among many Russians on this subject difficult to explain and unworthy of a great nation. True there has been a pessimistic note all through Russian history of the last two hundred years, but it is my impression that it did not really go that deep. The Russian intelligentsia talked and wrote about the coming apocalypse, but in the meantime they acted as if it was still far away. However, there is no room for excessive optimism either. Russia's road to prosperity and free institutions will not be like Germany's after 1945. It will be a very long road with many detours and setbacks. And it is precisely against this background of inevitable economic and political crisis in the years ahead that the extreme right, in collaboration with the neocommunists and perhaps with military circles may get its chance.

Since the appearance of the English edition of this work history has not stood still, some of the trends that could only be dimly perceived can now be seen more clearly. No great monarchist revival has taken place, nor have the Cossacks emerged as a major political force nationwide. During the crisis of September/October 1993 the Church called not for the shedding of blood but tried to mediate between the two sides though without much success. Quite irrespective of the extent of the religious revival, a majority of Russians do not look to the Church for political guidance and with some notable exceptions the Church, wisely no doubt, has not been in a hurry to volunteer such leadership, instead merely insisting on its moral authority. Some servants of the Church have openly come out on the side of the extreme right, one of them was Metropolitan Ioann of Petersburg and Ladoga. His appeals were openly chauvinistic and anti-Semitic; before 1990 he was not known as an outstanding patriot. Perhaps, this old man is a recent convert, or perhaps he thought it too risky to make known his true convictions. Some of his colleagues continue to be cautious even though their sympathies might not be that far from Ioann's.

The future on the extreme right seems to belong to much younger leaders such as Mikolai Lysenko, Nikolai Parlov, to Sergei Baburin and Gennadi Ziuganov, the Communist party leader, whose appeal would have been even greater had he decided to change the name of his party, to drop the old slogans, to forego the Lenin and Stalin portraits (which are quite popular except among some members of the older generation).

It is very difficult to assess the strength of the various factions on the Russian right and they mostly do not know it themselves. They all have pockets of influence but no one has a country wide organization so far. While the results of elections are of interest, they do not necessarily convey a full picture. These results have more to do with the success (or failure) of their leaders on television than the number and dedication of their cadres. Some, obviously are better financed than others, but money alone cannot provide strength as Sterligur, the KGB general found out during the October 1993 showdown when he could not send any "fighters" to the White House and Ostankino whereas Narkashov the fascist karate expert could mobilize a few hundred. It will be recalled that neither Pamyat nor Zhirinovsky's people took part in the fighting, and many other leaders and groups also had no wish to get involved. Those who did, such as Konstantinov and General Makashev came to regret it for they no more became martyrs than had the leaders of the earlier coup of August 1991.

Not many facts are available as to the finances of the extreme right. A considerable amount comes, no doubt, from among the new breed of businessmen in Moscow and also the provinces. Some may give because they genuinely sympathize with the patriots, not belonging to the "comprador bourgeoisie," others, because of the time honored practice of *perestrakhovka.* It is most unlikely that any of these groups exist mainly from membership dues. Are other sources involved such as the funds of the former Communist party that have mysteriously disappeared? It took the revolution of March 1917 to find out details about sources of income of the Black Hundred and it is unlikely that we shall soon have hard facts on this account.

The ideological quarrels continued on the extreme right. Even such impeccable stalwarts like Shafarevich and Kozhinov found themselves under attack which, given their committment to the patriotic cause, struck outside observers as wholly unjustified.[1] Their attacker, Ms. Glushkova, was not exactly an ideological heavyweight, she reminded one of a small but very aggressive lapdog who would be the terror of postmen and casual visitors, barking and biting passers-by quite indiscriminately. But there was some logic in her strictures. Her basic point was that some of the leading right wingers had gone too far in their anti-Communist critique, and that it was perfectly possible to combine extreme right wing views with streamlined and updated Stalinism, anticommunism, she maintained, was the most obvious manifestation of Russophobia. As if to prove this point the issue of *Molodaya Gvardiya* which featured Glushkova's polemics also published, not for the first time, the full text of the *Protocols of the Elders of Zion.* Another stalwart of the extreme right who found himself under fire was the indefatigable Mr. Dugin, who had introduced obscure or forgotten West European neo-Fascist thinkers to Russian as well as his own brand of geopolitics.[2] He was taken to task by Kseniya Myalo and others from the right poking fun at the strange synthesis of an ideology combining Hitler and Dostoevsky, Mussolini and Leontiev and other wholly incompatible elements.[3]

Sergei Kurginiyan, the theater expert, who has been one of the more innovative and certainly the most productive ideologist of the new right, expressed concern about the growing fascination of the extreme right, and launched a lengthy polemic against Dugin, but predominantly against Dugin's patron Prokhanov, the editor of Den. Den had certainly become during the period before the events of October 1993 the leading organ of the extreme right, more widely read and more often quoted than any other. It also became shriller with each issue and irrational—not to say downright crazy—a fact that displeased the more moderate and saner elements of the right. Prokhanov, its editor was essentially a *gosudarstvennik* (statist), to what extent did he believe the stories published by his own weekly about horrible plots and crimes, planned and carried out, about black magic and satanism? Yuri Vlasov, no doubt believed this stuff but did Prokhanov? Probably not, but he must have thought that a great number of his readers did.

One could go on commenting on the quarrels and splits in these circles for a long time. All that matters is that there were some fundamental differences between the "integral nationalists" (such as Shafarevich) and the National Bolsheviks who want to preserve a good part of the old system and the Stalinist tradition. There was a conflict between the believers in the restoration of the Soviet Union and those who regard the old Union as a burden and would see their future in a Slavonic Union based essentially on Russia and the Ukraine. Some only see the future for Russia in an alliance with Muslim fundamentalism and a reawakened Asia; others, on the contrary, regard aggressive Muslim fundamentalism and an expanding China as the main threat facing Russia in the decades to come. Some want to keep the old agricultural system, others believe that it could not survive in the long run. Most of these bones of contention were mentioned, even if only briefly in the present book. During the last year these differences have become more pronounced. During a certain period they were papered over because of the need to fight the common enemy—the democrats and the reformers. But sooner or later these issues would crop up simply because they concerned real, fundamental problems.

My book has been criticized by certain Western reviewers for not making it crystal clear what the extreme right was, which groups belonged to it, where borderlines run between it and other movements. To a certain degree I must plead guilty. I was mainly preoccupied with the ideas, sentiments and motives of the extreme right, much less with their organizational structure. Russian politics are very much in flux, and will remain so for a long time to come. Groups and individuals who belonged to the center have moved to the right as the result of current events—and vice versa. Some have become more moderate. I have written elsewhere that, not surprisingly, the whole spectrum of Russian politics has moved to the right. In these circumstances it seems to me impossible, and indeed misleading, to draw rigid dividing lines between "extremists" and "moderates." Strange alliances have emerged—and will emerge in future, and any attempt to "classify" such as botanists, zoologists, or chemists do is quite futile (and even in these fields, the dividing lines are sometimes anything but rigid).

The constant changes on the Russian right are regrettable, but any attempt to impose an artificial order on an essentially disorderly situation would not clarify the state of affairs, on the contrary, it would cause even greater confusion. At the present time, and probably for a long time to come, it is simply impossible to draw a clear dividing line between the extreme right and the moderate, "respectable" wing. Just as there are great differences among the Cossacks or within the monarchist camp, so there are substantial differences between, say, various *gosudarstvenniki*. Furthermore, in a fluid situation people tend to change their opinion, sometimes radically. If Alexander Zinoviev wrote in his preface to Kiril Hankin's *Okhotnik verkh nogami* that the Soviet system wanted to conquer the world, ten years later he attributed to America everything he had written earlier on about Moscow's crimes. Yuri Vlasov began his public career with a massive attack against the KGB and within a few years had joined the camp of the Black Hundred. Maksimov and Sinyavsky found a common language at least with regard to Yeltsin after the event of October 1993—there are countless other examples for massive changes in orientation in Russian politics. Nevertheless, there are certain characteristics as far as the extreme right is concerned, which are almost foolproof and I have pointed to them once or twice in the course of this book: The absence of self-criticism for whatever went wrong in Russia, the constant harping on the crimes of traitors within and outside plotters (Americans and the West in general, the liberals, the Jews, and Masons, the Catholic Church, etc.) Whether such groups and individuals are fascist (or para- or protofascist) or simply in the tradition of the old extreme right, is yet another question. Not every chauvinist or antidemocrat or antisemite is necessarily a fascist. Historical fascism, that is to say the movements launched by Mussolini and Hitler are dead and done for. But this does not mean that in different historical conditions fascism cannot make a comeback as recent events in some West European countries have shown. In post-Communist Russia a fascist, or semifascist upsurge is bound to contain strong Soviet (Communist) elements. I do not claim that such a future is the most likely in store for Russia; as of now a strengthening of the right rather than the extreme right seems more likely.

But the historian is not a prophet, the future is not predestined, and, in any case, there can be no doubt that the extreme right will play a political role of importance in Russia for years to come.

My name will not be known in Russia except to a few specialists. I am not a professional Sovietologist, my field of interest has been, above all European history in the nineteenth and twentieth centuries, and I have been particularly interested in extremist movements of the left and the right, political violence, and the question of generations in politics. Two of my books (possibly more) were translated into Russian but few Russian readers will have seen them. The first, *Russia and Germany*, appeared in Washington, the other *The Long Road to Freedom* (on *glasnost*) was one of the last books, if not the very last, to be translated and published in about 300 copies for the benefit of members of the Central Committee of the CPSU and a few other dignitaries, ordinary mortals had no access to it. The anonymous writer of the preface said that Professor Laqueur was pessimistic (too pessimistic) about the reforms of 1988/90—I wish he had been right, and I had been wrong but history decided otherwise.[4]

Notes

1. *Molodaya Gvardiya,* 9 and 10, 1993.
2. Dugin edited several journals such as *Elementy* and *Mili Angel,* published countless articles in *Den* and elsewhere. A summary of his theories appears in *Konspiratologiya* (1993). He is also head of the Center for "Special metastrategic research."
3. Y. Bulychev, in *Moskva,* 5, 1993.
4. I noted in my book that there was hardly any literature in Russia about fascism. Recently some biographies of Hitler have been published but fascism per se remains terra incognita. The situation with regard the Black Hundred and similar movements is better. Among the books recently published I would like to single out two, S.A. Stepanov, *Chernaya Sotnya v Rossii 1905–1914,* Moscow 1992 and R.S. Ganelin (*Natsionalnaya Pravaya, prezhde i teper.* St. Petersburg, 1992, vol I. There has also been a translation (from the English of John Stephan's book on Russian fascism which deals mainly with Charbin.

15

In Praise of Menshevism

Tatyana Tolstoy wrote somewhere that she never knew anyone who believed in communist ideology, and that this observation referred also to the generation of her parents. I have no reason to disbelieve her as far as her own age cohort is concerned, but I suspect that she either was not very interested in the beliefs of the previous generation, or did not try very hard to find out: Solzhenitsyn, Alexander Zinoviev, Lev Kopelev and many other could have told her that it was quite easy to be an ardent believer, that in fact, it was almost unnatural for young people not to be one. True, to be a party member became progressively more difficult after 1936 for those not ready to do without their critical faculties. The recently published protocols of the communist German writers' party cell in Moscow are mindboggling as a case study in self-flagellation. I am sure many must have read them. But this does not mean that people did not believe in the cause; on the contrary only belief made such exercises possible.

The question why individual intellectuals became members of the Communist party, and why they left it continues to intrigue us more than forty years after the *God That Failed* first appeared. It will continue to preoccupy not only the historians for a long time to come.[1]

I would like to deal for a little while with the fellow travellers rather than the party members. If I remember correctly, the Congress of Cultural Freedom was much more preoccupied with confronting them than the party members with whom no dialogue seemed possible. It is useful to remember that neither Brecht nor Ernst Bloch, nor most members of the Frankfurt school nor Ilya Ehrenburg, not even Kim Philby were ever party members. They were not subject to strict discipline, did not have to denounce each other, engage in ridiculous self-criticism, and were not even expected to welcome with great enthusiasm every minor twist and turn of the party line. In brief, it was much easier to be a fellow traveller than a party member.

For the fellow travellers there were in each period good reasons to defend the Soviet Union against its detractors, while admitting that not everything in the "Socialist Sixth" was quite comprehensible, let alone perfect. During the first decade after the revolution, in the pre-Stalinist period, there was admiration, or at the very least sympathy and interest in the revolutionaries who wanted to "storm the heavens" to create a just society by means of social engineering and a new and higher type of human being—in Europe's most backward country.

With the end of the romantic-revolutionary period other motives appeared that induced many Western intellectuals to ignore what later became known as the "cult of personality," political and cultural regimentation, the purges, the trials, and the terror. Some more sources are now at our disposal shedding light on the behavior of figures such as Romain Rolland or Lion Feuchtwanger; they do not radically change the traditional picture, but tend to confirm what had been suspected several decades ago.[2]

Stalin's Russia was not a particularly attractive place for visitors from abroad, least of all intellectuals. But many of them thought that the West was either too weak or too deficient in political will to resist the rise of Nazism; if the choice was between Stalin and Hitler the fellow traveller would opt without hesitation for the former. As Brecht put it, the most dangerous, the only real enemy of fascism is communism, as fascism knows. After the Molotov-Ribbentrop pact it became difficult for a while to defend Stalin, but the honeymoon between the dictators lasted for less than two years, and thereafter the Russians were the allies of the Western powers, and any criticism was considered in bad taste—if not outright sabotage of the antifascist war effort.

Another inhibiting factor should be mentioned in this context—Nazi anti-Soviet propaganda. True, most fascists movements showed very little interest in the Soviet Union one way or another; under Mussolini, for instance, hardly any books were published about this subject—there was intense anti-French and anti-British but virtually no anti-Soviet propaganda. However, in Nazi Germany anti-Bolshevism was for much of the time a major issue, and the antifascism of the left saw this as confirmation of their beliefs—a system attacked with such fervor by the Nazis could not be all bad. While much of the Nazi propaganda was clearly mendacious inasmuch as facts were concerned (Stalin as the running dog of world Jewry), it was not always lying—there was no need to do so. As a result the antifascists of the left missed out some key issues, two of which I would like to mention. The most detailed and accurate description of the Gulag archipelago was given by one Karl Albrecht (*Der verratene Sozialismus*) a high official in the Soviet administration who defected to Germany.[3] His book was circulated in two million copies, but the anti-Stalinists of the left ignored it. Another example: in the Nazi literature the confessions extracted in the Moscow trials were explained with reference to the application of torture, physical and mental. This, as we now know from Soviet sources, was the correct explanation, at least in most cases, not Koestler's *Darkness at Noon* version. But at the time, in 1936–38, even those on the left very critical of Stalinism tended to rule out torture as an explanation. The fear of "applause from the wrong side" (as Rohrwasser put it) was crucial; Feuchtwanger's main charge against Gide was not that Gide had been spreading calumnies—but that he had published his book at the wrong time.

With the outbreak of the cold war, the cause of peace, the prevention of a third world war appeared as the central issue. As the Soviet Union turned a little less dictatorial after Stalin's death, it became less inconvenient to defend the Soviet system in the West. But after the Khrushchev speech, the Soviet system could no longer be idolized as it had been earlier on.

In fact, general interest in Soviet affairs, particularly in Soviet culture, faded—some former fellow travellers transferred their loyalties to China, Cuba, or even Albania but these were unlikely places to generate enthusiasm for any length of time. Others became preoccupied with a variety of intellectual fashions, or simply turned against the policies of their own governments.

With all this, a future post-Soviet fellow travelling trend cannot be ruled out. While the collapse of Communism came as a shock, the kind of political regimes likely to emerge in Eastern Europe will not have many admirers in the West. While Tito was in charge, Serbs and Croats and Bosnians at least did not kill each other in the thousands. I can well imagine that there will be a certain nostalgia, not to put it any stronger, for an autocratic, Titoist regime. I do not think that fascism will prevail in the former Soviet Union and Eastern Europe, but at least some of these regimes may well be autocratic, aggressive, intolerant and generally speaking unattractive. While Soviet imperialism seemed unaccept-able, disintegration into many dangerously unstable and nonviable small units may seem equally unwelcome. I would not be surprised if in the West as in the East there will be a longing for a return to a more stable regime, to law and order, even if it means drastic cuts in the freedoms gained in recent years.

II

While fascism was a threat, liberal anticommunism was under con-stant attack from the left—as "objective supporters" of Hitler and Mussolini. After 1945 they were accused of having opted for the wrong, reactionary, side, that is to say, for the imperialist West in the great con-frontation of the age. It is entertaining to review now the old battles of 1937–38 and of the 1950s; eventually dissertations and monographs will be written on this subject. But at present revisiting the old controversies is hardly a matter of great priority; no elaborate commentaries are needed to prove who was right in the quarrel between Sartre and Aron, it is sufficient to reprint the pertinent sections from their writings.

More recently liberal anticommunism has come under fire from differ-ent quarters, namely from the Russian right, and also on occasion in the West. Its historical role has been ignored and its position has been misrep-resented. Solzhenitsyn belongs to this trend; he persuaded himself that until he appeared on the scene the Western liberal intelligentsia had a field day in the media misleading the public with its apologies for Stalin and Stalin's successors. Solzhenitsyn also made it known that while he was not the very first to write about the camps, his predecessors had been ignored and the public had not been aware of the existence of the gulags.[4]

Then *glasnost* came and with it a new theory according to which Stalinism had been as popular among the Western intelligentsia as in the Soviet Union. Vadim Kozhinov, an influential literary critic and essayist in a seminal essay entitled "Pravda i Istina" published in *Nash Sovre-mennik* argued that if such sophisticated Westerners as the Webbs, Shaw, Wells, Einstein, Romain Rolland and Feuchtwanger had believed in Stalin and defended him, it was grossly unfair to put any blame on the Russians who had ben cut off from outside information, who did not know any better. Stalinism was a global phenomenon "from Madrid to Shanghai," there was nothing specifically Russian about it. Furthermore, Russian liberal critics of Stalinism had no moral legitimacy because their pangs of conscience awoke only at the time of the purges in the 1930s when communists had killed other communists. They had not spoken out against the collectivization of agriculture in 1929–30, when many more people had perished: simple Russian and Ukrainian peasants, no intellectuals among them. Subsequently the argument was taken a step further by Academician Igor Shafarevich, a noted mathematician and an ideologist of the Russian right who argued that Western liberals had been procommunist while Stalin was alive. They turned anticommunist (or rather anti-Russian...) only after Khrushchev's famous speech, that is to say at the very time when many people were released from the camps and, generally speaking, the Soviet human rights record greatly improved.

This theme has been widely belabored in the last three years in the publications of the anti-Western party in Russia, and one tries to look for mitigating circumstances for those responsible broadcasting this kind of higher lunacy. It is, of course true, that fellow travellers like Feuchtwanger, Rolland, the Webbs and others were given immense publicity in the Soviet Union (but even Feuchtwanger's book was banned after a first printing!) and Soviet citizens were cut off from the mainstream of Western intellectual thought. Who, except a few experts had even heard of, say Souvarine, Orwell, Koestler or Aron. (True, Koestler and Orwell were circulated in *samizdat,* but this was only much later.) But even the reader of the Russian mass media knew that there were wicked intellectuals, defectors, and traitors in the West such as Andre Gide and other jackals and hyenas who dissented from the praise heaped on Stalin and Stalinism. Furthermore, if Soviet intellectuals were cut off from Western thinking in the 1930s and 1940s, this is certainly no longer true today, and not much effort is now needed to establish that Feuchtwanger, Rolland, and Howard Fast (the early Fast...) were not the only Western intellectuals signing manifestoes at the time. Thus the suspicion obtrudes itself that ignorance of the true state of affairs is not the only, probably not the main, explanation for the denial of the role of liberal Western anticommunism, there seems to be a deliberate intention behind it. The new version tends to absolve Russia from any specific responsibility for Stalinism; if all were guilty, no one was. But the new version does not explain why Stalinism prevailed in Russia and not, say in France, America, or Japan. These arguments tend to play down the whole issue of Stalin and Stalinism which is not surprising, because the ideologists of the new right are often

National Bolshevists who do not reject communism in toto. Even those who do, prefer Stalin (who made Russia great and powerful) to Lenin and Trotsky (who tried to destroy it).

III

The Congress of Cultural Freedom did not have a party line on communism, the Soviet Union, or indeed any other subject. But there is no denying that the impact of Menshevism in this context was greater than that of any other group. With Menshevism I mean not only card-carrying members of the Russian Social Democratic party in exile, but the whole liberal wing of the Russian emigration, including the Social Revolutionaries who edited *Sovremennye Zapiski,* the most important periodical in Russian published outside Russia between the two world wars. Few in the Congress read Russian, but they all were, of course familiar, with *The New Leader* edited for many years by Sol Levitas. The story of the *New Leader* remains to be written; I doubt whether there ever was another small and impecunious weekly which had indirectly so much influence.

The debt which liberal anticommunism owes to the Mensheviks is immense, but to the best of my knowledge no one has drawn attention to it in recent years, least of all in Russia. Since *glasnost* Russia has rediscovered all kind of thinkers who were suppressed for many decades. The monarchists have reprinted Ivan Ilin and Ivan Solonevich, the extreme right has republished the *Protocols of the Elders of Zion*, the memoirs of Denikin, Wrangel, and even Trotsky have been reprinted, *Vekhi,* that famous collection of essays has been reissued and quoted countless times; it is difficult to open a Russian journal these days without facing an essay by, or at least a quotation from Berdyaev. Despite some misgivings, even General Vlasov has been rehabilitated, and the brochures and books of the emigre National Labor Union are widely available. But there is a massive white spot, and this refers to the Mensheviks and the anticommunist Russian left. Most Russians have only the haziest notion who these parties and leaders were, and in the West some highly misleading references have been made by writers who should know better. Thus Professor Malia in an article containing much that is true about fellow-travelling views and "revisionism," in Soviet studies refers to "neo-Menshevism," laboring under the strange delusion that this was something akin to Bukharinism, situated somewhere between Carr and Deutscher, a doctrine based on the belief that Bolshevism was essentially a progressive phenomenon. It had played a positive role in the past, and was to be defended against its detractors at present. In brief, a caricature of Menshevism. No political group is perfect, and there were some hesitations on Julius Martov's part during the revolution and its immediate aftermath even though he was always sure that "Asiatic Bolshevism" had to be combatted to the utmost.

Until shortly before his death (he passed away in 1923) he stuck to the notion that since it was a working-class party, the Bolsheviks could not be all wrong. But Martov also wrote early on that he had no sympathy for Asian police socialism which negated political freedom, that Bolshevism was a senseless utopia which would end in disaster. Towards the end of his life he became more and more hostile to Bolshevism, which he called the "party of the executioners: As soon as they came to power, they began to kill."

It is also true that Fyodor Dan under the impact of the Soviet victory over Nazi Germany in 1945 suffered a relapse into pro-Sovietism and misjudged the future turn of events in the Soviet Union. But mainline Menshevism in the 1920s and thereafter was not in the tradition of Martov and Dan but rather of Pavel Axelrod who wrote Martov in a famous letter in 1921 that

> it was not in a mere outburst of polemical ardor, but from deep conviction, that I described the Leninists ten years ago as a Black Hundred gang of double dyed criminals within the Social Democratic party.[5]

There were people who assessed Bolshevism correctly on all sides of the political spectrum, from the monarchists on the right to Bertrand Russell and Rosa Luxemburg. But as a group the record of the Mensheviks and the Social Revolutionaries in exile was unrivalled in its perspicacity and consistency. Whereas a great many Russian emigres of the center and the right, including high churchmen and tsarist generals, made peace with Stalin, were penetrated by the GPU, became Soviet agents of influence and even returned to Russia, there was not a single Menshevik, and only one Social Revolutionary (Sukhomlin) who turned traitor. Even Miliukov and Maklakov, even Berdyaev and Timasheff towards the end of their lives found much to admire in Stalinism, which they had sharply denounced only a few years earlier. The only ones who did not waver were the liberal anticommunists. They were also the most prophetic. After a mere three years of Soviet power, Marc Vishniak, a right Social Revolutionary and editor of *Sovremennie Zapiski,* noted that Bolshevism would disappear but its legacy of unfreedom was pernicious and profound and would not easily vanish. While the thousands of kilometers that separated Russian Bolshevism from the West had given it "features of sublimity and grandeur," he saw no reason for optimism as far as the future of freedom in Russia was concerned.[6]

Today the Russian right points with pride to its consistent stand in the past. In truth, the behavior of many of them was far from admirable; even some of the Russian fascists chose ultimately to return to Russia and wrote grovelling letters to Stalin. There were some outstanding thinkers among the Russian emigres such as the theologian G.P. Fedotov who was fully aware of the weakness of the position of the Russian nationalists who had rejected Bolshevism above all because of its internationalist, antipatriotic character. He wrote in 1935:

> A liberal knows why he is against Soviet power: because it destroys freedom. Democrats also know, because Bolshevism oppresses the people, because it falsifies the national will and suppresses all forms of self-government. A socialist opposes it because Soviet power exploits the people and invokes in vain the very term socialism, which becomes a synonym for a giant state prison. Honest individuals who do not belong to any political party are against Bolshevism because Soviet power educates people to dishonesty and lack of moral conscience. Religious people have every reason to oppose Sovietism which has made atheism the state religion.[7]

But why should a nationalist *pur sang* oppose Soviet power except for personal rancor? His opposition was based on a misunderstanding; once this misunderstanding is cleared up the nationalists will return to Russia as similar groups such as *Smena Vekh* (Change of Landmarks) and the Eurasians did before. If Fedotov's prediction did not literally come true, it was mainly because Stalin did not want the emigres to return. But by and large, he analyzed the situation correctly; and it is, no doubt, for this reason that he remains among the thinkers who are still ignored in Russia.

The Mensheviks were few in number, they had no financial means at their disposal, no radio station, no secret channels to penetrate the Soviet Union, only a small monthly. But they did what they could to inform the West about the true situation in the Soviet Union, first among their fellow social democrats, the Second International, later among the public at large. In this respect their role was unique. Their opposition did not begin with the trials and terror of the 1930s but many years before 1917. Their quarrel was not with Stalin but with Lenin. As Abramovich told the Second International in 1928:

> However much fascism and Bolshevism may differ in their social ideals and class contents, they are alike as blood brothers in their method and ways. Fascism and Bolshevism are the two great dangers threatening the working class from opposite sides but equally strongly. It is imperative that the Socialist International fight them, in different fashion but with all the energy and strength it can muster.

Fifty years later Abramovich would have been drummed out of a meeting of American Sovietologists for uttering such crude and primitive anticommunist views, yet history has born out the dire analysis and prediction of the Mensheviks. It is quite untrue that they did not care about the fate of the peasants (as Solzhenitsyn and Shafarevich claim); on the contrary, in countless resolutions and publications they denounced the collectivization, demanded that it be discontinued forthwith because it was leading not only to untold suffering but to the ruin of Russian agriculture.[8]

It would be too facile to compare the record of the Mensheviks and their allies among the liberals with the extreme right in the Russian emigration—say with Kazem Bek who with great sound and fury established a fascist movement, only to crawl back to Moscow in the 1950s to end his days as employee of the Moscow patriarchate. Vasili Shulgin, a leading and highly intelligent spokesman of the Russian right before the war and in the 1920s, found himself in Russia after 1945 as an involuntary guest—he had been arrested in Yugoslavia at the end of the war. For this reason one should perhaps not judge his subsequent declarations too harshly. But it is still a historical fact that no Menshevik ever recanted ideologically in such an abject way as Shulgin, praising the achievements of Sovietism, admitting that his ideological beliefs had been all wrong.

Among the Mensheviks there were no outstanding thinkers of international renown—theologians such as Berdyaev, political philosophers such as Peter Struve, sociologists such as Timasheff, historians such as Miliukov. But their political track record was still infinitely better; they never claimed that Western democracy was bankrupt (like Berdyaev and Struve), there were no kudos for Mussolini, no predictions about Stalin's "great retreat" (Timasheff), no genuflections to the Soviet system towards the end of their lives (Miliukov and Berdyaev).

The Mensheviks were right where so many others went astray because they had deeply held democratic convictions which made it impossible for them to compromise either with fascism or Bolshevism. They also had a good deal of political experience and common sense. These hopelessly old fashioned Social Democrats were greater realists in their political assessments than more clever and erudite ideologists; these "cosmopolitans" were also better Russian patriots. None of them lived to see their views born out by history.

History does not award prizes to people who have been right prematurely; in the intellectual climate of contemporary Russia the Mensheviks are as unfashionable as they were seventy and fifty years ago. No statues will be erected in Moscow to Abramovich, even not to Nikolayevsky. If it had not been for the *New Leader* they would have been forgotten also in the West, except among some academic specialists. Time has come to accord to the Mensheviks at long last their rightful place in Russian political and intellectual history, before mythology takes over. Politically they were bound to fail for there was no future for their ideas in Russia in 1917. But they realized more acutely than others that the Bolshevik coup would lead to total disaster; as warners to the world they were farsighted and consistent. They never compromised with the dictatorship which made them as popular among the Western left as Cassandra was among the Trojans. It should be hoped that they will be remembered as long as Cassandra.

Notes

1. One of the most interesting and certainly the most systematic attempt to come to terms with the phenomenon is Michael Rohrwasser, *Der Stalinismus und die Renegaten*, (1991).
2. I have commented on these sources—Rolland's unpublished diary and the Russian reports on Feuchtwanger's stay in Moscow—in the *Partisan Review*, Fall 1992, reprinted in this volume, see "Feucht Wanger and Gide", below.
3. There were some predecessors such as Ivan Solonevich, who fled from Russia in the early 1930s.
4. Could he really not have been aware of David Rousset and the Kravchenko trial?
5. Quoted in A. Ascher (ed.), *The Mensheviks in the Russian Revolution* (1976), p. 132.
6. Jane Burbank, *Intelligentsia and Revolution* (1986), pp. 90 et seq.
7. "Novyi Idol," *Sovremennye Zapiski*, 57, 1935; reprinted in *Tyazhba o Rossii* (1982).
8. Simon Wolin in L.H. Haimson, *The Mensheviks* (1974), pp. 324 et seq.

16

The Long Goodbye

Soon after the Revolutions of 1917 a British observer stationed in Russia predicted that a verdict on Bolshevism will be possible only after the final curtain will have come down. Martin Malia believes that this is now the case: "Soviet history is at last real history." I am a little less certain, we have not heard the last of 1917. The consequences of the French Revolution which lasted a mere four years dominated French history for another century until a new equilibrium emerged. The consequences of the Russian Revolution are likely to be at least as enduring. But there is no reason to postpone the verdict any longer.

These two books* are among the most important in the Russian field published for many years. They are also angry books, uncompromising verdicts, bound to give rise to bitter controversy. For almost two decades ending with *glasnost* the field of contemporary Russian history (and of Sovietology) had been dominated, to a considerable degree, by a school of thought according to which October 1917 had been a popular, democratic movement expressing the fundamental interests of the masses of the Russian people. True, the movement had some blemishes from the very beginning and in later years the essentially liberating character of the Russian Revolution had been diluted as a result of Russian backwardness, of civil war, of the hostility of the West, of the excesses of Stalinism and other causes. But despite certain economic difficulties and human rights shortcomings Soviet society was steadily improving in most respects, moving towards a civil society, a new brilliant dawn, the return to pristine Leninism (or Bukharinism), to true socialism and the arrival of democracy was therefore

---

*Martin Malia, *The Soviet Tragedy. A History of Socialism in Russia in 1917–1991* and Richard Pipes, *Russia under the Bolshevik Regime.*

only a question of time. Some even thought that *perestroika* had already taken place before Gorbachev came to power.

This school of thought was called "revisionist," a label that some of its adherents resented. They thought that their views were not just an antithesis to cold war doctrine with its biassed, anti-Soviet approach, but altogether on a much higher level of detachment, objectivity and scholarly quality. It was "scientific," not "folkloristic," academic, not partisan.

The breakup of the Soviet system came as a great surprise to everyone. But it was particularly painful for the revisionists for reasons that do not have to be spelt out in detail. Under *glasnost* it became exceedingly difficult to locate in Russia anyone who had a good word to say on the Russian Revolution and its aftermath. In Moscow everyone was talking about the totalitarian character of the old regime—a term that had been anathema to revisionists in the West. While Russian authors published accounts and studies showing that the cost in human lives of the Soviet experiment had been truly staggering, Western experts from Australia to California continued to prove to their satisfaction, that while regrettable, the impact of the terror had been much narrower than thought by Solzhenitsyn, Conquest, and other cold warriors. While American authors continued to say that the cold war was largely America's fault, and had been avoidable, Russian experts took a much less categorical view. While the first volume of Pipes' *History of the Russian Revolution* (a book harshly attacked in American professional journals) and Malia's essays were published in Russia in huge editions, Russian interest in Western revisionist literature is virtually nonexistent.

These anomalies provide the background for an understanding of these two books—and their likely reception in American academic circles. It is their view that the Bolshevik seizure of power was an unmitigated disaster for Russia and mankind, leading to the direst consequences. There are certain important differences in both the scope of these works and the views of the authors. Pipes' new volume on the history of the Russian Revolution ends with Lenin's death in 1924, whereas Malia's work spans the entire Soviet era. Malia believes that it was not Mother Russia (i.e., Russia backwardness) that perverted the noble and pure idea of socialism, but vice versa. He says that at long last the awful truth has now to be faced that socialism was the source of all evil; it was bound to lead to totalitarianism. Pipes, on the other hand, points to the fact that the Russian patrimony did play a great (and destructive) role in this context. Nowhere in the West did Marxism have such negative consequences.

But in their essential verdict on the balance of seven decades the two authors see eye to eye, it was a profound tragedy. With all their negative comments on Russia's past, they are hopeful with regard to the future. Malia writes that the "furies unleashed in 1914" have now been "finally appeased" a commendable sentiment but in my view a premature one. Pipes, on another occasion has gone on record with the belief that Russia will follow the road of Germany after 1945—towards prosperity and democracy. How to explain Malia's and Pipes' optimism? For many years there was little, if anything inspiring to report about the Soviet Union and it is understandable that inveterate critics of the Soviet system should now welcome Yeltsin and overrate the prospects of his policy. But it seems at best a little premature: Yeltsin and his ever-changing crew have made major mistakes. And even if they would have committed no errors whatsoever, even if Russia were now run by a cohort of statesmen of genius, could they succeed without strong popular support?

Pipes concentrates on the period of the Civil War and the New Economic Policy. He adduces a number of good reasons why Bolshevism should have prevailed in the Civil War, above all the fact that the communists were united while their enemies were not. Nevertheless, he goes too far arguing that the victory was more or less foreordained. It is true that the Bolsheviks could maneuver with greater ease because they could make use of interior lines of communications. But this did not help the Republicans in the Spanish Civil War. Could it have been that the Red Army was by and large more highly motivated—as well as better organized?

The two books are long overdue correctives to the kind of "scholarship" peddled in the 1970s and 1980s. As such they deserve the highest praise; the Soviet experiment (as it was called in the early years) was a tragedy and Pipes is absolutely right when he argues that there is no virtue (as many revisionists have claimed following E.H. Carr) to view such an unprecedented calamity with dispassion and ethical neutrality.

However, at a certain point something does go wrong. Like competitors still running even though the race is over, they continue relentlessly, not knowing where to stop. Pipes' book should end chronologically with Lenin's death, but he continues his narrative and his reflections well beyond, wandering off in various directions, such as long discussions on Bolshevism's impact on Nazism.

In the case of Malia the broadside against Bolshevism turns into a wholesale attack against socialism in all its forms, which, as he sees it, inexorably led to the totalitarian monstrosities. Thus the poor, ineffectual Second International becomes responsible for Stalin. This approach involves the author in various difficulties; he claims on the one hand that there is no such a thing as socialism, and on the other hand he maintains that it is the main key towards an understanding of the totalitarian system. He puts most of the blame for the tragedy on communist egalitarianism. But whatever the sins of communism, excessive egalitarianism was never one of its main theoretical tenets, and it was certainly far from Bolshevist practice—viz. the lifestyle of the *nomenklatura.*

There is room for disagreement on detail. *C'est la lutte finale,* is not, as Malia believes, the first line of the *Internationale;* the impact of Andrei Sakharov inside Russia was infinitely deeper than that of Alexander Zinoviev (whom Malia seems to prefer), a gadfly rather than a serious, consistent thinker.

In 1991 the Communist party was destroyed (Malia writes) and a superpower dismembered, socialism was renounced and capitalism restored. The most enduring fantasy of the twentieth century, the pseudoreligion cum pseudoscience of Marxism-Leninism simply evaporated. Nor could any of these things have occurred as a gradual process. Marxism-Leninism, to be sure, did vanish in the former Soviet Union. But can it really be argued that capitalism has been restored in Russia (let alone in the Ukraine and White Russia) what with all the old *nomenklatura* in place? It could be even premature to talk about the destruction of the Communist party. And can one be quite sure that a gradual process was impossible? It seems unlikely, but as long as we do not know the outcome of developments in China, there can be no final verdict.

Having relegated socialism to the lower depths of hell, Malia's resolve weakens towards the end and he suddenly mellows. Yes, he says, utopias are dangerous, but they are also necessary: "The overstatements of visionary socialism were necessary to produce the welfare state." Yes, the lion of "capitalism" and the unicorn of "socialism" will continue to contend inconclusively until the end of modernity. Much ballast will have to be jettisoned if the socialist aspiration is to survive. Social democrats may agree with such sentiments. Mises and von Hayek (quoted with evident approval by Malia) would have taken a dim view of such weakening of resolve.

"Utopia," even though more narrowly defined also plays a central role in Pipes' "Reflections on the Russian Revolution" his last chapter. His basic philosophy is expressed in a paraphrase of a comment by Hippolyte Taine on the French Revolution—that precisely because modern society is vast and complicated and thus difficult to grasp, it is neither proper nor feasible to impose on it patterns of conduct, let alone to remake it: What cannot be comprehended cannot be controlled: There is truth in this argument, Marx's actionism, his endlessly quoted appeal to change the world rather than continue interpreting it in different ways, was in retrospect not such a good idea.

And yet, such categorical injunctions against tampering with the social and political order are unfeasible. There is a considerable grey zone in the real world, neither fully understood nor entirely terra incognita. On many occasions decisions have to be taken without ultimate certainties concerning the consequences. If it were true that what cannot be comprehended cannot be controlled, much of modern medicine would have to go out of business. For while the effect of many drugs is, broadly speaking, known, the way they do act is often subject to surmise and speculation.

As for Bolshevism's impact on fascism there can be no doubt that there was such an influence. The revisionist school of history has labored hard to prove that similarities between the communist and fascist regimes were either accidental or of no great consequence, but this is simply not true. The one-party, one-leader, one-doctrine structure was no coincidence, nor was the intensive use of terror and propaganda. Unfortunately, European revisionists have virtually succeeded in banishing "National Socialism" (Nazism) from the professional dictionary—the politically correct term is now "fascism." This helps to obliterate the important differences between Italy and Germany on one hand and to ignore the populist, anticapitalist inspiration of Nazism on the other. "Fascism" in this light is the creature of big business. The political purpose of this exercise is obvious, the evidence nonexistent.

Pipes makes these and other useful points, but he tends to overshoot the target. We all know that Mussolini was once a Revolutionary socialist, and that he made some favorable comments on Lenin in the early 1920s. But it is an exaggeration to say that Mussolini "never concealed his sympathy and admiration for Communism." After he came to power he was no longer interested in the subject and the communists ended up on the Lipari islands. It is true that the Nazis (whatever their feverish propaganda slogans) did not regard the communists as a mortal threat to the German nation. But it is not true that relations between the two parties were "friendly." On a few occasions, even in wartime Hitler expressed (grudging) admiration for Stalin—which he never did for Churchill or Roosevelt. But Pipes makes too much of such asides, he overstates the affinities. They did exist, but they were not as all important as he thinks. One of his main sources is Hermann Rauschning, a former Nazi leader, whose testimony is now taken by most German experts with great reservations, an entertaining and sometimes prophetic book of doubtful authenticity.

It is true that Stalin relied more on terror than Hitler and Mussolini, but it is another overstatement to claim that "whereas the Bolshevik leaders relied almost exclusively on coercion, Mussolini and even Hitler followed Pareto's advice to combine coercion with consent." Did Hitler and Mussolini really "learn a great deal from Bolshevik techniques"? They were in no need of such inspiration and made no effort at all to learn. They understood that the appeal of nationalism was crucial well before Stalin did. Pipes concludes that "the Jewish holocaust thus turned out to be one of the many unanticipated and unintended consequences of the Russian revolution." This is certainly true in the sense that all history is a seamless web. Seen in this light, Kerensky and, of course, Tsar Nicholas II are partly responsible for the Bolshevik takeover and thus, indirectly also for the Holocaust. There is a German nationalist school of historians headed by Ernst Nolte, asserting that Hitler got his inspiration for mass murder from the Gulag which is pernicious nonsense. Pipes does not go that far, but statements such as the one just mentioned come close to it.

Pipes makes the valid point that while communism derived its inspiration from the enlightenment, fascism is rooted in the counterenlightenment, but that in practice the distinction got blurred. But later he puts the blame for communism's failure on "Enlightenment's most pernicious idea," that man was merely a material compound devoid of either soul or innate idea. This was indeed the view of some diehard materialists such as La Mettrie, but not of Locke and Hume, of Kant or the French Encyclopedists. True, Nietzsche has been made responsible for Eichmann, and Mazzini for Mussolini, but such searches for intellectual parentage are more often misleading than enlightening; Voltaire as Stalin's godfather does not make sense.

All this is a pity because it detracts from the value of two important and valuable books. Psychologically, the exaggeration is intelligible. The misleading literature about communism and the Soviet Union put out over a quarter of a century was enough to try the patience of saints. Anger and irritation accumulated and as the Soviet Union collapsed almost superhuman restraint would have been needed commenting on so many books and articles combining great scientific pretensions with profound lack of understanding of the true state of the Soviet Union. One understands the reaction but one still wishes it had been more measured. These two books are of enormous value as an antidote to two decades of revisionist writing, they should be read by everyone even vaguely interested in this subject. But they could have been more than an antidote and this is a matter of regret.

Part IV

Writers and Fighters

17

Maxim Gorky

I

It is difficult to think of another great European writer of the last century whose reputation has been as much subject to ups and downs as Alexei Peshkov, a.k.a. Maksim Gorky. Tolstoy, Chekhov, Korolenko, and Chaliapin befriended him; Repin drew his portrait; his plays were staged all over the world. He became the virtual poet laureate of the Soviet Union and something like an institution. Stalin said of one of his poems that it was greater than Goethe's *Faust*. His native city was named after him—for some forty years. His books were printed in many millions of copies. He was surely the only writer in history whose funeral in 1936 was attended by 800,000 people. There were several editions of his collected works.

Yet his works were as uneven as his political judgment, and though many Soviet writers of the older generation have written fondly of him, his literary influence began to wane even in his own lifetime. The official status of his works underlines the fact that he had become a classic in his lifetime and this had a negative effect on his reputation.

The emigres loathed him as a Bolshevik fellow traveller, for the national communists inside Russia he was not sufficiently patriotic and his views about Russian peasants were anathema. Though he wrote bitterly about America and France he was a Westernizer at heart and disliked Dostoevsky. Despite his many good deeds the liberals never forgave him his support for Stalin ("If the enemy does not surrender, he is destroyed" and similar slogans). With *glasnost* Gorky's standing has fallen to an all time low. Gorky, the city has been renamed Nizhny Novgorod, Gorky Street in Moscow is again Tverskaya and even the Gorky metro station has lost its name. Gorky's standing can only rise, but it may take a long time.

Gorky was born in Nizhny Novgorod in 1868. His grandfather had been an officer who had been dismissed from the army for cruel treatment of soldiers at a time when excessive humanism was not the rule in these quarters. His maternal grandfather began his working life as a barge hauler on the Volga but later became a trader and succeeded in business. Both Gorky's father and mother died when he was a child, and he was brought up by his maternal grandfather. At the age of eight he became an apprentice in a shoe shop, later,on a Volga steamer, he was assistant to the cook who had many books and encouraged Gorky to read. During the years that followed he worked on the railways, as a baker, sold icons, traversed much of southern Russia on foot, mingling with the kind of people Russian writers seldom met in the flesh. His first short story, "Makar Chandra," was published when Gorky lived in Tiflis in 1892, the year after he settled in Nizhny Novgorod. With the publication of his collected short stories (1898) his fame spread all over Russia, and his plays, above all *The Lower Depths* (1902), conquered the stages of Europe and America.

Suffering from tuberculosis Gorky divided the rest of his life between Italy and Russia. He lived in his villa in Capri from 1906 to 1913, and again from 1921 to 1930. The circumstances of his death in 1936 are not entirely clear to this day. At the time of the Moscow trials the official version was that he had been killed by his doctors following instruction given by Yagoda, the chief of the NKVD. Under *glasnost* it was alleged that Stalin had been instrumental in hastening his death.[1]

II

Gorky's literary merits and demerits have been discussed in considerable detail during his lifetime and after. He figures prominently in the recollection of contemporaries, friends and enemies alike.[2] Having enthusiastically welcomed him, the critics turned against him after a few years. But having written him off he confounded them with works that were in most respect better and more mature than his early books, Gorky's politics were probably the chief reason for his mixed fortune as far as the reception of his works was concerned. From an early age his sympathies were with the downtrodden and the revolutionaries. But he had seen too much of the Russian peasantry, the proletariate (and the *Lumpenproletariat*) to be an uncritical admirer of the poor. Side by side with straightforward propaganda (above all in *The Mother*), there were in his works realistic, merciless descriptions of the evils he had observed among the lower classes as well as the upper. And his attitude towards the intelligentsia was equally mixed and inconsistent; he saw them as the salt of the earth, the only force capable of saving Russia, and he would at other times reveal their weaknesses without pity. He was a "socialist realist," using the hackneyed literary term, *avant la lettre* but incurably romantic in other respects. There are Nietzschean elements in his writings, contempt for the stupidity, insensitivity, and the base instincts of the multitude. Yet at the same time he was motivated by deep humanist impulses. There is Gorky visiting the Solovetsky island and other gulag labor camps and the White Sea canal where many thousands of forced laborers perished as the honored guest of the NKVD. And there is the other Gorky who after the revolution saved hundreds from starvation, prison, and execution through his close contacts with Lenin and other communist leaders. In brief, a complicated and contradictory figure. The fashionable total contempt with which he has been treated outside the communist ranks is not deserved; there was more to him than the servant and apologist for Lenin and Stalin.[3] The book *Nesvoevremennye Zapiski* (Untimely Notes) is evidence to this effect.

III

Gorky's sympathies were with the left from the very beginning of his literary career. He supported the revolution of 1905, joined the Bolsheviks in the summer of 1905 and was on friendly terms with Lenin. He dropped out of the party not long after and his views in the prewar period were anything but Marxist. ("I was a bad Marxist" he disarmingly told Lenin when the Bolshevik leader visited him at his Italian villa). He contributed money to the Bolsheviks even after he was no longer a member but he also gave to other political causes. He had been arrested and exiled by the tsarist police for having been connected with an illegal, underground printing house. Yet with all this the fanaticism of Lenin and the emphasis on violence repelled him. Gorky was a socialist but he also believed in freedom and human dignity. Through his close relations with Lenin he intervened after 1917 on behalf of many victims of the revolution—including several grand dukes and members of the family of the tsar, for whom he had no political sympathy.[4] Gorky was not a politician, though he frequently wrote about politics, he had no ambition to be consistent in his views and to advocate a party line. How to explain that Gorky preferred life in Fascist Italy in the 1920s to staying in Soviet Russia? The brief answer is that he was not in good health, that he preferred the calm, warm, and beautiful landscape of Capri to the harshness and constant tension of Russia, and that he had lived there before Mussolini appeared on the scene. There were other parts of the Mediterranean (or the Crimea) that had as much to offer as Italy, but politics seldom played a crucial role in Gorky's personal decisions.

Gorky continued to write articles on politics (and cultural politics) almost weekly even during the last years of his life, when his health was bad and deteriorating and when his main literary ambition was to finish his *Life of Klim Samgin* that he had started writing in 1925 and that in the end remained incomplete. Yet his most interesting political journalism by far were his comments on the Russian revolutions of 1917 that appeared in the Petrograd newspaper *Novaya Zhizn* between May 1, 1917 and July 16, 1918. This newspaper was not an organ of any specific political party though it was close in orientation to the Mensheviks.

His articles were often astute, sometimes prophetic, and while they were wholly in support of the overthrow of the old regime, they were very critical of the Bolsheviks. Consequently, they were not reprinted in the Soviet Union for more than seventy years after 1918. They were not included in the many volumes of Gorky's collected works; in the "full lists" of Gorky's books and manuscripts there is no single reference to these articles—even though they had actually been published as a book in Petrograd in 1918.[5]

Gorky's great fear all along was the spread of barbarism in Russia— the democratic revolution had prevailed but the deeper Russian illnesses had not been cured: "We Russians are anarchists, a cruel beast, in our veins the dark and evil slave blood is still flowing, the poisonous heritage of the Tatar yoke and Serfdom." Only the spread of culture could cleanse the people of the dust and the dirt of the past, only enlightenment could put an end to the bitter hostility between Russians.

This basic concept runs like a red thread through his writings. The general deterioration of mores was in part the result of a senseless, destructive war—hence Gorky's hope that it would soon end. Culture was in danger, and culture was the only hope for recovery.

Such views made the Bolsheviks dismiss Gorky as a "petty bourgeois utopian"—and the right bitterly attacked him for calumniating the Russian people. Gorky notes that after the February Revolution valuable, good, honest books almost entirely disappeared from the shops which reminds one of the situation in 1994. He fought for women's rights, for the emancipation of Jews. But from July 1917 (when the first abortive Bolshevik coup took place) most of his writings deal with the "anarchist" and "adventurist" danger: he does not yet single out the Bolsheviks but rather the "stronger, more dangerous enemy," namely Russian stupidity, the dark instincts. Only with the Bolshevik seizure of power in October, does he come out in the strongest possible terms against the "thieves and professional killers," creating, as it were, the history of the Russian revolution under the leadership of Lenin and Trotsky. At the bottom of Lenin's madness Gorky discovers anarchist inspiration à la Bakunin and Sergei Nechaev. Hence the bloody crimes committed by those who usurped power, hence the introduction of censorship, and the gradual liquidation of freedom and democracy. Gorky does not doubt for a single moment that the Russian people will pay a heavy price for the sea of blood spilled by the "socialist Napoleons." Lenin, as Gorky sees him, is a strong leader but wholly amoral in his attitude towards the popular masses, a "master" (*baryn*) dealing with his serfs. He does not know the people, never lived among them, he uses them as raw material like a chemist in a laboratory. Gorky has no doubt that the horrible experiment is bound to end in tragedy. The proletariat was now in power and what were its achievements? Random killing, kangaroo courts, arrests of leading liberals and social democrats.

These attacks made difficult reading not just for communist historians according to whom the October revolution was the greatest most progressive achievement in human history, but also for some Western historians, in particular those in the Unites States, who on the basis of their studies reached the conclusion that the October uprising was not just a great and good event, but that it had mass support, or at least the support of the most educated part of the working class.

In the *glasnost* and post-*glasnost* era Soviet historians have modified their views and stressed the role of army deserters and sections of the *lumpenproletariat* in the uprising. Gorky expressed a similar view at the time. As the result of the war educated workers had been decimated, tens of thousands had been killed in military action, and their place had been taken by people alien to proletarian psychology, lacking political consciousness and mainly interested in escaping army service. These people had nothing in common with socialism or Marxism, their actions reflected the dark instincts of an amorphous mass finding expression in "zoological anarchism," a new form of a "Pugachev revolt."[6]

Gorky's attacks against the Bolsheviks reached their height, when in February 1918 the new masters of the Kremlin dissolved the Constituent Assembly that had been elected well before the communist coup and that consisted not of "bourgeois elements" and counterrevolutionaries but of members of socialist parties—with the Bolsheviks a minority. As Gorky saw it, this was the end of political freedom in Russia, there was no hope anymore, only dictatorship and terror.

Gorky continued to write his articles for a few more months, but he commented less and less on politics and there were fewer attacks against the Bolsheviks. On the contrary, he defended himself against charges of collaborating with the dictators. Nevertheless, he was frequently threatened by the authorities with the closing of his newspaper; most other noncommunist papers had already been liquidated. Zinoviev, the Leningrad party boss who did not share Lenin's admiration for Gorky (or at least the belief in his usefulness) had Gorky's home searched.

Yet it was not only, perhaps not mainly, out of fear that Gorky decided to surrender. By July 1918 he was, as he wrote his wife, physically and mentally exhausted. It seemed pointless to engage in negative criticism, he decided to "collaborate with the Bolsheviks on an autonomous basis"—whatever that meant. One had to transfer one's efforts (he wrote) where the action was—in the middle of the revolutionary movement.

While he did not rejoin the Bolshevik party and while he applied (in January 1919) for permission to publish again *Novaya Zhizn* (permission was refused), he began to make speeches in praise of Lenin and his party. Communism was a tragic experiment, a lesson for the whole world. If mankind could be saved (and Gorky did not feel sanguine about the prospects) only the Russian people could accomplish this. Gorky saw in the backward peasantry the main enemy to social and cultural progress in Russia, and since he thought the Bolsheviks shared his antipeasant prejudice (an assumption which was not far from the truth), he could give them critical support. Gorky's negative attitude to the Russian peasantry also explains his decision more than ten years later to return to Stalin's Russia. Whereas others were deeply shocked by the enforced collectivization of agriculture and its millions of victims, Gorky seems to have had no such qualms. He regarded the destruction of the traditional Russian village as a blessing, not a disaster.

It is not quite clear in what light Gorky viewed in later years his writings of 1917–18. For the Bolsheviks these were, of course, major ideological mistakes, and on a few occasion Gorky conceded later on that his relation with Lenin was not close at the time. But being a nonparty person he never engaged in "Bolshevik self-criticism."

In 1921 Lenin advised Gorky in friendly fashion to move to Italy, given his weakened constitution, and the difficult living conditions in Russia. Gorky welcomed the proposal; since the State Bank was to cover his expenses abroad, it meant that he was from now on largely financially dependent on the Soviet government.

At Capri, the father of socialist realism wrote some more novels, as well as a long essay about Lenin (after his death in 1924) and a report about his visit to the Soviet Union in 1927–28.

What did he really think towards the end of his life about the situation in his native country? There is no clear answer. His letters, especially to foreigners like Romain Rolland were permeated with the spirit of Leninism-Stalinism, and his scandalous involvement with the NKVD (the predecessor of the KGB) was, of course, indefensible. He would not have been in personal danger had he been a little less sycophantic.

But there is reason to believe that side by side with the professed belief in the progressive mission of the Russian revolution, there was deep pessimism as to the ultimate outcome. He collaborated with Lenin and later Stalin because he thought that this was the price that had to be paid to do some good, to help individual victims. To a certain extent this assumption was correct, but in the final analysis it caused irreparable harm to his moral standing and his reputation. In any case, Stalin did not keep his part of the bargain. Articles critical of Gorky were published in the Soviet press throughout 1935. Gorky became a virtual prisoner, a fact noted even by Romain Rolland, not one of the world's most astute political observers. When he wanted to travel to Italy in 1933, the request was refused, and Gorky's secretary kept him in virtual isolation.

On June 18, 1936 Gorky died, either of natural causes, or was killed on Stalin's order as others claim. Two years earlier his son Max had died; the circumstances of his death are equally unclear.[7]

Whatever we make of Gorky's moral and political aberrations in later years, his essays of 1917–18 are of enormous interest in view of his unrivalled vantage point as an observer. They show that a sympathetic observer of impeccable left-wing convictions could still feel that the "Soviet experiment" (as it came to be called) was bound to end badly. Gorky's writings are in the tradition of Bertrand Russell and Rosa Luxemburg who—from a distance—reached similar conclusions at the time. Gorky was one of the most Russian writers of his, or any other, time; there was no need to flaunt his love for the people because it was innate and self evident. Yet at the same time his writings were exceedingly honest: Unlike other, louder and more self-conscious patriots, past and present, he did not dream of making foreigners responsible for the misfortunes of the Russian people in his time. In brief, an important book of as much interest now as at the time it was written.

Notes

1. V. V. Ivanov, "Pochemu Stalin ubil Gorkovo?" *Voprosy Literaturi,* 1, 1993 pp. 91–134.
2. There are many biographical studies of Gorky in Russian and other languages and it would be invidious to single out any one or two. Some of the most interesting evidence about Gorky is contained in the recollections of fellow writers, particularly Vladislav Khodasevich, Nina Berberova, Kornei Chukovsky, Konstantin Fedin, and Evgeny Zamyatin.
3. As Anna Akhmatova said in the 1960s: "It is now fashionable to curse Gorky. But without him we all would have died of hunger." V. Ivanov, loc. cit. p. 95.
4. On Gorky and the Russian left, B. Wolfe, *The Bridge and the Abyss: The Troubled Friendship of Maxim Gorky and V.I. Lenin* (1967) and, more recently, N. Katzer, *Maksim Gorky's Weg in die russische Sozialdemokratie* (1990).
5. Other editions include a German selection (*Süddeutsche Monatshefte,* October 1918), a more comprehensive French edition (1922); a first English edition appeared in 1970 which was prepared by Herman Ermolaev of Princeton. A full German translation was brought out in the 1970s (1972, 1974). A Russian edition (also by Ermolaev) was published in Paris in 1972 which was sponsored by the NTS journal *Posev* and mainly scheduled to be smuggled into the Soviet Union. A *glasnost* edition appeared in Moscow in 1990, but the book was subject of debate in the Soviet media even earlier, see for instance Aleksandr Ovcharenko, "O nesvoevremennykh Myslakh M. Gorkovo," *Literaturnaya Gazeta,* September 14, 1988.
6. Pugachev was the eighteenth-century peasant rebel whose revolt threatened Tsarist rule briefly but was eventually suppressed with great cruelty. The term "Pugachevism" is used to this day as a synonym for a violent rebellion, mainly destructive in character, lacking purpose.
7. According to the charges in the Moscow trial (1938) Yagoda, former head of the KGB instigated the murder because of his love for Max' wife. The charge was brought in one of the few closed sessions of the trial. Stalin and his acolytes combined cruelty and profanity with great prudishness. Anyway, the accusation was ludicrous.

18

Andrei Sakharov

For those who had the good fortune never to experience a totalitarian regime, it is exceedingly difficult even to begin to understand the meaning and the implications of dissent in these circumstances.[1] For the essence of totalitarianism is not just (as Mussolini once put it) that antistate activity is a priori forbidden, but that there should be no activity outside the state, that identification with the official view ought to be complete, that standing on the sidelines is almost as great a sin as opposition.

In the heyday of totalitarianism under Stalin from about 1932 (the destruction of the last vestiges of opposition inside the party) to his death, and under Hitler, dissent was unthinkable; men and women were killed even though they had been fervent supporters of the regime. True, under the Nazis there were some rare exceptions; a well-known bishop could make a speech condemning euthanasia without being arrested. But such cases of dissent referred to certain specific policies of the regime not to the regime per se.

But communism existed also before and after Stalin. Even the staunchest communists agreed that under the rule of the Georgian tyrant too many innocent people had been killed and that, generally speaking, excesses had been committed. No one, least of the *nomenklatura,* wanted to live in permanent fear. The era after Stalin was not quite communism with a human face, nor did anyone consider restricting the power of the KGB and the whole machinery of repression. But it was assumed among those ruling the country that the regime was able to get along without executions and that the population of the gulag could be drastically reduced. The thaw after 1953 manifested itself in literature and the arts and to a lesser extent in the social sciences. No one would dream as yet to speak frankly to strangers, but discussions among friends in the Moscow kitchens would become markedly freer.

Such liberalization was strongly resented by the orthodox communists; there were ups and downs in the party line and eventually, after Khrushchev, de-Stalinization, which had been hesitant and partial in the first place, was halted and even reversed. However, even a partial retreat from Stalinism created a dilemma for the communist authorities that was to plague them to end of their rule. For while according to the constitution and the laws anticommunist activities were forbidden in view of paragraph 70 (anti-Soviet agitation and propaganda) and 190/1, it was also true that many human rights were accepted on an abstract level including the freedom of expression, of conscience and of assembly; there was no *habeas corpus* but trials were to be open, not secret. Those fighting for human, national and religious rights were demonstrating under the slogan "Respect the Soviet Constitution." In other words, the system rested on the assumption that people would not invoke the rights which they did have in law.

This proved a miscalculation, for time and again courageous people appeared who tried to make use of these abstract freedoms. They did not constitute an immediate threat to the existence of the regime. Their number was small, they could be intimidated, blackmailed, arrested, sent to lunatic asylums and labor camps, exiled. But they constituted a permanent irritation at home and abroad; the alternative would have been to abolish the constitution and to change the laws. But this would be an admission of failure, a heavy blow to the reputation of the regime and its legitimacy.

When Valery Tarsis, one of the first dissidents was threatened with a road accident by the KGB, he told his interrogators, that no one would believe that he had died under such circumstances, and that for this reason he was convinced that state security services would do their utmost to prevent any such accident. The KGB had to accept the logic of this argument, but it is also true that enormous courage was needed to voice an argument of this kind talking defiantly to the all-powerful KGB. It was a gamble, Tarsis and those who came after him could, after all, have underrated the ingenuity of the KGB. And, in any case, short of killing people, the KGB could do a great deal to make life miserable. It could destroy lives and careers, arrest people for many years on trumped up charges, divide families, exercise moral terror and even drive people to suicide.

Who were the dissidents? Among the first wave were writers who published their works abroad, circumventing Soviet censorship. Some of them used pen names (such as Sinyavsky and Daniel), others like Pasternak, a wholly unpolitical writer and poet by Western standards, published *Doctor Zhivago* under his own name. Pasternak was merely hounded, isolated, ostracized and forced to decline the Nobel Prize; the less known ones were arrested and sent to the gulag. But there had been other dissidents even earlier on such as Yesenin-Volpin, son of the famous poet, and Vladimir Bukovsky, who quite independently had turned into bitter opponents of a regime which represented to them the worst forms of injustice.

Seen from a Western point of view there was little rhyme and reason in the practice of persecution. It was not surprising that the KGB should take a dim view of young Andrei Amalric's brilliant and prescient essay "Will the Soviet Union survive until 1984?" for which he received the remarkably lenient sentence of three years internal exile. But the young apolitical Leningrad poet Joseph Brodsky received a five-year sentence as a "social parasite," ostensibly for not having a regular job, but in truth for writing unauthorized verse on John Donne rather than the future of the Soviet Union. Another Leningrad writer got a four-year sentence simply for writing a preface to Brodsky's poems. Less than twenty years later the parasite received the Nobel Prize for literature. The leading bards of the period such as Aleksandr Galich, Vladimir Vysotsky, and Bulat Okudzhava were never arrested—Galich was, however, forced to emigrate—though their songs and poems were far more political in character than Brodsky's. Perhaps they were too popular, perhaps the KGB thought they could be redeemed.

The list of those who joined this movement in later years is long and impressive. According to the KGB and the Communist party spokesmen these were mainly Western-style liberals of Jewish origin. Such statements were made to disparage dissent, but while there were indeed many Jews among them, there were also many others. They included Germans who wanted to emigrate; Tatars who wanted to return to the Crimea from where they had been exiled under Stalin; Ukrainian, Armenian, and Georgian nationalists; Zionists eager to emigrate to Israel; advocates of workers' rights and free trade unions; religious believers of various denominations, Baptists, and Pentecostalists and also some Old Believers who were persecuted.

Solzhenitsyn, for a while the best-known dissenter inside Russia, was hardly a liberal and certainly not a Jew. Among the best-known names among the contemporary Russian right, and extreme right, not a few were at one time dissidents, including Academician Igor Shafarevich, Father Dudko, Vladimir Osipov, Leonid Borodin, Evgeni Vagin, Skuratov (Anatoli Ivanov), Vladimir Maksimov. One should not, perhaps, include two of the most famous, Eduard Limonov and Alexander Zinoviev, for while they emigrated they had never been active in Russia among the dissidents. Roy Medvedev, a marginal but vocal dissenter, rejoined the Marxist-Leninists after it was all over.

The dissidents believed that communism was a disaster though few would say it in so many words. Beyond this, their ways parted: Some thought the regime could be reformed, others did not. Some put the idea of a great, united, and strong Russia uppermost, others were fighting primarily for freedom and human rights. Most saw their future in Russia and would choose emigration only under duress, others were fighting for the rights of their ethnic groups; neither the Ukrainians, nor the Balts, neither the Zionists nor the Germans shared the dreams of the Russian patriots. There was a certain amount of solidarity but little if any cooperation between the various groups while they were all persecuted by the KGB. Once Soviet power collapsed, they soon found themselves on opposite sides of the barricades.

Allowing for all this diversity (and antagonism) it remains true, however, that the most important group by far in the public eye was the human rights movement advocating political freedom. Those on the right and most religious believers had little, if any, support from likeminded people who had opted for collaboration with the regime: Religious believers were disavowed by their bishops, the samizdat Russian nationalists were held at arms' length and denounced by the establishment nationalists, who subscribed to National Bolshevism and thought that the regime would gradually develop in the direction they wanted. Typical in this respect was the treatment of Solzhenitsyn. He was published by *Novy Mir,* the chief organ of the liberals, even though he had very little in common with them. For the National Bolsheviks Solzhenitsyn was a traitor and renegade besmirching the good name of the fatherland. Even *Pamyat* preferred to work within the regime.

How quickly would these collaborators of the right change their colors after the breakdown of the regime, claiming that they had always been against a regime founded and maintained by Jews, freemasons, and Russophobes of every persuasion. There is no gratitude in politics; only yesterday they had been among the most faithful supporters, the most insistent beneficiaries of a regime which they now denounced so bitterly. The human rights dissenters, on the other hand, had the backing of the liberal intelligentsia. This was not surprising, because the majority of the intelligentsia, certainly in Moscow and Leningrad, tended towards a more liberal orientation than the party authorities, hence the negative attitude of orthodox communists toward the "unreliable" and "wavering" intelligentsia. The dissent movement consisted mainly of members of the "creative" and "technical" intelligentsia. True, most of the establishment liberals were afraid for their positions and did not want to become too deeply involved in dissident activities; one should perhaps not blame them for the system had a great many sanctions at its disposal and did not hesitate to use them. Considerable courage was needed to engage in relatively minor gestures of defiance such as the refusal to condemn Pasternak or asking for freedom for Sinyavsky and Daniel, or to extend material help to an unknown dissenter or to express solidarity in small ways. There were such expressions of support and they were of psychological importance; without them the dissenters would have felt wholly isolated. But in the final analysis the liberal intelligentsia counted for very little, they were not calling the shots in the party and state apparatus, let alone the KGB. They could request, urge, and argue, up to a point, but they had no power of decision.

The activities of the dissenters were innocuous enough as seen through Western eyes. They did not plot against the Soviet government nor did they intend to establish new political parties to compete with the communists. They merely protested against cases of gross injustice and tried to alert the public to such incidents. They signed petitions, monitored human rights violations after the signing of the Helsinki protocols, in which the Soviet government had committed itself to observe these rights. They published the *Chronicle of Current Events,* a register of human rights violations, and to the best of their ability assisted the families of the prisoners of conscience. Perhaps the most political action was the demonstration by a handful of dissenters against the invasion of Czechoslovakia on Red Square in August 1968.

Lastly, there was the publication of dissident works of literature abroad that could not pass Soviet censorship. They included some of Solzhenitsyn's works such as *Cancer Ward* and *The First Circle,* Viktor Erofeyev's *Moscow-Petushki,* Evgenia Ginzberg's and Nadezhda

Mandelstam's autobiographies, Vasili Grossman's *Forever Flowing,* Maximov's *Seven Days of Creation* and other works were published abroad in Russian and frequently also in English. Again, KGB practice in this context was not consistent; some *tamizdat* (published abroad) authors were not touched be it because they were too old or infirm or had already spent many years in prison. But if a copy of one of these books was smuggled back to the Soviet Union, and if it was found in the possession of an undesirable individual, this could well lead to arrest and a lengthy prison term.

The position of human rights activists outside Moscow and Leningrad was particularly weak and dangerous, for in the metropolitan areas thousands of foreigners lived and visited and this indirectly imposed a certain restraint on the security organs. There was no such restraint in the provinces; some of these cities were closed to foreigners in the first place, and even those that were not, were virtually cut off. No one would know about the activities of a courageous individual or a small group outside Moscow, except by accident and with considerable delay. Foreign radio stations would not cover their activities; there was a network of human rights activists but of necessity it was not well organized, nor was there much support for the dissenters outside Moscow and Leningrad.

One of the main tasks of the KGB was to monitor these human right activities and to stamp them out. This was the job of the Fifth Directorate set up after the Prague Spring. It was later renamed, ironically, the "Protection of the Constitution" directorate. There were subdepartments dealing with intellectuals, religious believers, Jews, nationalists, and the KGB psychiatrists also came under this roof. A great variety of methods were used by the KGB to combat the human rights activists; including provocation, infiltration and systematic psychological warfare. While it was always possible to arrest dissidents and to bring them to trial, it was thought to be preferable that the dissidents should be broken, giving up their activities on their "own free will," having reached the conclusion that they were totally isolated, could not trust anyone, that their activities were wholly pointless because the overwhelming majority of the Soviet people resented and actively opposed them. To demoralize the dissidents the KGB faked letters, planted rumors about the activists (ranging from being CIA agents to beating their wives or husbands) and even employed a little stable of "writers" to publish scurrilous pamphlets about leading dissidents such as Sakharov and Solzhenitsyn.

These measures were effective only in part: The informers were relatively few, and, in any case, the dissidents had few secrets to hide. The pamphlets of the professional antidissident writers were given little credence, decent people, even if they disagreed with the dissidents would not lend themselves to such dirty work. The activities of the KGB psychiatrists backfired inasmuch as they led to great scandals abroad and the suspension of Soviet psychiatrists from international organizations.

The human rights activists tended to regard the KGB as its main antagonist, just as a street demonstrator would see his main enemy in the policeman beating him. But the KGB was not an independent organization with a policy and a will of its own. It operated under the guidance and leadership of the Politburo, it carried out orders, sometimes with excessive zeal, sometimes with less enthusiasm. Within the KGB those combatting the "internal enemy" did not enjoy the highest prestige; no great distinction was to be earned from driving an elderly lady or a young poet to suicide. It was considered a necessary job but not a glamorous one, no television films would glorify these brave Chekists on the intellectual and human rights front.

Some of the memoirs of KGB officials in later years tended to show that there had been little enthusiasm among them. The policy of the party leadership in this respect was affected to a considerable extent by the international situation. It goes without saying that they did not want to lose control over their own people. But at the same time they wanted to create the impression that the Soviet Union was a free and civilized country in which no one was punished for his opinion. Furthermore, while detente lasted, the sensitivity of Western public opinion acted to a certain extent as a brake on full scale persecution. True, the arrests continued during the seventies and leading dissenters such as Bukovsky, Sinyavsky, and Maximov (not to forget Solzhenitsyn) were forced to emigrate. But the *Chronicle of Current Events* continued to appear for a long time and the Helsinki work groups still operated even if on a reduced level.

The authorities could have arrested the dissidents at any time and effectively stopped all their publications. But they could not easily ignore public opinion abroad—including friendly pro-Soviet circles in the West who were protesting against the arrests, the trials and the persecution. As the human rights activists did not constitute an immediate danger, the authorities were willing to permit a minimum of activity while detente lasted. Like all police forces the KGB probably assumed that it was better to have these activities under control, rather than drive them totally underground and make supervision more difficult. In any case, it would have been next to impossible to isolate the Russian public entirely, putting an end to smuggling out manuscripts to the West, jamming all Western radio stations all the time.

The KGB had to play a delicate game vis-a-vis its political masters. On one hand they had to exaggerate the threat to the communist regime for reasons that are obvious. Unless there was a challenge to the regime, how to justify the existence of the enormous apparatus of control and suppression? Thus in a paradoxical way they may have had a vested interest in not seeing dissent totally disappear because this could have cost them their jobs. On the other hand the KGB wanted to impress the party leadership with their competence and efficiency. So they tried to create the impression that while the dissenters were a dangerous enemy and that internal vigilance was needed, the brave Chekists were perfectly able to cope with them.

In 1973 a major campaign was launched against Sakharov and Solzhenitsyn. Early that year, as it emerges from the KGB files, Andropov suggested that Sakharov's name be deleted from all Soviet publications and also made a number of proposals as to how he could be most effectively isolated.

The KGB had lost hope with regard to Solzhenitsyn, in January 1974 *Pravda* published an article entitled "The Path of a Traitor" foreshadowing the deportation of the writer. The campaign against Sakharov, on the other hand was tuned down, at least for a while. Did the award of the Nobel Peace Prize (1975) play a role? If so, it did not play a decisive role for the literature award a few years earlier had not saved Solzhenitsyn.

Major repressions against the dissidents came under way again in 1977 as detente waned. During that year Yuri Orlov as well as Ginzburg, Father Yakunin, Sharansky and others were arrested. By 1979 detente was virtually over, in December of that year the invasion of Afghanistan took place, and the following month Sakharov was exiled to Gorky without the benefit of a trial. This measure had been envisaged several years earlier. According to a document already referred to it had been decided in November 1975 to exile the Sakharovs to Sverdlovsk, where they would have made the acquaintance of Boris Yeltsin. But only with the change in the international situation was the decision carried out. A few dissidents remained at large in the 1980s, several issues of the *Chronicle* and some other Samizdat publications appeared.

By 1980, the human rights movement, was in a state of agony with most of its members deported from Russia or exiled or arrested and with few new recruits to take their place. But it was precisely during this period, during Brezhnev's last years and then under Andropov and Chernenko that the self-confidence of the rulers rapidly declined, that pessimism prevailed not only among the public in general but even among the party leadership, and that some of the ideas of the dissenters were gaining ground. They had been the keepers of the flame in dark times, a small flame, but one that owing to their courage was never allowed to be entirely extinguished.

* * *

Andrei Dmitrievich Sakharov who played such a crucial role in the human rights movement was not the first Soviet dissenter but he became the most famous. He was born in Moscow on May 21, 1921; his ances-tors on the paternal side had been village priests in the vicinity of Arzamas near Nizhny Novgorod, later Gorky, yet later again Nizhny Novgorod. His father was a gifted musician who graduated with honors, an ami-able, decent, educated but not very ambitious man who eventually be-came a mathematics and physics teacher and the author of a number of popular science books. His mother's family, the Sofianos were Greek-Russian; his maternal grandfather had been a Russian army officer who became a member of the (lower and landless) nobility. Andrei's forma-tive years in the late twenties and thirties were a stormy period in Soviet history; like most others, the Sakharov family was also affected by the purges and the terror. His father's brother Ivan was arrested and eventu-ally starved to death, his mother's brother was arrested and died during the course of the investigation. Sakharov writes in his autobiography that every family he knew suffered casualties. But he also noted that the era marked by tragedy, cruelty, and terror was also one of persisting revolutionary elan, hope for the future, fanaticism, all-pervasive propa-ganda, enormous social and psychological changes: "I was content to absorb communist ideology without questioning it."[2] In any case, Sakharov's main interest was not politics but, in the footsteps of his father, physics and mathematics. He had tutors during his early years and when he went to school first at the age of twelve, he was well in advance of his class and found it a waste of time. When he was in the seventh grade, aged about fourteen, he began to engage in physical experiments at home. Aged seventeen, he enrolled in Moscow University. When war broke out in June 1941 he was in his first senior year. Sakharov failed a medical test for recruitment in the army, but he might not have been drafted in any case because the more promising students of his department were evacuated to Ashkhabad, the capital of Turkmenistan, far away from the front. However, studies were not resumed and Sakharov worked for the next two and a half years in the laboratory of a cartridge factory. There he met Klava who became his first wife.

It was only during the last year of the war that he could return to Moscow. Owing to the intervention of his father he was accepted as a graduate student by Igor Tamm, one of the greatest names in the history of Russian physics. Tamm was to remain a crucial influence in Sakharov's life for years to come, as a man and as a scientist.

The next three years Sakharov spent reading the standard works in the field of advanced theoretical physics such as Wolfgang Pauli's *Theory of Relativity* (which took him three months) and his *Quantum Mechanics*; he taught himself English in order to read the *Physical Review*, took part in Tamm's seminar and even began to teach. The young Sakharovs could not find a room in Moscow and living conditions were miserable. But in retrospect Sakharov wrote: "Recalling that summer of 1947 I feel that never before or since have I been so close to the highest level of science—its cutting edge." Aged twenty-six, he was a young man in a hurry; the war years had been lost years as far as his education as a scientist were concerned. (Pauli had written his famous book at the age of twenty one!) But he had already emerged as one of the most promising physicists of his generation. In late 1946 he was first contacted with the proposal to join a working group preoccupied with a "special project." He managed to get out of it, but when in June 1948 Tamm was mobilized for the same purpose, Sakharov was not even asked and together with others, he began to investigate the possibility of building a hydrogen bomb. Sakharov moved first to Dubna near Moscow and later to Arzamas-16, some 400 kilometers east of the capital, the center of the Soviet work on nuclear weapons, not far from the region whence his family originated.[3]

Sakharov's prominent role in the development and refinement of the Soviet thermonuclear bomb is known. If the Soviet nuclear bomb was a copy of the American, the first hydrogen bomb was constructed on the basis of an independent theoretical concept, and it was in this context that Sakharov's ideas (the "layer cake") concept constituted a break-through. As a result the Soviet Union exploded its first such device much earlier than anticipated in the West—in August 1953. In December of that year Sakharov, not a member of the communist party became a "Hero of Socialist Labor," and the next year at the age of thirty two, a full member of the Academy of Sciences.

During the years that followed Sakharov worked on a design of second generation nuclear weapons, on nuclear fusion and on other projects, together with the other leading scientists and managers such as Kurchatov, Zeldovich, Khariton. The members of this group were awarded twice more the "Hero of Socialist Labor" each, until, in the end only Brezhnev had more of these, and in Brezhnev's case they were a butt of jokes. Such recognition was only deserved from the Kremlin's point of view for the Soviet nuclear effort was a huge success. Owing to it (and the military build up in general) the Soviet Union became a superpower; not only Soviet science but the system in general gained great prestige. True, these achievements had been made owing to a singleminded outlay of resources in one specific direction and the neglect of most others. But in the end only the results mattered: The Soviet Union had been first in space travel and at least the equal of the United States in the nuclear field. Could there be any doubt that eventually the political and economic system would also show its superiority? The achievements of Sakharov and the other scientists decisively contributed to the optimistic mood that despite all hardships prevailed in the country up to the late 1960s.

Yet another aspect should be mentioned. The "laboratories and installations" were an island of freedom in a harsh dictatorship.[4] There was a constant struggle of ideas and concepts not only among scientists, but also between them and the political supervisors. This was the only way progress could be made and results achieved. There could be no party line in physics, theoretical and experimental, at almost every stage there were two, three or more approaches that had to be explored. Thus the years in Arzamas-16 became a unique training ground in citizenship. Not all availed themselves of the opportunity; other leading scientists restricted their dissent to purely scientific issues—such as protesting against the Lysenko charlatanism that had established a virtual monopoly in the field of Soviet biology. But Sakharov went further; it is unlikely that but for his experience in Arzamas-16 he would have dared to send notes to Khrushchev suggesting that the test ban which had been in force for three years should be continued, whereas the political leadership wanted to resume testing. This made Khrushchev angry: "I can see Sakharov got illusions.... Leave politics to us, we are the specialists, we have to conduct our policies from a position of strength."

Independence of mind was Sakharov's most outstanding characteristic and there was also an element of obstinacy, but he was neither pugnacious, nor aggressive, looking for a quarrel. What he wrote about his first marriage (which was not a happy one) was true, *grosso modo* for his public persona up to the 1960s—that he tended to avoid confrontation and chose the line of least resistance, except, of course, where it really mattered—in science.

How then did he become involved in public affairs? During the fifties and early sixties he had been wholly absorbed in his work but once the great breakthroughs had been made Sakharov found more time to think about the wider implications of the bomb. This led him to searching thoughts about war and peace, the consequences of nuclear war, and the general state of his country.

In 1966 he began to read *samizdat* books such as Yevgenia Ginzburg's memoirs, he first met critics of Stalinism such as Roy Medvedev and Ernest Henri, and he began to sign letters of protest against the impending re-Stalinization. He wrote a letter to Brezhnev in defense of the Ginsburg-Galanskov group which had been arrested and put to trial. He phoned Andropov, head of the KGB, with a request to help Yuli Daniel (Sinyavsky's co-defendant) sick in a Mordovian labor camp. He also became involved in an attempt to save Lake Baikal which had been heavily polluted owing to reckless and irresponsible industrial policies. However, up to 1968 Sakharov had not played a prominent part in the human rights movement, his main interests had been scientific rather than political. In his autobiography he writes that by the beginning of 1968 he felt a growing compulsion to speak out "on the fundamental issues of our age:

> I was influenced by my life experience and a feeling of personal responsibility, reinforced by the part I played in the development of the hydrogen bomb, the special knowledge I'd gained about thermonuclear warfare, my bitter struggle to ban nuclear testing, and my familiarity with the Soviet system.

This resulted in a long paper entitled "Reflections on Progress, Peaceful Coexistence and Intellectual Freedom" alerting readers to the many perils facing mankind and making a case for convergance, a rapprochement of the capitalist and socialist system and ultimately world government. This paper was sent to Brezhnev for Sakharov had no wish to engage in "covert" activities. It was circulated in Moscow and ultimately published first in a Dutch newspaper, later in the United States and elsewhere—altogether in 18 million copies.

Publication coincided with the invasion of Czechoslovakia, the Marchenko trial, and a first meeting with Solzhenitsyn. This in turn led to Sakharov's deeper involvement in human rights affairs above all with Valery Chalidze, in whose home he met Yelena, his future wife. He also became one of the cofounders of the Moscow Human Rights Committee.

As a result of these activities Sakharov was fired from the "Installation" which made it easier for him to pursue his social-political activities in Moscow. The communist authorities did not easily give up their attempt to save Sakharov's soul. After all, he had done a great deal for his country, and perhaps his ideological confusion could be dispersed. The KGB submissions to the Politburo with all the slander and insinuations betray from time to time a measure of embarrassment and annoyance, not so much with Sakharov but with the fact that they had to deal with it. After all, he was not a prisoner, he had been deported to Gorky but was free to move there, was it not the task of the Academy of Sciences, and perhaps other organizations to deal with Sakharov's reeducation and the other problems arising out of his exile? (Andropov's memorandum of 9 December 1981) The issue was surely not that the resources of the KGB were unduly strained as the result of their accepting responsibility for Sakharov. The feeling is that for whatever reasons they felt somewhat uneasy about the whole affair: Not many laurels were to be gained on this field of battle.

In Moscow Sakharov had become a frequent visitor at the seminars of the dissidents and he attended, not without great difficulty, the trials against them. He supported the Tartars and the Jewish activists. He had discussions with the leading liberals of the day such as academician Peter Kapitsa, and the movie director Mikhail Romm. But no one wanted to go as far in their protest as Sakharov who had become increasingly pessimistic about the state of his native country. The "Reflections" of 1969 had been the work of a social democrat convinced that the Soviet government was still his government. In 1973, in an interview with a Swedish correspondent, he said that he was skeptical about socialism in general, it was neither a novel nor a better way to organize society. He had become, in his own words a liberal, a gradualist.

Ideological issues apart, Sakharov's many activities were one of the reasons for the estrangement with Solzhenitsyn. Solzhenitsyn's biographer describes the different approach and style as follows:

> He [Solzhenitsyn] felt that by his innumerable appearances in public trials and his numerous open letters Sakharov was needlessly expending his energies and exhausting himself. Sakharov's important statements, such as his *Postscript* [of 1971] tended to get overlooked in the welter of less important declarations and thereby lost their impact. Whereas Solzhenitsyn meticulously planned each public statement and carefully abstained from getting mixed up in the affairs of other dissidents, Sakharov continually fired off declarations and letters in all directions and kept open house for anyone who cared to visit him. As a result of this "incorrigible urge to champion the persecuted" as Solzhenitsyn wrote to him, and of his extraordinary generosity and humility, Sakharov had become the people's tribune. Solzhenitsyn, on the other hand, was proud, suspicious, secretive and aloof.[5]

There was a grain of truth in these observations, but seen in retrospect both approaches were needed, and Solzhenitsyn's aloofness was by no means more effective. There was no one to replace Sakharov at the time just as Solzhenitsyn played a unique role with his political manifestoes and the *Gulag* books. In later years the two men were to drift even further apart. Sakharov was first and foremost a democrat and fighter for human rights. Solzhenitsyn was a Russian patriot on whose agenda the issue of individual freedom, democratic institutions and a pluralist society did not figure highly. In his American exile Solzhenitsyn was to publish bitter attacks against the Russian democrats at home and abroad.

By 1972–73, however, this conflict had not yet come out in the open. Sakharov and Solzhenitsyn had not just become a major domestic irritant for the Soviet authorities but an international scandal. Once Solzhenitsyn was settled in the backwoods of Vermont writing his historical novels he ceased to be a victim of the Soviet regime whereas Sakharov was still a prisoner. Not only Western scientists were rallying for the defense of Sakharov, leading American politicians made it known that there would be no substantial improvement in U.S.-Soviet relation as long as Sakharov was persecuted by the Soviet authorities. Since Soviet foreign policy was orientated towards *détente* at the time, it was decided in the Kremlin to tune down the campaign. This did not save Solzhenitsyn from deportation in 1974—but his fate might have been worse. And it gave Sakharov another six years in relative freedom in Moscow, until he too, was exiled to Gorky.

The KGB file on Sakharov probably dates back to his student days; at the very latest he was submitted to a thorough security check when he was enlisted for work on the nuclear project. Such operational files have not, of course, been released. The present collection contains only documents submitted on the very highest level by Andropov and his successors to the Politburo or the first secretary in person. On occasion Rudenko, the Soviet attorney general and Rekunkov, his successor, were brought in. From time to time there are reports by Andropov's assistants, heads of KGB departments (the second and fifth directorate) to individual members of the Politburo such as Suslov, who was for years the chief ideological supervisor. Even on this rarified level there must have been documents which were not declassified or are kept in other archives or may have been destroyed.

The references to Sakharov are in repetitive, routine, bureaucratic terms "A.D. Sakharov, born in 1921 in Moscow, Russian by nationality, full member of the Academy of Sciences, etc."—as if anyone did not know that Sakharov was Russian by origin and a member of the Academy. The charges against Sakharov were also phrased in what the East Germans called "party Chinese"—Sakharov had made himself the mouthpiece of "anti-public moods," "hostile elements" pursuing demagogical aims were trying to exploit the authority of Sakharov for their purposes such as "improving socialism" and to counteract the alleged excessive interference of the party in scientific and cultural affairs. Even in their internal communications they heavily used circumlocution and state security refrained from calling a spade a spade, referring to an agricultural implement instead. The language concerning Sakharov's activities became harsher around 1975. In the document in which Andropov, Rudenko, and Ustinov (the overlord of the military-industrial complex) proposed to exile Sakharov to Sverdlovsk, it was alleged that whereas in earlier years Sakharov had merely given currency to various calumnies and inventions, had opposed domestic and foreign policy of the Soviet state and had inspired a variety of "anti-society" initiatives, more recently he had stepped up his campaign, openly fighting Soviet Power, revealing to the enemy state secrets concerning the most important defense problems of the country. The same document also alleges that Sakharov's hostile actions had been inspired to a considerable extent by his wife, Yelena Bonner. But according to internal evidence the KGB had its eyes on Sakharov back in 1966 as a leading human rights activist, and it was only well after 1968 that the name Bonner first appears.

There is no attempt to understand what might have induced Sakharov to take an uncompromising stand in the defense of his principles—which was to cause so much deprivation and suffering. Obviously, the KGB officials could not have believed that this was Sakharov's preferred way to pursue personal happiness. They could have argued that he was a Herostratic figure in search of publicity, they could have thought of some other psychological explanation, however spurious. But there was no such attempt at all which makes one wonder what went on in the heads of those in charge of the security organs. Perhaps they thought him childish, confused and misguided, but if so, how to explain his incredible obstinacy to persist in his impractical dreams?

From time to time suggestions were voiced that a leading political figure should meet Sakharov for a discussion. (Sakharov did look for a meeting with Brezhnev for a long time.) The KGB and the Politburo probably assumed, not without reason, that Brezhnev would not have been a suitable interlocutor for Sakharov. But there were other party leaders who could have met him. Perhaps they thought that this would have been against all protocol, especially in view of the fact that Sakharov was not even a party member. Perhaps they believed that it would set a dangerous precedence. The suggestion seems to have come primarily from the KGB. True, the KGB did not think that such an initiative would show results, but it agreed that it was still of some importance just for the record, because Sakharov's treatment by the authorities had provoked attacks not only in the capitalist countries, but had generated criticism also among the Western communist parties, and even within the ranks of the communist party of the Soviet Union. If any additional evidence is needed to the effect how rigid a body the party leadership was in the 1970s and 1980s, the present file presents such evidence.

More often than not, the KGB reports about Western reactions with regard to the Soviet treatment of Sakharov were mendacious or at least misleading. Western diplomats and journalists are quoted to the effect that public opinion in the West was fed up with Sakharov, and that Westerners believed that the Soviet government was acting correctly depriving the scientist of the various orders and awards which had been bestowed on him in earlier years. Even if some misguided Western attache had expressed views to this effect, Andropov must have known that such opinions were by no means representative. The head of the KGB was either misinformed by his aides or he deliberately misinformed his colleagues in the Politburo. While the obiter dicta of unnamed Western attaches cannot be checked, the quotations from Western newspapers used in the KGB summaries were far from the truth concerning the intensity of Western outrage, and Sakharov's moral standing and prestige outside his homeland.

The members of the Politburo received detailed reports about Sakharov's mood and state of health. This included even such details as the name of the (foreign) medicine (Tarkan) which he had taken against the advice of the Gorky physicians and which, being foreign, had caused a deterioration in his state of health.

Much as the Politburo and the KGB chiefs preoccupied themselves with the details of the case there is a feeling that they could not make up their mind how to treat Sakharov. On one hand it was reported that but for the evil influence of Yelena Bonner, a *status vivendi* could have been reached with the Academician resulting in his return to his scientific work and his desisting from political activities. If so, one should have assumed that the authorities would have been overjoyed by the prospect of getting rid of his wife, at least for lengthy periods. (The couple had requested that Bonner should be permitted to travel to Italy and the United States for medical treatment.) But the KGB was most reluctant to give such permission; it came only after Sakharov had declared a hunger strike.

The routine reports to the Central Committee about the nefarious activities of Bonner and Sakharov (with special emphasis on the hunger strike) continued right up to his release. But on August 10, 1985 a handwritten note by Gorbachev appears in the archives requesting "once again" Comerades Chebrikov (head of the KGB) and Shevardnadze (the foreign minister) to "rethink everything attentively in particular with regard to the present state of affairs" and to express their considerations. We do not know exactly what preceded this cryptic note, but the subject was Sakharov and the "present state" referred obviously to the beginning of the new course, of *glasnost* and *perestroika*. Gorbachev had been in Paris in February of that year and in an interview with *Humanité* the French communist daily, had declared that there were no political prisoners in the Soviet Union. Whereupon Sakharov and other names were immediately brought up, acutely embarrassing the visitor from Moscow. We do not know whether it was on this occasion or earlier on that Gorbachev decided to liquidate this unfortunate chapter in recent Soviet history.

Soon after Gorbachev became first secretary in 1985 a new wind was blowing in Soviet policy at home and abroad. Increasingly, there was talk about the need for reform, there were meetings with Western leaders on the highest level (Geneva and Reykjavik) pointing to the fact that a new era in East-West relations was dawning and that there was an attempt on Moscow's part to retreat from the confrontational style of the late seventies and early eighties. There was Western readiness to meet them halfway, but all the time Sakharov was still in Gorky, a bone of contention and clearly an anachronism. But it took Gorbachev more than a year to accomplish his aim.

The report for which Gorbachev had asked, signed by Chebrikov and Shevardnadze, dated August 28, 1985 was still hostile—people in the West were no longer interested in Sakharov. Sakharov himself was tired. But Gorbachev was not persuaded and asked the head of the KGB to comment on a letter sent him by Sakharov concerning the fate of political prisoners in the USSR. Chebrikov who must have thought this more than a little naive replied as had been the custom for many years, that those detained had been sentenced on the basis of the criminal code, and on concrete charges.

But this was followed by the report of a subcommittee appointed by the Politburo consisting of Ligachev, Chebrikov and Marchuk, the new head of the Academy of Sciences. Dated December 12, 1986 it reviewed the deportation of Sakharov in 1980 and reached the conclusion that the "preventive measures" taken against Sakharov since 1980 had been successful to a certain extent, inasmuch as Sakharov had been isolated from Western secret services, his contact with anti-Soviet organizations abroad and at home had been cut. Furthermore, he had returned to his scientific work. In the circumstances his return to Moscow could be envisaged even though there was the danger that owing to Bonner's influence, once in Moscow, Sakharov would again become the focus of "negative elements" advocating human rights. But all things considered, it was preferable that he should return rather than remain in Gorky. On December 15, 1986 Gorbachev called Sakharov in Gorky telling him that the decree of January 8, 1980 had been rescinded and that Sakharov was now free to return to Moscow. On December 23, Sakharov and Bonner arrived at Moscow's Yaroslavl station, where they were welcomed by hundreds of friends, acquaintances, and well-wishers.

Marchuk, the president of the Academy, had come to Gorky even earlier on to give Sakharov good advice: many members of the Academy were feeling that Sakharov was wasting time worrying about problems that "we are in the process of eliminating anyway." Marchuk forgot to mention that if there was such a change in attitude among the leadership, it had been, last not least, Sakharov's merit, who had contributed to the spirit of reform, more than any other individual inside the Soviet Union.

The following three years—Sakharov died in Moscow in December 1989—were a time of hectic activity. Sakharov continued his work in the Academy, (having been made a member of its presidium), he was elected a member of the Soviet parliament, participated in countless meetings, made speeches and gave interviews, he travelled to America, France, Italy several times, found time to see old friends and new. He made speeches in little places outside Moscow to help other candidates in the election campaign. He went on fact-finding missions to Armenia, where war had broken out, and to other parts of the Soviet Union. He supported Gorbachev's reform policy even though he stressed time and again that it was not radical enough. With others he prepared a draft for a new constitution and did not hesitate to make unpopular speeches on subjects such as the war in Afghanistan.

The KGB continued to be interested in him even after he had returned to Moscow. On the occasion of his funeral it noted that only 40,000 people had come (on a cold day in December), not hundreds of thousands such as had been hoped by certain circles who had wanted to exploit the funeral for "speculatory political purposes." And a few days later in a KGB report about the views expressed by American diplomats about Sakharov's death: Of late Sakharov had become more and more "idealistic" (?) in his political mood and in certain cases had preached a destructive radicalism. But he had enjoyed esteem even among his political opponents including inside the communist leadership. Altogether he had been a unifying symbol, an integrative rather than a real political figure. (December 23, 1989, signed by V. Kriuchkov, the then head of the KGB). This had not been the opinion of the Politburo and the KGB when they had arrested Sakharov in a Moscow street ten years earlier and exiled him to Gorky. They had not been bothered by a symbol (though he was, of course, also a symbol) but a real political figure.

Sakharov did not live to witness the chaos, the disintegration of the Soviet Union, and the antidemocratic backlash. But this will hardly affect the judgment of posterity, for Soviet communism did not only fail miserably to carry out its promises, it also bears the historical responsibility to have made the transition to a new way of life so excruciating difficult. Authoritarian regimes such as Kemalist Turkey, Franco's Spain and even Chile under Pinochet adopted democratic systems without great difficulties. In the Soviet Union such smooth transition had become impossible for seventy years of communist rule had left a moral wasteland and an exhausted people. After a few years of relative freedom the pendulum was swinging back to a nationalist, or to be precise a nationalist-socialist mood, to authoritarian practices, to corruption and anarchy. Despairing of politics and politicians many paid no longer attention to public affairs, others claimed that the bad old days had not been that bad, after all; as the French had said in a bygone era, how beautiful was the dream of the republic under the empire. There is a Yeats poem about the beggar upon horseback lashing a beggar on foot; then the revolution occurred: "The beggars have changed places but the lash goes on" (and it was not even sure whether the beggars had indeed changed places).

Was it for this kind of society that the dissidents had fought, suffered, starved, were arrested and, in some cases driven to their death? The very same question was asked in another Yeats poem. Summing up the achievement of the Irish freedom movement:

> Was it for this the wild geese spread,
> The grey wing upon every tide;
> For this that all that blood was shed
> For this Edward Fitzgerald died,
> And Robert Emmet and Wolf Tone
> All that delirium of the brave...
> —"September 1913"

If Sakharov were still alive he would be deeply saddened by all that has gone wrong in Russia in recent years. But would he be greatly surprised? Hardly, because only the most inveterate optimist would have assumed in 1987 that the transition to a free and civilized society would be quick and smooth.

Writing in 1988 assessing the prospects for a free Russia, I compared it with the traditional procession in northern Germany in which the unfortunate participants have to retreat three steps after every four they have advanced. As an afterthought I recalled the exodus from Egypt of the children of Israel. The geographical distance between Egypt and Palestine is not great but it took Moses forty years to cross the desert.[6] But there is every reason to believe that Sakharov would not have lost faith despite the setbacks that have occurred and the dire prospects facing Russia at present. In the dark nights of 1982–83, and indeed all the years right up to his release from Gorky success in his own lifetime must have seemed seemed a distant possibility. It is the mark of a truly great individual that he (or she) will persist in the struggle for what is right, following a moral code, a categorical imperative, not because victory in the foreseeable future seems more likely than defeat.

Notes

1. "Dissent" and "dissidents" are imperfect terms for the struggle for human rights under the Soviet regime and Sakharov never liked them. But they became part of the language and even those who felt uneasy about their usage had to accept them.
2. A. Sakharov, *Memoirs* (1990), p. 23. The Russian edition, *Vospominanya* (1990) is somewhat more detailed. Other sources for Sakharov's life are Andrei Sakharov, *Gorky, Moskva, dalee, vezde* (1990) and Elena Bonner, *Alone Together* (1986).
3. Secrecy was such that even in Sakharov's autobiography published in 1990 this place always appears as the "Installation," it is never called by its real name. Sakharov lived there for eighteen years. Arzamas-16 is situated next to the little town of Sarov, known to students of Russian history as the home of Serafim of Sarov, one of the chief figures in the annals of the Russian church.
4. There was a heavy concentration of Jewish scientists in the field of nuclear research, at a time when cosmopolitans were actively persecuted (under Stalin), and discriminated against in many other fields (under Stalin's successors). About the physicists' community as an "island of intellectual autonomy" see David Holloway, *Stalin and the Bomb* (1994), p. 363.
5. Michael Scammell, *Solzhenitsyn* (1984), pp. 798–99.
6. W. Laqueur, *The Long Road to Freedom* (1989); Russian (restricted) edition— "for official use only" (1989).

19

Feuchtwanger and Gide

The motives of those prominent Western fellow travelers visiting Moscow in the 1930s have been a source of fascination and puzzlement for a long time. I want here to concentrate on the trips that two of them took, Romain Rolland in the summer of 1935 and Lion Feuchtwanger in December of 1936. Because of *glasnost* (and the passing of time), one can now write about their motives and impressions with some greater authority than before. There was a fifty-year embargo on Romain Rolland's personal diary, which has become accessible only recently; his Moscow diary was published in three installments in *Voprosy Literaturi* in 1989. As for Feuchtwanger, the daily reports his guide and translator D. Karavkina made to VOKS (and ultimately the NKVD) are now available. (VOKS was the society for cultural ties with foreign countries; the NKVD was the predecessor of the KGB.) The reports on the Feuchtwanger stay were published in *Sovietskie Archivy* in 1989. Feuchtwanger's own book *Moscow 1937* was republished in 1990 in the Soviet Union together with Gide's *Return from the USSR,* with a long informative preface by A. Plutnik.

A few words about the *dramatis personae*: both were major writers; their works seem to have stood the test of time. There is too much gushing, naive idealism in Rolland's *Jean Christophe* for many tastes, and his last novels, *L'âme enchantée,* are now virtually unreadable. But his *Colas Breugnon* is certainly one of the great masterworks of twentieth-century French literature. Rolland was always more popular in Germany and Russia than in his native country, which may have to do with his unpopular pacifist stance in World War I. The Nobel Prize he received in 1915 was small comfort for the disdain of many of his fellow countrymen and the fact that for years he could not return to France, eventually settling in Villeneuve, on the shore of Lake Geneva. Feuchtwanger was a master in a genre more popular with the reading public than with the critics, namely the historical novel. The histories of literature have not had much to say about him, but his best works are still widely read and enjoyed.

Both became aware early of the danger of fascism, Feuchtwanger because he lived in Munich where Hitler first appeared on the political scene. He described the early Nazi movement in a *roman de clèf* called *Erfolg* (the English title, for unknown reasons, was *Power*, rather than *Success*). Rolland had always closely followed events in Italy, and he became an early opponent of Mussolini. Neither Rolland nor Feuchtwanger were ever members of the Communist party; they were not even social democrats. Though they wrote a great deal about politics, they did so because politics was so heavily in the air; deep down they were unpolitical men. I ought to mention a third, even more famous writer, André Gide, who visited the Soviet Union in between Rolland and Feuchtwanger; his negative impressions, published as *Retour de l'USSR,* became a major scandal. Reread now, it seems rather tame and to have been written in anguish rather than anger, but it deeply offended the communists. Both Rolland and Feuchtwanger attacked Gide's book in *Pravda,* and it is doubtful whether Feuchtwanger would have been invited had it not been for the feeling that something ought to be done to repair the damage. Feuchtwanger was handed his invitation, which led to a three-hour visit with Stalin, by Mikhail Koltsov, who was, next to Ilya Ehrenburg, the most famous journalist of the day. Koltsov was arrested the year after and later executed. Ehrenburg was on the list of the spymasters but for some reason escaped a similar fate.

Rolland's diary, some 150 printed pages, covers the period between June 17th and July 23rd of 1935. The mood that year in Moscow was more optimistic than ever before or after. It is true that there had been mass arrests after the Kirov murder, but the mass executions had not yet started. The economic situation had improved and a new constitution, "the freest in the world," had been adopted. There was a feeling of achievement in the air—at least among the people whom Rolland met in Moscow.

He spent much time with Gorky but also talked with Stalin, Molotov, Kaganovich, and Yagoda, head of the secret police. Unlike Feuchtwanger, he was not entirely dependent on a translator; his wife, Masha, was Russian and had family in Moscow. He was a sick man but also a great hypochondriac. Among his most frequent interlocutors were Dr. Levin and Dr. Pletnev, the Kremlin physicians soon to be arrested and executed. Pletnev tried to explain to Rolland that he should not have come in the first place and ought to leave Moscow for a place where the air was healthier. The present period in Soviet history, he said, was unhealthy; he himself would have preferred to live forty years later. Rolland either did not understand or pretended not to understand.

Many of the things Rolland disliked in Fascist Italy he enjoyed in Moscow—the feeling of purpose, the youthful idealism, the parades, even the cultural conformism. Above all, he was impressed by Stalin, his "absolute simplicity, straightforwardness and truthfulness." Stalin admitted to him that the execution of some hundred people after Kirov's murder had been precipitous and a political mistake but rationalized that it had been necessary as a deterrent. Stalin told him that it was a dirty business and much better not to get involved. But, he continued, once one had decided to liberate the exploited, one did not have the right to opt out. Stalin explained that the Soviet leaders had to take not only world opinion into account but also the domestic situation. Many Russians were very angry that he, Stalin, had spared the lives of people such as Zinoviev and Kamenev. (The interview took place after their first trial.) Did Rolland know that there had been a conspiracy of young women of aristocratic background who aimed to poison the whole Soviet leadership? One young lady librarian had attempted to poison Stalin.

Rolland asked about the introduction of capital punishment for minors from the age of twelve. Stalin answered that such a measure could not be understood by the West. He muttered something about yet another conspiracy and concluded that Rolland should rest assured that death sentences would be passed only in very rare cases. Rolland wrote in his diary: "When I heard about these horrible crimes committed by women and children, I understood that we in the West tend to forget these realities. The Bolsheviks still have to fight for a long time against the cruel, barbaric old Russia."

For every negative feature, Rolland found an excuse or at least some mitigating circumstances. And yet, one has a sense of underlying uneasiness, a lack of enthusiasm. Rolland disliked some of the movies he watched; he disliked the Moscow weather; and he regretted that Esperanto had been banned in the Soviet Union. He fought hard for the release of Victor Serge—a French-Russian oppositionist who had been in a Soviet prison for years. He explained to Stalin and Yagoda that he had no sympathies for Serge's views, but that they should realize Serge's continued detention was grist for the anti-Soviet mills in the West. Serge was released the following year, no doubt due to Rolland's intervention. Rereading his diary after his return from Moscow, Rolland concluded that he had been perhaps too critical and written with too much haste. In retrospect, the negative aspects of the Soviet regime were outweighed by the positive features: "I have no shadow of a doubt that the best hopes of the world rest on the assumption of a Soviet victory."

However, Rolland apparently did have some dire forebodings. He would not have dreamed of uttering these doubts in public, but he did write to Stalin in 1937 asking for clemency for Bukharin, whom he had met in Moscow two years earlier. About the mass terror, he wrote at the end of 1937 in his diary: "I defend not Stalin but the Soviet Union, I stand for freedom, for people who are masters of their own destiny. Idolatry be it of Stalin, Hitler or Mussolini is a most damaging thing."

It is more difficult to find mitigating circumstances for Feuchtwanger's book—except one perhaps; the subtitle was "a report for my friends." This was a propagandistic work which the Soviet authorities produced in record time. The manuscript was translated within a few days, typeset in twenty-four hours, and printed within two to three weeks in Moscow, Amsterdam, and New York. Two hundred thousand copies in Russian were produced, but *habent sua fat libelli,* soon after withdrawn. It was never reprinted and was excluded from the Russian edition of Feuchtwanger's collected works. It was thought that Feuchtwanger's approach would be very effective for Western consumption, yet for the Soviet public he was too objective, even critical. After attending the Radek-Pyatakov trial, for instance, he wrote that for people in the West the basic motives of the accused and their behavior in court could not be wholly comprehensible. He also wrote that the deification of Stalin could not be comprehended as long as one looked at the Soviet Union through Western eyes.

His Soviet hosts were in a great hurry to get some statement out of him even before his book was to appear, and thus he was invited to write an article for *Pravda.* It appeared on December 30, 1936, and was titled, "An Aesthete in the Soviet Union." In it, he dealt with André Gide's allegations that there was a cult of the individual in the Soviet Union. It is true, Feuchtwanger wrote, that Stalin was honored in the Soviet Union in a way not customary by Western standards. But if one looked at the phenomenon closely, one would find this had nothing really to do with Stalin as a person, rather with Stalin as the embodiment of socialism. It was not an artificial cult; it had developed as the result of real socialist achievements. People were grateful to Stalin for their having bread and butter, education, law and order, and for creating a strong army. When the people said "Stalin," it meant prosperity and enlightenment.

Was Feuchtwanger aware of the real situation in the Soviet Union? Up to a point, yes, although sometimes for the wrong reasons. He constantly complained about the lack of material comforts there; the light in his hotel room was insufficient, the furniture ugly, the service inefficient and unhelpful. He even suggested that Gide, a sensitive man and an artist, had been similarly irritated and offended by the Russians. In brief, much of the time there Feuchtwanger was in a foul mood, though somewhat appeased by the enthusiastic ovations he received in the theater and by his interview with Stalin. However, he continued to complain: he did not get his mail on time; the editor of *Pravda,* Mekhlis (a particularly unsavory character) had asked him to make some changes in his article about the Stalin cult.

Feuchtwanger's Soviet companion complained that despite all the precautionary measures and controls that had been made, Feuchtwanger was seeing all kinds of doubtful characters. Thus, Erwin Piscator's wife had told him about the housing situation in Moscow; last summer she had spent several weeks in the street because she had no shelter. He wanted to know whether it was true that Pasternak was in disfavor and no longer printed. Why, he asked, did the Russian leaders publish only the nineteenth-century classics,and why were they afraid of modern writers? He had long conversations with Soviet officials about democracy and freedom of speech, but he told his companion that they had not persuaded him. Yet unlike Gide, he was not an aesthete, so he went on to defend Stalin's policy and, above all, the trials.

Gide was politically more naive than Feuchtwanger. He had taken the news about the new democratic constitution seriously, and he was bitterly disappointed when he realized that, far from becoming more democratic, the Soviet regime was turning more and more tyrannical. Feuchtwanger was not disillusioned, since he had no illusions in the first place. A Russian commentator, Plutnik, writing in 1990 exaggerates when he observes that "Feuchtwanger was not deceived. He saw everything and understood everything." He saw very little in his three weeks in

Moscow, and he did not, of course, understand everything. Above all, the behavior of the defendants in the trial he attended and the accusations against them remained a riddle to him. It is doubtful whether he was convinced by his own explanations. Why did the accused not defend themselves? He reported what the Soviet people were saying, but this was not quite persuasive. Perhaps he had missed something in translation? He concluded that probably a major Russian writer was needed to explain this psychological mystery. But there was no such writer. After his departure, Feuchtwanger ceased to be interested in Moscow, Stalin, and the trials. He remained a fellow traveler and signed various appeals in defense of the Soviet Union. He did not write the series of profiles he had promised his hosts about the outstanding leaders he had met such as Molotov, Voroshilov, and so on. Instead, he went back to his historical novels about Goya, the American Revolution, and the last part of the Josephus trilogy.

In recent years, the Feuchtwanger affair and the writings of other Westerners who had whitewashed Stalin and the trials have provided ammunition for a number of Russian writers on the extreme right of the ideological spectrum. Their argument runs, in brief, as follows: The Russian people cannot be made responsible in any way for the "cult of the individual." Stalinism was a worldwide phenomenon "from Madrid to Shanghai." If such humanists and astute observers of human behavior like Barbusse, Rolland, and Feuchtwanger, who were under no compulsion and pressure, totally misjudged the real state of affairs, why blame the poor Russians who were living in a totalitarian dictatorship?

The real explanation, as I see it, is simpler. Rolland, Feuchtwanger, and the others were indeed students of human behavior, but their experience was limited in the main to France and Germany. I don't think they ever understood England and America—let alone the Soviet Union. Their political interest was not very deep, although they did sense that Europe was on the eve of a war. This theme occurs repeatedly both in Rolland's *Diary* and in Feuchtwanger's *Moscow 1937*. Having to choose between Hitler and Stalin, they opted for the latter. Seen in this light, any criticism of Stalin and the Soviet Union was tantamount to weakening the anti-Fascist alliance. Feuchtwanger feared that the West was no longer capable of resisting Hitler. At the end of his book, he wrote that Western civilization was in decline, that it could no longer take decisive action and was cowardly and hypocritical. The very air in the West was poisoned; in Russia it was fresh. So he concluded this "report for his friends" with three cheers for the Soviet Union, despite all the problems as yet unresolved there. Stalin and his people were the only hope for stemming the tide of Nazi barbarism. The argument is a little shaky. The decapitation of the Red Army was certainly not the best way to prepare the Soviet Union for war, and in any case Stalin did not believe that a military conflict with Nazi Germany was near. The real enemy was the West.

It is not my assignment here to examine the validity of the arguments of our two fellow travelers. All that matters in this context is that they genuinely believed that the West was finished and that the Soviet Union was the only bulwark against a Nazi victory. As for the rest, Romain Rolland died in 1944 at Lake Geneva; Feuchtwanger moved to Pacific Palisades, California, despite the fact that he had so much liked the Moscow air. He never went back to the Soviet Union, but he never recanted either. In a sampler of his work that Feuchtwanger published in Germany in the 1950s, excerpts from the "report to my friends" were included. He died in 1958.

Part V
Public and Private Affairs

20

The Congress for Cultural Freedom: A Memoir

I visited the headquarters of the Congress for Cultural Freedom in Paris for the first time in May 1953. It consisted of a small office of three or four rooms in Avenue Montaigne, a distinguished street not far from the Champs Elysees, better known for haute couture (Chanel, Givenchy, Ungaro, Valentino, Dior, Louis Vuitton, and Cartier) than for high culture. (Which is not literally true, Stravinsky's *Sacré du Printemps* was first performed at No. 15.) The secretary general was Michael Josselson born in Reval (Tallinn), educated in Berlin who had worked in Paris as chief buyer for a major New York department store prior to enlisting in the American army. He was truly polyglot and at the same time a man of substance, not an academic but a manager in the best sense; he had good judgment and a great deal of common sense. To me he seemed almost always on the verge of an emotional explosion; at the same time he was a charming man and good at public relations.[1] I was a little overawed by him in the beginning and we became friends only much later, whereas his associate and nominal boss, Nicholas Nabokov (a composer and the cousin of the writer) did not impress me greatly. I remember him rushing in and out of rooms, always in a hurry. He was preoccupied with celebrities and since I was quite unknown and unimportant, he took no interest in me. This was my first visit to Paris ever, I had not published a single book and the few articles I had written had appeared under a pen name out of consideration for Naomi's family living in the Soviet Union.

The Congress had been established a few years earlier, and I had been recommended by George Lichtheim, who did not belong to Congress and was critical of Josselson's strategy of approaching the literary intelligentsia.[2] He had told Josselson that I was some latter-day Rastignac, a young man from the provinces, unpolished, a self-made man but of a certain promise, eager to continue his education in Europe. Josselson liked to act as a talent scout and introduced me to some of his gurus, friends and colleagues. But I spoiled at least two such meetings; at lunch with Irving Brown, the European representative of AFL-CIO who singlehandedly did much to prevent the takeover by the communists of the European trade unions, I spilled a plate of very hot soup over his pants which Brown took in good spirit but which still caused some slight resentment. At tea with Raymond Aron, there was a famous American sociologist, but since my knowledge of American sociology was even less then than now I mixed him up with a comic actor very popular at the time on American television. This amused Aron (whom I came to admire greatly in later years) but the American sociologist was outraged.

That hot summer of 1953—we went to swim in a piscine in the Seine every afternoon—was quite memorable. I met some of the French thinkers and writers, of whom I had heard so much in previous years, we went to coffee houses in St. Germain des Pres, which appear in countless books, the museums, and the bookshops. There were interesting visitors such as Richard Loewenthal and Franz Borkenau, a young New York editor about to launch *Encounter* named Irving Kristol, Herbert Lüthy a young Swiss historian about to publish a famous book on France, and many others.

Paris in 1953 was a very different place from ten years later, more picturesque, far shabbier but intellectually much more exciting. Most people still drove around in the old Citroens familiar from old movies; in every other building there was a tiny BOF shop (selling butter, eggs and cheese), in our little hotel in the rue Jacob there was no elevator, and our room had neither shower nor toilet.

Mike Josselson offered me to become the correspondent of the Congress in Israel which I gladly accepted. My work was neither arduous nor well paid. I remember acting as host to Edmund Wilson who was interested at the time in one subject only, the Dead Sea Scrolls about which I knew little and cared less, ever though I had been present at the small meeting in December 1947 when Professor Sukenik had announced the original discovery. I invited Wilson to tea together with my neighbor Abba Lerner a distinguished if somewhat eccentric economist. Wilson had quoted Lerner at considerable length in *To the Finland Station* but that afternoon he pretended never to have heard of him. From a history of the organization, I learn that I recommended that the Congress should not be active in the Middle East since it was bound to remain unpropitious ground for cultural freedom.[3] The Congress disregarded my recommendations and sponsored certain activities, including a cultural magazine in Lebanon. They were not successful. I was equally skeptical about Congress activities in India and not only because, as George Kennan put it at the time, in Asia Americans were always thought to be acting from power-lusting, money-grabbing or war-mongering motives. Indian intellectuals had their own agenda, either they sympathized with communism (not very deeply, admittedly) and disliked America and the West, or they were Hindu nationalists combatting Muslims and Pakistan and keeping the Untouchables in their place. Internal Western quarrels between Marxists, non-Marxists and anti-Marxists were of little interest to them. The Congress was essentially a Western enterprise and the attempts to expand its activities to Asia could not be very successful.

I tried to persuade Josselson to launch a journal devoted to the study of Soviet and East European culture in London. It was an uphill struggle, the need for such a publication was doubted. At long last a compromise was reached; I received permission to bring out a monthly documentary newsletter of sixteen pages, something in between a typewritten sheet and a printed newsletter in a few hundred copies. George Lichtheim helped me, so did Jane Degras, the Russian expert of Chatham House, the Royal Institute of International Affairs, a warmhearted, impulsive, and tough lady, perhaps the best editor I ever knew. In the 1920s she had worked for the Marx-Engels-Lenin Institute in Moscow, her name was respected by everyone in the field. There was no editorial office, no secretary, the newsletter was put together in our small Hampstead apartment. After a few months, *Soviet Culture* became *Soviet Survey*, it grew from sixteen to thirty-two, to sixty pages and more; after a year or two it became a bimonthly and later still a quarterly. It had not yet been accepted as a permanent fixture by Josselson, and during its early years its existence was more than once in jeopardy. But neither did they want to kill it and thus *Survey* became a journal of history, sociology, and politics of some consequence; it continued to appear for almost a quarter of a century after I left it.

My association with the Congress lasted up to 1964–65, when my interests shifted to other directions. Soviet affairs had become much less exciting; I must have felt instinctively that the intellectual confrontation was over. Until 1965, Naomi and I visited the Soviet Union every year, after that there was an interval of twenty years. True, the Soviet Union was steadily gaining in military strength. But my interest was not in the strategic-military field, and while I continued to follow the great confrontation from afar, I was even more interested in other aspects of contemporary history and modern culture.

My involvement with the Congress thus lasted for about ten years; I was never a full-time employee and while I participated in some of its conferences I never belonged to the inner circle and my knowledge of the decision making was only second hand. Still, I experienced the excitement of those early years, the feeling of being involved in an enterprise in which I wholeheartedly believed and which, given the imperfections of all human endeavors, seems to me in retrospect to have been eminently worthwhile.

The Congress for Cultural Freedom played a part in ideological confrontation between communism and the West; its overall impact will be known only after there will be full access to the Soviet and East European archives. Thousands of studies have been written in the West about the political and military aspects of the cold war, but in the final analysis the contest for the hearts and minds of people was more important than the strategic blueprints. Yet historians have paid little attention to the "liberal conspiracy" (as one author has called it) which was not really a conspiracy at all, but a small organization operating with a tiny budget and a handful of administrators. It was a strange coalition of antitotalitarians of the left, right, and center which through a network of periodicals, conferences and work groups tried to influence the intellectual climate of the 1950s and 1960s.

How effective was it? Only now, twenty years after the Congress ceased to exist, ten after the communist empire disintegrated, is it possible even to begin drawing a balance sheet. While it existed, the Congress was bitterly attacked not only by Communists, but by third world radicals, European neutralists, anti-Americans of every possible hue. For those who believed that the cold war was entirely (or mainly) the fault of the West, the Congress was, of course, an abomination, a war-mongering institution, a major obstacle on the road to world peace and a sworn enemy of the forces of progress. When the Congress was disgraced as the result of the revelations about CIA financing, its fall seemed complete; it never recovered its initial impetus even though it continued to exist under the auspices of the Ford Foundation for more than another decade.[4] When it was finally dissolved in January 1979 it seemed to have been a failure. But perspectives and assessments tend to change in the light of subsequent events. As I see it, the Congress had outlived its usefulness in Europe by the 1970s but as one now rereads its publications of the 1950s and 1960s and if one compares them with what its critics had to say there is no doubt who was right in that historical confrontation.

Two histories of the Congress have been written so far, one by Peter Coleman, a former Australian member of Parliament, and a more recent one by Pierre Gremion, a French academic.[5] In addition there have been several essays by Edward Shils in the *American Scholar* and in *Encounter.* Both books are judicious, well informed, and reliable, they bring much that is new even to those, who thought they knew all that there was to know. Neither author was present at the creation; those who were may not agree with all their observations and comments. All history is based on documents, but documents seldom contain the whole story, and this is true even with regard to a relatively small organization such as the Congress; those who wrote many letters and memoranda now figure more prominently than others who did not write memos but who were of equal importance. As so often, those who knew most did not write diaries or publish their recollections and are unlikely to do so.

The Congress was founded at a conference in Berlin in July 1950 following the Soviet takeover in Eastern Europe and a major Soviet campaign to establish procommunist popular fronts among Western intellectuals including the World Peace Movement, the Wroclaw Conference of intellectuals, and similar initiatives. The moving spirit during this early stage was Melvin Lasky, subsequently editor of *Der Monat* and *Encounter.* Others who took a leading part were Arthur Koestler, Carlo Schmid (a leading German Social Democrat), Ignazio Silone and Sidney Hook; none of whom was an organizer by vocation or training, nor had they any ambitions in this direction. Thus leadership passed to Michael Josselson and his makeshift offices in Paris.[6] (Whether Paris was a good choice is not at all clear in retrospect.) From recently published CIA documents it emerges that there was a strong body of opinion that preferred Berlin to Paris, since Paris seemed too "ethereal, evanescent and neutralist in the struggle between liberty and tyranny" (Michael Warner, "Origins of the Congress for Cultural Freedom, 1949–1950," *Studies in Intelligence,* Summer 1995). Two other more important facts emerge: According to received wisdom, the initiative to establish the Congress came from the OPC (the Office of Policy Coordination, which was the covert action arm of the CIA, headed by Frank Wisner). But in fact the impetus had come from a small group of European intellectuals and the OPC was at the time doubtful and reluctant. Again, it has been widely believed that the central figure in these initiatives had been Melvin J. Lasky, an agent of American intelligence and the editor of the first *Der Monat* and later *Encounter*. The documents show that Lasky was anything but persona grata in Washington. Wisner issued an ultimatum—unless Lasky was removed, the CIA would not support the Congress. At the same time Lasky came under attack as a left-wing radical by the Papal Nunzio in Germany, an American citizen who had considerable influence among the U.S. occupation leadership in Germany. Thus it was decided to terminate *Der Monat* which had been financed by the military authorities. If the journal survived nevertheless, it was owing to the support of John McCloy and some others who had known Lasky in Berlin during the postwar years. The KGB thought *Der Monat* of sufficient importance ot infiltrate an agent. This was Eric Nohara, a seemingly inoffensive young man, the son of an official in the Berlin Japanese embassy. It did not become known until many years after the event. To the best of my knowledge there was no agent at *Encounter*, but this could be a scenario for a quality thriller.

The Congress consisted of a substantial number of intellectual prima donnas; politically it was a coalition of social democrats, ex-communists, liberals, conservatives; unpolitical philosophers (such as Jaspers); erratic figures such as Bertrand Russell vacillating between nuking the Soviet Union and submitting to Stalinism; men of the left such as Silone; British, German, and Scandinavian social democrats; liberals in the classical tradition (such as Raymond Aron), robust anticommunists such as James Burnham and Sidney Hook, who otherwise had almost nothing in common. Thus it came as no surprise that a sizable number dropped out sooner or later and that it was next to impossible to draft platforms and resolutions—except in a very vague way. The Congress had no party line and its publications followed more or less their own approach; a vitriolic article by Dwight Macdonald on American culture and politics which was refused by *Encounter* appeared in Silone's *Tempo Presente.*

These divergences concerned not only ideological issues; there were fundamental differences among the major political issues of the day: some supported the Vietnam war, others opposed it from the beginning. Some were among the fiercest opponents of the student revolt of 1968, others wrote about it with sympathy. If so, what held the coalition together? A commitment to the defense of cultural freedom which was still threatened.

It is easy to dismiss in retrospect the totalitarian challenge; the very concept was denied by many in the 1970s and 1980s when the war had already been won, but not owing to the efforts of the neutralists and fellow travellers. The *Zeitgeist* of the 1950s and early 1960s was definitely "progressive" that is to say neutralist and even defeatist. Sartre's politics, those of *Le Monde* and *Esprit,* prevailed in France, the situation in Italy was not very different and the British and Scandinavian intelligentsia also gravitated toward "equidistance." Those unwilling to admit that they misjudged the world situation now claim that the Congress overrated the danger, but nothing could be further from the truth.

The strength of the Congress was not in political resolutions but in the ideas it generated and discussed in its workshops and publications. This refers to issues of economic development and planning, the idea of the postindustrial society, the "end of ideology" debate, modernism in the arts, the essence of totalitarianism, the social responsibilities of scientists. These issues discussed in small gatherings played a crucial role in the intellectual life of postwar Europe and also in America; later conferences such as the Princeton jamboree in 1968 when the Congress had changed its name were gatherings of distinguished people, and celebrities (including some very curious attendants such as Lillian Hellman), but they lacked clear focus. The theme was America's place and image in the world, an interesting theme but far removed from the original purpose of Congress. It could have been sponsored by a dozen other well-meaning foundations.

Of the journals sponsored by the Congress, *Der Monat* and *Encounter* were for years the most successful. *Der Monat* found least difficulties because Germany had been cut off for twelve years from the outside world and there was a great wish to retrieve what had been missed (*Nachholbedarf* in German). *Monat,* an international magazine, was in the 1950s the most influential magazine in Germany and the most consistently interesting in Europe. There was an openness and freshness to new ideas in Germany in the early postwar period that disappeared in later years when the economic miracle had taken place and large sections of the German intelligentsia turned towards radical chic, when the old German provincialism, self-righteousness, and *Besser Wisserei* prevailed again. (There has been not a single even modestly interesting German periodical ever since.) If America could do no wrong in 1950, in 1970 many intellectuals in Germany had become anti-American and this brought about the decline and demise of *Der Monat*.

Both *Preuves* and *Tempo Presente* faced an uphill struggle. The mood of the intelligentsia in France and Italy was *progressiste* and fellow travelers dominated key positions in cultural life. The Gaullists and the right also disliked *Preuves* because of its"Anglo-American" connections, its lack of enthusiasm for the Algerian war and other reasons. Silone had been a political emigrant under fascism, one of the very few major Italian cultural figures, who had never collaborated or compromised with fascism (so had Nicola Chiaromonte, his associate) but it was precisely for this reason that they were not liked by *gli indifferenti* who had produced films and written books under Mussolini. Silone and Chiaromonte reminded them of their own misdeeds.

The record of many French intellectuals, including Sartre, was similar; very few had been resisters and they wanted to atone for their sins of omission by joining the front rank of antifascism—after fascism had ceased to exist. They persuaded themselves that Communism—purged of its specifically Russian excesses—was the wave of the future, that Stalin was an enlightened, if somewhat harsh ruler, that the Gulag did not exist, and that the Soviet system was making enormous progress in economic as well as in most other respects. These delusions faded only in the late 1960s and early 1970s when Solzhenitsyn's books became bestsellers, when Raymond Aron who had been ostracized for decades was at long last recognized as the most prescient French thinker of his age and when Sartre and his *compagnous de route* were put on the dumphill of history they had so often invoked, writing on their foes of earlier years.

To what extent did *Preuves* contribute to this change in the French mood? It had a certain influence but probably not a very large one, the period was simply not propitious. The French were not ready for an international journal of liberal persuasion.[7] It had a major impact in Eastern Europe, in countries such as Poland. *Encounter* in London faced difficulties of a different kind. It succeeded to a much larger degree, for a while it had the largest circulation of all serious British magazines and became the flagship of the Congress. Irving Kristol was in many respects an ideal editor, yet with all his anglophilia he did not quite succeed in overcoming the antagonism of the British literary intelligentsia, which resented America (and foreign influences in general). Many still sympathized with the *New Statesman* (still going strong in the 1950s), others pretended to be eccentrics; the mixture of superciliousness and negativism, of snobbism and arrogance was not promising for a journal like *Encounter*. It tried to accommodate itself to this mood, its most famous article in the early years was Nancy Mitford's *British Aristocracy* (on U and non-U), and while Evelyn Waugh and Graham Greene did not, of course, become contributors, Malcolm Muggeridge was one of the stalwarts. Whatever the place of these figures in the history of literature, for a movement devoted to the cause of cultural freedom they were useless. Kristol mixed with the wrong crowd—but there was no other crowd, at least not among the literati.

This was not, of course, the whole story, and if the Labour party has distanced itself in recent years from public ownership, much of the spade work had been done by *Encounter* in the 1950s and 1960s. There were some immensely gifted writers among the academics, but there was no real support for a cosmopolitan journal; intellectual fashions preferred *Private Eye* and occasionally *The Spectator*. For serious magazines such as had existed in earlier generations there was no longer much demand. *Encounter* provided more entertainment than message (or messages) for which there was not much interest. It published interesting and widely read articles but as in the case of *Preuves,* its influence and reputation was greater outside the country in which it was published. And, as in the case of *Der Monat, Encounter* did not find a successor; since its demise there has been no serious political-literary journal in Britain.

I did not regularly read the other Congress magazines. *Quadrant* in Australia was among the more successful and *Forum* in Vienna was pretty much the work of one author, Friedrich Torberg one of the greatest satirists in the German language, splenetic, largely devoted to his private feuds with other writers. Neither Silone nor Torberg paid the slightest attention to what the Congress Secretariat in Paris thought or wanted or objected to; they were quite independent.

The story of Torberg and the Congress has been recently told in a critical, even unfriendly biography of Torberg by Frank Tichy (1995). Aged nineteen, he had written a novel on the suicide of a high school student (*Der Schueler Gerber hat absolviert*, 1930) an astonishing work, followed five years later by the best ever German novel with competitive sports as a background (*Die Mannschaft*)—Torberg had played on the team that won the Czech water polo championship. In later years he was more successful as the author of short satirical sketches; the great novel he wanted to write he never wrote. He introduced me to Dehmel's, the famous Viennese *Konditorei* and other such local institutions and I owe him a great debt of gratitude. But he was a quarrelsome man, one of the few friendships that lasted was with Marlene Dietrich who called him from Paris whenever she felt lonely and sad which was quite often.

For an organization such as the Congress Torberg became an embarrassment and thus their ways parted. Silone I knew less well. On the few occassions when we met he was, for one reason or another, ill-humored and taciturn and no real conversation developed. As a writer in his native country he was overshadowed for a long time by more fashionable figures, but toward the end of his life three Italian biographies appeared and there have been more since his death in 1978.

I was most familiar with the affairs of *Survey,* at least in the early years, and also the foundation of the *China Quarterly* founded in 1960.[8] There was a constant battle with Paris to obtain greater allocations to publish a more substantial magazine, there was so much interesting material and so few pages at our disposal. (I do not remember whether there were author's fees in those days, if so, they must have been a mere pittance.) By the late 1950s and early 1960s some of the best issues of *Survey* were published—on Marxist revisionism, on the state of Soviet studies, on China, on personal recollections of the early, "heroic" period of Soviet history. George Lichtheim, writing his books on socialism, had dropped out and I also wanted to have more time for my own work.

One day Jane Degras mentioned Leopold Labedz who, like Faust, had studied just about every subject under the sun in four countries for twelve years, who had never graduated but knew everything. Born in Simbirsk (like Lenin and Kerensky) of Polish parents, he was thirty-five at the time. I asked him to contribute an article on Soviet sociology to *Survey,* talked to him for many hours and eventually asked him to join *Survey* as associate editor. Leo was a man of amazing breadth and depth of knowledge, at home in the social sciences as much as in the humanities, a thinker of greater stature than more famous men I came to know. His critical faculties were admittedly more developed than his creative, he never wrote a book, those he edited were mainly conceived and prepared by others. He lacked the patience of a teacher.

The best essay he ever wrote was a devastating critique of Isaac Deutscher, a Jewish-Polish author who had settled in Britain. A former communist, Deutscher had a phenomenal success as a commentator in Europe on Soviet affairs which lasted for years; to this day his *Stalin* biography is treated in some books as a classic. (For instance, in the *Oxford Encyclopedia of the Second World War*, 1995). Deutscher was not an uncritical admirer of Stalin, but an admirer he was and his seemingly "objective" approach, very much in contrast to the official communist absurdities, made the Soviet Union and its leaders a democratic and progressive, humanitarian force. If there had been deviations from the erstwhile ideals, a breathtaking Leninist revival was just around the corner, restoring the pristine values of the Russian revolution, the best thing that had ever happened in the history of mankind.

Deutscher wrote exceedingly well, he would have been even more successful as a novelist than a historian; he had started his career in fact as a literary figure. Against this very talented purveyor of snake oil, Labedz went to field and his essay was so devastating that Deutscher threatened the author with a lawsuit if he would publish (as announced) the second part. This installment could be published only after Deutscher's death in 1967. In a small circle Leo was a most formidable critic, his judgment of articles was excellent, and we usually shared the same dislikes. Leo's name never became widely known outside the small circle of *cognoscenti* but those who knew him greatly respected him. In his native Poland he became a legendary figure; shortly before his death, an invalid, he revisited Warsaw for the first time in fifty years and was given a hero's welcome.

I found Leo in those years immensely stimulating and we used to talk almost every evening for an hour over the phone not only about editorial business at hand but about world affairs in general and books we had read. As I mentioned, Leo read so much that there was no time left to write anything of much consequence except some brilliant polemics. He also found it physically impossible to discard manuscripts, newspapers, magazines and books, as a result of which his little house in East Finchley became a storage place in which there was hardly room for a bed and a table. When I was looking for a copy of an article, his immediate reaction was that he had it, as well as many others, but hard as he tried he would never find it.

Leo's habits drove Jane Degras to distraction. Not only were his own articles never delivered on time, he was not willing to pass on contributions by other authors; trivial considerations such as deadlines set by the printer did not exist for him. Things went from bad to worse and reluctantly I asked Paris to dismiss him. But Leo promised to mend his ways, which he did to a slight degree, and I was overruled. In the circumstances I suggested that he should be made co-editor, thus sharing the responsibility for the appearance, more or less in time, of *Survey*.

After I left, *Survey* continued to grow in size and to a certain extent changed its character. Leo obtained and first published in English some of the key texts of Russian and other dissidents; his merits in this respect were enormous and have not been fully recognized. He also persuaded himself that he had been the founder of *Survey*, that until he had arrived on the scene there had been a mere newsletter which he had transformed into a major magazine. Later, this version found its way into some books; I thought it amusing rather than annoying because Leo had been in the front ranks of those preaching the gospel of truthfulness to communist historians, he did not always practice what he preached. I was not angry because I had moved on to other fields whereas for Leo *Survey* was the center of his life, the cause of endless, heated debates, of sleepless nights and of friendships which were broken off. It could well be that but for such a singleminded editor with his utter lack of discipline the magazine would not have lasted as long as it did and not have made such a noble contribution. What did it matter *sub specie aetenitatis* that the magazine appeared once or twice a year rather than four times, and often with a year's delay?

For years after 1964, I saw him but rarely, but whenever I was in London he would come for dinner. He did not mellow with age but became more rigid and this also affected his judgment. Political discussions became difficult but we still had many common interests such as literature and French movies of the 1930s and 1940s. On Israeli affairs Leo became a hawk in the 1970s without ever having been interested in Jewish affairs. He died in 1993 after a long and painful illness which he bore with great fortitude. The last issues of *Survey* were guest edited by friends of Leo. At the very time when the Soviet empire collapsed and about everyone in Moscow made it known that what the authors of *Survey* had been saying for decades had been correct, the publication ceased to appear.

There had been rumors for a long time that the Congress for Cultural Freedom was CIA financed, or, to be precise, received a considerable part of its budget from grants channeled by the CIA through various American foundations to Josselson in Paris. It is my impression that no more than three or four people knew about this. Like the rest I did not know, nor did I try very hard to find out. It seemed not really a crucial question at the height of the cold war, financial aid was needed, where would it come from? Similar allocations were made by governments in every major (and many minor) country in the world but these countries were less open than the United States and affairs were handled more discreetly.

It seemed not to matter because there was editorial freedom even on such issues as Vietnam. Mike Josselson and other leading figures opposed the Vietnam war from the beginning ("I agree with Senator McGovern..." Mike wrote in one of his letters), others were Vietnam hawks. The Congress played a role of some importance in the destabilization of the Franco regime in Spain, it published a journal called *Censorship,* denouncing political and cultural censorship all over the globe. The sums involved were small, the salaries anything but princely. Congress had great difficulty in finding and keeping first-rate editors at the salaries it could pay, nor could it provide tenure; quite a few switched over to magazines that paid more and offered greater security. Peter Coleman's book states that the annual allocation for *Survey* in 1966 was a $45,000. I would imagine that in earlier years, while I was editor, it received little more than half that sum. I am not certain since I was not interested in the financial aspects. In 1965–67 with the shift of public opinion in America, revelations about the CIA were made in various American journals such as the *New York Times,* the *Nation, Ramparts,* the *New York Review of Books* and eventually there was an article by Tom Braden the senior CIA official responsible for the channeling of funds in the *Saturday Evening Post,* in May 1967 in which he said that he was far from ashamed having contributed to the appearance of the Boston Symphony in Paris, the founding of *Encounter* and other such ventures. ("I am glad the CIA is immoral.") I was no longer associated with the Congress in any way at that time, but the defensive tenor still seemed to me as idiotic as the accusations were hypocritical; what was immoral about *Encounter* and the Boston Symphony Orchestra?

George Kennan put it very well in a private letter to Shepard Stone:

[The] Congress is an institution of great value which should have a permanent place, it seems to me, in the life of our western world. The flap about the CIA money was quite unwarranted and caused far more anguish than it should have been permitted to cause. I never felt the slightest pangs of conscience about it....

This country has no ministry of culture and CIA was obliged to do what it could to try to fill the gap. It should be praised for having done so, and not criticized. It is unfair that it should be so bitterly condemned for its failures and then should get upbraided for when it does something constructive and sensible. And the Congress would itself have been remiss if it had failed to take money which came to it from good intent and wholly without strings or conditions.

The revelations caused much commotion especially in Britain and among some sponsors elsewhere who felt their trust had been betrayed. There was a stronger argument that what had been permissible and indeed inevitable in the 1950s in view of the immediacy of the danger and the urgency of the needs was no longer feasible ten years later. Greater efforts should have been made to obtain funding from other sources. But given the American system it seems unlikely that the Congress would have allocated funds to foreign operations over which it had no control; those on the far left would have opposed it because of the anticommunist orientation of the Congress for Cultural Freedom, others would have been reluctant to finance liberals and social democrats with whose ideas they had no sympathy whatsoever. Above all, there was the general aversion against spending on cultural diplomacy, the record of the White House and Congress in recent years shows this clearly. Public diplomacy was always the stepchild of American policymakers, deemed at best a luxury America could ill afford. Could the big foundations have stepped in? Attempts were made in the late 1950s but they were not successful. Furthermore, it is quite likely that under the tutelage of the foundations, Congress seminars and publications would have had less freedom than under the CIA. Such are the ironies of history. That there was such freedom seems difficult to accept even now to authors, firmly convinced that the freedom propagated by Congress "concretely meant submitting to American power in return for dollars." One of these deconstructionists writes that "intellectuals from America such as Hannah Arendt, Edward Shils, Arthur Schlesinger Jr., Daniel Bell, John Galbraith and others, took for granted the benign character of whoever they thought was subsidizing their travel to Milan and did not welcome having their discussions of principles disrupted by low minded charges that Western freedom concretely meant submitting to American power for dollars."[9] Milan in 1955 was one of the Congress' key conferences, however, even if we assume that the character of the ticket payers was malign and not benign, even if we take it for granted that a satanic force in Washington planned the agenda of the Milan conference ("The Future of Freedom") in all details, commissioned Professor Peter Wiles of the London School of Economics to present a paper in which he showed that Soviet industrial production was outpacing the West, commissioned Michael Polanyi of Manchester to give a paper arguing that state controls did not necessarily weaken freedom (which induced an angry Friedrich Hayek to declare that the real agenda of the Milan conference was not to plan the future of freedom but to write its obituary), even then the scenario of the Wellesley postcolonialist professor of English is not quite persuasive. For she shows that the Indian Cultural Freedom committee manipulated the Congress for its own designs (opposition to domestic authority), and it stands to reason that if the Indians were able to get away with this, Mess. Bell, Schlesinger, Shils and Galbraith were not less capable of having it their own way.

The Congress had been under attack all along but with the CIA revelations the campaign reached a crescendo. "Literary Bay of Pigs," wrote Alexander Werth in the *Nation* deriding the journals which had "done their best to keep the cold war going." There was Conor Cruise O'Brien in *Book Week,* Jason Epstein in the *New York Review of Books,* Christopher Lasch in a long article in the *Nation* (later included in a book), and countless lesser lights denouncing the deep moral corruption of the anticommunist liberal intellectuals, especially the ex-communists among them. The issue was no longer what the subsidies had been used for, let alone who had been right in the ideological debate; by accepting secretly government money Congress had automatically disqualified itself. It was no longer necessary to discuss seriously the political issues involved because any cause supported by the U.S. government was *a priori* reprehensible. As Alexander Werth put it, "that there was something fishy about *Encounter* should have been clear to any person of minimum intelligence." Others were equally scathing; the anti-anti-communists had regained the moral high ground. As for the lack of cultural (and other) freedom in the Soviet empire, all kinds of mitigating circumstances were advanced by Mr. Lasch; the Soviet Union was still underdeveloped, for penny-pinching (Soviet) bureaucrats culture was judged in utilitarian terms—these were luxuries they thought they could afford. And the bitter denunciations of Theodore Draper's "diatribes" that had dared to suggest that Castro was not a democrat but belonged to the Soviet orbit...

I missed most of these articles at the time and read them recently for the first time; what strange and embarrassing reading they make! How sure the authors were of their cause at the time, how triumphant, how mordant, and how mistaken from the perspective of thirty years! In each period there are tests according to which individuals and groups are judged, antifascism was one, anti-Stalinism another. There was, of course, much more to the Congress for Cultural Freedom than communism and anti-communism but this was the issue that most annoyed the critics. It seems not to have occurred to them that one day the Soviet archives would be opened and that the findings would undermine most of their cherished assumptions about the cold war, the aims and the character of Soviet policy. Soviet publications would not just confirm most of what the Congress publications had said at the time but go well beyond it. In fact, many opponents of Congress came to change their views well before. Christopher Lasch who died in 1994 is a case in point, Conor Cruise O'Brien another; he became a columnist for Rupert Murdoch's (London) *Times*. There were persistent allegations that Alexander Werth had been an agent of influence (not of his country but of another), he made damaging confessions and eventually committed suicide. And the *New York Review of Books* has not published diagrams of Molotov cocktails for many a year. Seldom in history has an organization been vindicated as fully as the Congress for Cultural Freedom by subsequent events.

One could conclude the story here, but there still are a number of loose ends. Mistakes were committed by the Congress but they were not those most frequently adduced in later years. The Congress was established hastily and the choice of some officials was far from ideal. There was a heavy concentration on well-known names and great reputations, some of them bogus. Some of the conferences were mainly for show and the attendants sometimes reminded one of the smart set commuting between St. Tropez in summer and St. Moritz or Gstaad in winter. There was snobbery particularly in Britain, the outward appearance of refinement, wit and sophistication combined with a lack of substance; college high table talk and Cafe Royal gossip. A figure like Labedz was kept at a distance in the 1950s, he was too uncouth, his English too heavily accented to fit into the polished company at inconsequential tea and cocktail parties. Such flippancy and lack of seriousness was very much in contrast to the European-Russian traditional image of intellectuals and the intelligentsia.

There were always mitigating circumstances, an organization aiming at a political impact could not only rely entirely on young, but so far unknown geniuses, it needed big names. But there was a tendency to overdo this and the efforts to attract certain literary figures were out of proportion, except perhaps in the case of a Camus and a Malraux. But in the overall balance such negative trends did not prevail; I have not met before or after such a concentration of gifted, stimulating and interesting individuals as in the workshops of the Congress during its best years.

The Congress was right in its basic political choices opting for the cause of freedom, or at least relative freedom; the true agony of the American left (C. Lasch) was not in 1965, but came two decades later when the full extent of its disastrous errors became clear.

But how influential was the Congress in affecting the politics of the intelligentsia in Europe and elsewhere—and politics in general? The impact of ideas on politics is always a complicated affair and there are no easy answers. Nor have subsequent developments been unequivocal, if many French intellectuals turned away from Leninism beginning in the late fifties (and the Italians in later years), the Germans discovered Marxism in the following decades only to turn to a new nationalism in the late 1980s. Solzhenitsyn had a tremendous impact in France, but little in Germany.

It is impossible to measure ideological influences but the impact of the Congress was considerably greater in Russia and Eastern Europe than in the West. A journal such as *Kultura* in Paris which did not belong to the Congress network but was very close to it ideologically, made a substantial contribution to the downfall of communism in Poland, and since the Polish example influenced the rest of the Soviet bloc, this was a matter of great consequence. A considerable amount of material published by the Congress was translated into Russian ("secret—for office use only") in a few hundred copies but was widely circulated. More was accessible in the so called *Spetskhrany,* the collections of ideologically harmful material available only for trusted researchers.

This literature had a great attraction and by the late 1970s all but the most hardened *apparatchiki* and the most simpleminded enthusiasts had ceased to believe in Marxism-Leninism; this was not unconnected with the ideological spade work done by the Congress in earlier decades. The Russian and Eastern European language radios in Munich provided up-to-date news coverage but more basic issues could not be discussed through radio and television. The disintegration of the Soviet empire was caused by a variety of crises including the exhaustion of the official ideology, if the system had functioned well the downfall would have taken much longer. But it did not function well, and even if the Russian intelligentsia played a relatively small part in the events of 1989–1991 it is also true that the self-confidence of the Soviet leadership had largely disappeared.

The full measure of the work of the Congress remains to be studied, wholly conclusive answers may forever remain out of our reach. Those who opposed the aims and activities of Congress at the time and their ideological descendants claim that its work was unnecessary because a real threat never existed or was grossly exaggerated. Amusingly, those who argued during the cold war that the Soviet system was working well, and that Soviet power was so strong that nothing should be done to provoke it because of the danger of war, have taken the opposite position once the cold war was over, claiming that Russia had been always so weak politically, economically and even militarily that it had been foolish ever to take it seriously. Similar arguments have been adduced with regard to Hitler and Nazi power—forty years after the war was over—the world had overrated the Nazi danger, Hitler had lost the Second World War the moment he unleashed it and so on. This is not misplaced hindsight, these arguments are as wrong now as they were then. According to the same logic, there was no need to spend much on defense since the Soviet system was so weak. But this is to confuse cause and effect, the Soviet system was not always weak, and Soviet propaganda, even among intellectuals, was not always ineffective. And if the regime collapsed it was not owing to the efforts of those who wanted to appease it and make major concessions.

All this now belongs to history, and yet it has a bearing on the present. The Congress was a coalition of disparate individuals and groups, a fact noted at the time even by a hostile critic such as Christopher Lasch who wrote that there was never really a united front as right wingers consorted with liberals (a "coalition of liberals and reactionaries") and the "reactionaries" gradually disappeared. Lasch thinks that it was in the final analysis "sham pluralism" but he was not well informed: Burnham and Koestler dropped out at an early date, so did Russell and Jaspers. Sidney Hook did not play a role of importance, whereas Raymond Aron became a key figure. The pluralism was genuine, so were the inconsistencies and the disorder.

Nor was the Congress for Cultural Freedom the breeding ground of neoconservatism. There has been a tendency in the media as well as in academic publications during the last two decades to describe the critics of Soviet and Communist politics as "neoconservatives"; in America (as distinct from the rest of the world) "liberal" became a synonym for anti-anticommunism. This, in historical perspective, may be flattering from a conservative point of view but it is untrue. Many conservatives (and some neoconservatives) were or became isolationists even though few were willing to accept this label, whereas the AFL-CIO was in the fore-front of the battles of the cold war. A recent writer on the rise of neoconservatism rightly notes that contrary to what the label implies, some cold warriors were liberal on social issues and favored governmental intervention in economic affairs, others were social and cultural conservatives reluctant to interfere with markets.[10] Having established this much, the author continues nevertheless to apply the useless and mis-leading labels. For while neoconservatism may make sense in domestic politics, what does it indicate in world affairs? (Nor does the epithet apply to Raymond Aron and Daniel Bell, the two people most central in setting the agenda of the Congress conferences and seminars.) Were Brezhnev and Andropov liberals or conservatives (and if so how to de-fine their opponents?), were the Chinese more progressive or more reac-tionary that the Soviet leaders, was Polish *Solidarity* a conservative or a liberal movement, did one have to be a neoconservative to oppose Honecker? If the critics of the Soviet system were neoconservatives, the Soviet leaders must have been radicals or at least liberals. But if any-thing, they were conservatives. To ask these questions is to demonstrate the absurdity of the labels. Yet they are used, and probably will be used in future, often out of laziness, ignorance, and want of another label, but sometimes simply to obfuscate matters. This was true forty years ago and it is especially true today; the fact that the Congress was right when many others had been wrong did not add to its popularity. As they used to say in Paris at the time, it was better to be wrong with Sartre than right with Raymond Aron. To this day many have not forgiven the Congress just as fascist fellow travellers could not forgive Silone.

   In the summer of 1991 a gathering took place in East Berlin of a few dozen cold warriors who had been involved in the activities of the Con-gress for Cultural Freedom. There were as is the custom on such occa-sions, a great many speeches, some long, others short, some interesting or at least entertaining, others less so. It was striking to see to what extent old colleagues had moved in different directions: some had become full-fledged conservatives stressing the importance of religion and other traditional values, while others felt more in tune with the heritage of the enlightenment, some were vaguely in sympathy with social democracy, yet others had moved towards some form of neoisolationism or had lost interest in foreign affairs altogether. Interests had shifted, all were aware that they were now divided in many ways but they had at least the past in common. The leading historian of the cold war, John Gaddis, wrote in 1992 that "many of us had become too sophisticated to see that the cold war was about the imposition of autocracy and the demise of freedom." The Congress for Cultural Freedom had not committed this mistake.

The story of the Congress will be told again in greater detail and with different emphasis. It was a fascinating historical episode and it offers a variety of lessons which will almost certainly be ignored. To put it in the simplest possible way, the initiative could be launched and the money allocated only because it was done behind the back of the Congress. A coalition of democratic and republican populists and isolationists always opposed cultural diplomacy root and branch; the attacks against NED (the National Endowment for Democracy), the virtual liquidation of the Munich radio stations and the budget cuts leading to the cessation of many USIA activities have shown this again in recent years. America now spends less on the support of arts on a per capita basis than any other developed country and it could be argued that it would be unreasonable to allocate to cultural purposes abroad funds which are denied to cultural Institutions at home. Cultural policy, unlike defense, has no domestic constituency; the villain of this piece is not however the American people, public opinion polls have shown that there is a willingness to give for purposes of this kind. But influential legislators know better, culture is elitist and the diffusion of culture abroad is a luxury as well as reprehensible because it constitutes interference in the affairs of other countries. Why invest in culture if CNN can be watched in many five-star hotels abroad? Having "cheap defense" hawks why not have advocates of cheap national heritage? Alone among all developed countries America has no ministry of culture (or arts or national heritage), the contributions made by the private sector have been sporadic and declining in recent years. But this is another story; as for the Congress, we shall not see the like of it again, except perhaps in another state of emergency.

Notes

1. Edward Shils wrote an excellent profile of Josselson several years ago in the *American Scholar.* I hope that Daniel Bell who knew him well will put his recollections on paper one day. Mike, as he was known to all, wrote one book but only in retirement, a biography of the Russian general Barclay de Tolly.
2. On George Lichtheim see my introduction to George Lichtheim, *Thoughts Among the Ruins: Collected Essays on Europe and Beyond* (1987).
3. "Laqueur warned the Secretariat in the early 1950's that the Congress office in the Middle East would be denounced by nationalists and Communists as a tool of Western Imperialism and Zionism (unless it joined the anti-Western chorus.)" And later on, "As Laqueur had predicted the attack on *Hiwar* (the Arab language Congress journal) by Communists, Baathists and Nasserites was relentless." Peter Coleman, *The Liberal Conspiracy* (1989), p. 189.
4. Among the many other recipients of CIA funds were various student organizations, the American Friends of the Middle East, the American Society for African Culture, the African-American Institute, the Synod of Russian Bishops Abroad, and the International Commission of Jurists. It is frequently forgotten today that during the critical years (1946–50) many European parties of the left, as of the center and the right, received American political and financial help to reestablish their organizational framework which had been destroyed during the war.
5. Pierre Gremion, *Intelligence de l'Anticommunisme: Le Congrès pour la liberté de la Culture a Paris 1950–1975* (1995).
6. Some documents on the early history of Congress have now been declassified. See Michael Warner "Origins of the Congress for Cultural Freedom, 1949–50" *Studies in Intelligence,* vol. 38, no. 5, Summer 1995.
7. Recognition came many years later when *Preuves* had ceased to exist. See P. Gremion (ed.) *Une revue européenne a Paris, choix de textes* (1989).
8. This grew out of a special issue on China published by *Survey.* It was edited by Roderick McFarquhar, who became for a short time a Labour member of parliament and later a Harvard professor. It is still published, but has been for decades under different management.
9. Margery Sabin, "The Politics of Cultural Freedom: India in the Nineteen Fifties," *Raritan,* Spring 1995, pp. 45–65. In this article the terms free and freedom almost always appear in quotation marks.
10. John Ehrman, *The Rise of Neo-Conservatism* (1995), p. vii.

21

Family Reunion

On March 19, 1994 a family reunion took place in Givat Haim (Ihud), a kibbutz about half way between Tel Aviv and Haifa. Such meetings are not unprecedented these days; a few weeks earlier eighty-five members of the Rothschild family, all descendants of Maier Amshel (1743–1812) had assembled in Frankfurt. But neither are they very frequent because there is not enough detailed, certain knowledge. As the result of the major migrations in modern Jewish history few documents have been preserved and the catastrophe that befell European Jewry did the rest. Few Ashkenazi families can trace their origins back further than three or four generations except perhaps in a very general way. The Diaspora Museum at the University of Tel Aviv regularly receives communications from individuals, claiming that they are the offspring of King David. But closer inspection invariably reveals one or more missing links.

In other cases the family name is so frequent that research is virtually impossible. There are about a hundred Rothschilds (not to mention Epsteins and Shapiros) in the Tel Aviv telephone directory and their total numbers have to be counted in the thousands.

The name Laqueur, on the other hand, is infrequent: despite much research its origins remain obscure to this day. Nevertheless, one hundred and five people from over a dozen countries who for the better part had not known of each other, let alone met before, came on that Sabbath afternoon to Givat Haim. All they had in common was documentary evidence that they were the progeny of a man named Elieser who lived in the Silesian village of Staedtel in the second half of the eighteenth century.

Family, even extended family, meetings are of concern mainly to those immediately involved. But I found the Givat Haim meeting of far more than ordinary interest. It reflected faithfully the fate of a very assimilated Central European Jewish family; furthermore almost everyone present had a fascinating story to tell—of survival, if not always of riches and fame. Not all Laqueurs came to the meeting for a variety of reasons, there are probably twice or even three times as many as those who attended. A quarter, or perhaps a third of them now live in Israel, another third has not been Jewish for generations. In fact, the first Laqueur who ever visited Jerusalem (in 1860) and wrote about it was a Russian man of letters and a faithful son of the (Russian Orthodox) Church. And it was the same man who first visited America (in 1859) and wrote a book about it. Others came to the United States to settle later in the last century, but their traces disappear in Chicago and San Francisco.

The idea to have a meeting first occurred to two women members of Givat Haim, about a year ago, but most of the preparatory work was done by a younger generation who showed great and unexpected enthusiasm in their search for roots. My own interest in younger years in family history had been strictly limited, and this was, I believe, quite typical. Attitudes in this respect have markedly changed in recent decades.

It was not easy to locate all those belonging to the tribe and there could not be full success. Women had changed their name through marriage, in some cases the name had been Hebraized (or Magyarized, or Russified), and certain branches of the family had vanished from purview altogether. However, having sent out chain letters, the organizers succeeded finding a surprising number of descendants of Elieser from Staedtel, and his three sons, David, Josef, and Moritz (later Boris). In fact, the response was overwhelming and in the end people turned up from places as distant as Chile and an Indian reservation in New Mexico. They ranged in age from four months to ninety-four years, they belonged to four religions, even though the Russian Orthodox Laqueurs could not come.

No detailed social survey was made that afternoon in Givat Haim but there were at least a dozen members of kibbutzim, as well as half a dozen physicists another half dozen computer scientists, about the same number of medical doctors and nurses, several professional army officers (Israeli), three university professors, a clergyman (Protestant), several housewives, a banker, two photographers, some retired people, a temporarily unemployed young Dutchmen, and others. There was no time to discuss the political views of those assembled which may have been all to the good. There was an equal number of males and females.

The family tree shows that relatively few members of the family—
perhaps ten to fifteen perished, less than in other European families in
the Nazi mass murder, but "Sobibor," "Belzec," "Theresienstadt" and
other such places do appear in the family tree. The survival rate was
relatively high partly because some were living outside Germany when
Hitler came to power and were able to assist others in emigrating. Several fought in the Allied armies during the Second World War, a number
were killed in the IsraeliArab wars beginning in 1948. I did not see any
physical similarity between those present, even though others claimed to
have discovered a variety of common traits. Whatever the truth, everyone seemed to enjoy him (or her)self.

When did the name Laqueur first occur and what were the origins of
the family? The search has been going on for about seventy years, and an
astonishing amount of material was uncovered during the last months
before the meeting, including old letters, archival material, and even the
poetry of Rabbi David (1770–1846). (Part was discovered in the archives of Bar Ilan University in Tel Aviv, part in Buenos Aires.) Auto-
biographical sketches, published and unpublished, helped with the
detection work, academic experts and diplomatic sources in Germany
and France, in Russia, Polen and Hungary were mobilized to help with
the search. But in the end we remained ignorant on some crucial questions concerning our origin albeit ignorant on a higher level of sophistication and knowledge.

* * *

With some well-known exceptions Jews received family names in the
German language areas of Central Europe less than two hundred years
ago. This process has been described in considerable detail and all that
need be said is that it caused endless confusion. In Kassel in 1808 four
brothers decided to call themselves Nordheim, Sudheim, Ostheim, and
Westheim respectively. Five others adopted the names Dalberg, Halberg,
Sahlberg, Stahlberg, and Traugott. The first Laqueur was probably called
Elieser Alexander, but this is far from certain. Jews lived in Staedtel
from the late seventeenth century, they constituted almost one third of the
population, and, in contrast to other villages, they engaged in a variety of
crafts. There were no urban guilds in this small place to exclude competitors from these professions.

According to legend Elieser and his three sons had come to Silesia
from Winzenheim, today a suburb of Colmar in Alsace. Ludwig Laqueur

reported in 1926 that his father had told him that the ancestors had come from Upper Alsace (place unknown). Independently, Anna Laqueur said that her grandmother (around 1870) had told her that "three brothers Laqueur" had come from the West, one settled in Prussia, another went on to Russia, a third to Hungary. But Professor Louis Laqueur who had the chair of ophthalmology at the University of Strassbourg in the late nineteenth century and wrote a textbook much used at the time, claimed in his unpublished memoirs that his grandfather had come from Kempen some fifty miles from Staedtel—a district town in what was then Russia, near the Silesian border.

According to legends, the Laqueurs had been invited by the Dukes of Wurttemberg (they became kings only in the following century) who had large holdings both in Alsace and in Silesia and were looking for competent people to help to develop their land in the east. According to the same legend, Rabbi David seems to have been a key figure in this context. He was a first-rate chess player and a frequent guest at the castle to play with the Duke, an intellectual of sorts who wrote books and even operas. (Carl Maria von Weber was another visitor.) As late as 1925 a visitor to the castle (Carlsruhe near Staedtel) was shown the cupboard in which the kosher dishes used by David were kept.

But there is no certainty that this version is authentic; on repeated visits to Winzenheim, I failed to uncover any records shedding light on this affair. The archives of this once sizeable Jewish community no longer existed; they could be in Paris or might have disappeared. The gravestones on the large cemetery near the mainstreet did not provide any clues either. There were many Weils, Blums, and Dreyfuses and a few other typical Alsatian Jewish names, but they all belonged to a later period.

According to another version the Laqueurs had originally come from the east, from Lachwa, a small town in White Russia, south of Minsk, or perhaps from Lak in central Poland. This version appears in Guggenheimer and Guggenheimer's *Etymological Dictionary of Jewish Family Names* published not long ago, a work of enormous erudition. When asked for further explanations, the authors reminded me that genealogy is a craft rather than a science. The family might have come from Lak (of which there are twoscore in Poland, mostly tiny hamlets). But there was, no certainty whatsoever. I started to make enquiries both in Poland and the now independent state of Byelorussia but gave up once it was established that proper archives did not exist. In any case we did not really know what we were looking for in view of the absence of a family name. Thousands of Jews who had originally come from France and Germany had settled in Eastern Europe several centuries earlier, reemigrated to the West in the later seventeenth century because of the almost constant fighting and pillaging in the east following the wars between the Russians and Poles, Swedes and Ukrainians. Perhaps the Laqueurs had been part of that wave, perhaps they had come from France, after all. It was only a legend but in our researches we found that legends were usually rooted to some extent in reality.

The name Laqueur appears first in Staedtel shortly after 1800, but it was spelled in different ways in the documents—Laquer, Lacquer, Laqueer, Lacoeur. Eventually two ways of spelling survived: the descendants of David became Laqueur, those of Josef—Laquer, and the children of Moritz (later Boris) who migrated to Russia became Lakier. As accident would have it a Laqueur and a Laquer were to collaborate in the 1920s in pharmacological research in Holland. The former went on to produce synthetic testosterone, the male hormone, the other (a professor at Temple University when he died in 1954) was the first to isolate vitamin B1.

French names were the fashion at the time, in Staedtel, and its vicinity family names such as Graveur and Translateur were quite common, pointing to professions; these names do not exist among Jews in France proper. Perhaps the application of Lacquer was at the origin of the name? The brief answer is that we do not know.

Life in Staedtel, a place surrounded by major forests at the time was hard. We know from documents that the community was desperately poor. There was never quite enough food and wood for heating, the purchase of a piece of clothing was a major event and one virtually never travelled except within the immediate neighborhood. There was not much of a future for Jews in Staedtel or indeed for anyone else. Economic prosperity and growth in the nineteenth century went side by side with the spreading of the railway net, and Staedtel somehow missed out. As a result, the number of inhabitants declined. There had been 241 Jews in 1842, fifteen years later less than a hundred were left. It lost its status as a city and became a village and a small one at that. While David, the rabbi was alive—he died in 1846—he refused to leave his flock, though he had some lucrative offers. He argued that they were too poor to get another rabbi,[1] and so he stayed on at one thaler a week and also some deliveries in kind. He was prophetic—he remained the first and last rabbi of Staedtel.

The detailed breakdown of the estate of a tradesman in the family who died in 1869 has been preserved: Gold and silver—nothing. Pictures and other valuables—nothing. A torah scroll was estimated at ten thalers. The summary showed that the deceased had more debts (doctor, pharmacist, gravestone) than assets and this seems to have been quite typical.

By the 1920s the last Jew had left Staedtel. Yet Jewish life did not cease altogether; an hours walk from Staedtel there was a sizeable farm which had been bought by a wealthy Jew, who in 1933 put it at the disposal of *He'halutz* the organization that provided agricultural training for young European Jews, preparing themselves for life in what was then Palestine. Ellguth, which was the name of that manor became one of the leading such centers in Germany. When the first group of *halutzim*, graduates of Ellguth reached Palestine in 1938, they went first to Givat Haim, the very kibbutz in which the reunion took place.

As the Laqueurs (and the Laquers) moved out from Staedtel to nearby towns such as Oels, Festenberg, Namslau, Brieg, and Medziborz (Neumittelwalde), their social and economic position improved. Around 1810 they had been peddlers or at best market dealers, selling leather goods, spirits and buying cattle. There was an occasional male nurse and a teacher. By the 1860s they had become "merchants," "traders," and, generally speaking, gained respectability even though most of them had not gained riches. Before 1800 the common language had been Jewish-German, a dialect in between Yiddish and German. Within one generation they acquired a perfect mastery of German as their letters showed; Hebrew was forgotten and Jewish-German frowned upon, even if some expressions survived. When only two generations later a member of the family explained to another that Reb David had been considered a *tsadik*, he had to explain what a *tsadik* was. Around 1830 one Laqueur went to Hungary for rabbinical training, but apparently never finished it. Twenty-five years later it was not thought uncommon to send a schoolboy to live as a paying guest at a vicarage in a nearby city, to prepare himself for his examinations. The first conversions to Christianity had (secretly) taken place around 1810 but intermarriage became frequent only towards the end of the century.

There was a Hungarian branch of the family. Early in the last century Josef Laqueur went to Budapest and married a lady named Maria Braun.

They had descendants, some of whom Magyarized their name to Laki, others kept the Laquer. Some contacts were maintained with the rest of the family up to the 1920s owing to the endeavor of one of the Hungarian relatives who seems to have had a propensity for languages (he was president of the Hungarian Esperanto society.) But after that all links were broken. Quite recently one of us discovered in the archives of the Mormons of Salt Lake City a Hungarian Laquer in Florida, who had not the faintest idea about his ancestors but was greatly interested. Since there are more than sixty Lakis in the Budapest telephone directory and probably some Laquers elsewhere, chances are that the one or another will be in contact sooner or later.

About the Russian line we now know much more, at least up to 1917, and in a few cases up to the present time. They were ennobled and thus found their way into the Ikonnikov, the Russian Gotha, the manual listing the aristocratic families. But the Russians did all they could to obliterate their origins, and as a result the story that follows became known only recently.

Reb David had a brother named Moritz who was trading in leather goods in Staedtel. He had a wife named Sarah, and a son but one day around 1810 he suddenly disappeared and was not seen again. According to legend he was converted, studied medicine in Berlin and Dorpat (today Tartu in Estonia), settled in Russia to become eventually the personal physician to the Tsarina. This story is correct but for the last part. Moritz became Boris and went to the Black Sea port of Taganrog where he served as head of the local quarantine station. He would probably have lived out his days in this backwater, about which Chekhov wrote that he doubted whether three honest people had lived there—but for an accident. In 1825 Tsar Alexander I visited Taganrog, fell ill, and died. (The circumstances of his death are shrouded in mystery.) Dr. Boris Lakier signed the death certificate and as a reward was ennobled. He married a second time and had to think of a background fitting his new elevated station in life. He came up with a cock-and-bull story about his descendance from a French judge named de Laquierre from Clermont-Ferrand who had fled to Russia at the time of the French Revolution. But on an earlier occasion, when he registered at the University of Dorpat he had to provide the true story of his provenance. Thus in the various works of reference the Russian Lakiers appear with two wholly different stories concerning their origins. The compilers of the works of reference expressed mild surprise, and refrained from comment. The family was not particularly eager to shed more light on it. By the end of the century the descendants no longer knew about the awful secret; they thought that they were Russian nobility of impeccably pure origin. Since most of the Russian nobility was of Tartar, Polish, or German origin they were right in a way.

Boris had three sons and one daughter; they married into the Russian nobility of rank or money. Among their relations and descendants were several well-known men of letters, one or two tsarist ministers, a commander of the Black Sea fleet, a governor of Kiev. One did not do well; he had a piano factory in Moscow and went bankrupt. In the 1880s letters from him asking for help were received by the Laqueurs in the West; this was the first sign of life in seventy years and there were none thereafter.

One who interested me professionally was Alexander Borisovich, Moritz' third son. I have written elsewhere about his strange fate[2] and need therefore only to summarize. He trained as a lawyer and was, for a while, secretary of the committee preparing the enfranchisement of the serfs. But he left government early on; a man of great intellectual curiosity, an inveterate traveller, his accounts of foreign countries appeared in the leading Russian journals of the midcentury. Some years ago the University of Chicago Press published a very much abridged translation of his book on North America, which was, by and large, the first serious account in Russian on American political and social conditions, with vignettes about Broadway, Washington's Pennsylvania Avenue, Harvard College, life on a steamer and so on. He married (for the second time) a very wealthy lady of Greek origin and became a country squire of rank. He looks brooding in his wedding photograph and died young. He was forgotten in his own lifetime but has been rediscovered in recent years, especially among the Russian right as the author of the leading Russian textbook on heraldry, a topic that has again become fashionable with the Russian nationalist revival. When I mentioned to some Russian acquaintances that Alexander Borisovich was of German-Jewish origin, they were a little shocked, even though neither Pushkin nor Lermontov, neither Herzen nor the Romanovs had been of pure Russian stock either. One of Alexander's sons was a godchild of the tsar—but ended his days around 1890 as a political emigre in Switzerland. He is buried in a forest cemetery overlooking Lake Geneva at Montreux; there must be an interesting story buried with him.

Alexander's grandchildren witnessed the revolution, lost their wealth and emigrated. They could be found in Paris in the 1920s, others went by way of Turkey to Yugoslavia and now live in Argentina. One of them a fluent Russian speaker, serves in the Argentinean embassy in Moscow. There are probably others, but because of the dislocation caused by the revolution, and the various other misfortunes that befell Russia, their tracks have been lost. On a recent trip to Taganrog, a very old lady was located who as a young girl had worked as a domestic servant in the Lakier household and was full of stories about the good old days.

As the Laqueurs left Staedtel, relations between the various branches of the German family became distant and gradually ceased. Members of the core families would, of course, meet from time to time, at weddings, and other family affairs, unless they happened to be involved in one of those horrible family quarrels, which, it is said, are the worst kind of quarrel. By the end of the last century they lived at considerable geographical distance from each other, their interests and their stations in life were different; they belonged to different clubs and confessions. Some were not particularly eager to remember their humble origins nor the religion practiced by their great grandparents. But there was a remnant of curiosity; in some of the letters of seventy years ago it is mentioned that when they travelled to other cities they were checking the local telephone directories whether any Laqueurs or Laquers were listed there. Whether they would call on these relations (by now distant) is not clear.

Those who continued to reside in Silesia would visit once a year, usually in early June the old Jewish cemetery in Staedtel together with some other families hailing from there. Since there had been a great deal of intermarriage in the village in the olden days, they were all somehow related. This went on until 1937, after that date it was reported that the local synagogue had been destroyed as was the cemetery. Consequently, no one ever made the effort to revisit Staedtel (now part of Poland and called Miejsce) after the end of the Second World War. But the reports were not correct, and last night I watched a poetic and very moving Swedish film[3]) which had been photographed in part in Staedtel. The synagogue where Reb David had officiated still stood though it now served other purposes and the local people were a little reluctant to have it photographed. It was a dark and rainy day, but there could be no doubt that between the bare trees, covered by brown leaves was the cemetery with the graves of Reb David, and the neighbors such as the Decros, the

Schiftans, and others. It looked quite neglected but no tombstones had been overturned; apparently the cemetery, like Staedtel itself, had been bypassed by history. It was in no one's way and therefore forgotten.

Other than these annual excursions to Staedtel there was no contact. I do not remember as a boy ever having heard of other Laqueurs except the closest relations, and I was told at the family reunion that the experience of others was similar. This changed only after Hitler's rise to power with the sudden necessity to leave Germany when remnants of solidarity and mutual help reemerged. But this belongs to a later date of family history.

The tribe disintegrated not only for reasons of geographical distance. *Standesbewusstsein*, the awareness of one's status in society, pride, and snobbery also played a certain role. Those who had not quite made it became an embarrassment to the others. It was not primarily a question of income and property—there was no one very rich in the family at the time—but more one of social standing. Someone with an academic title, say a physician or a lawyer, was more highly respected than a mere merchant, unless of course, he was very well off. Someone working for the government, state or regional official, however lowly his position, was a person of authority at least prior to 1914, far more presentable than, say, a commercial traveller. In this respect as in others the family reflected prevailing values and notions in bourgeois European society.

In my searches I came across the letters of Nanny Drewitz (1859–1932) who lived in Goldberg, a medium-sized town in Silesia. She had been born a Laqueur and married an assistant postmaster (and part-time accountant), a veteran of the Franco-Prussian War of 1870–71. She converted when she married and in her letters deals at considerable length with her prayers and thoughts on the occasion of Christian holidays. She must have been a fine, godfearing person, proud of her husband, her daughter, and grandchildren. In a way she was also proud of her ancestors. In a letter to the wife of a cousin living in Holland and non-Jewish by origin she wrote, "Isn't it amazing that from one source, [meaning Elieser in Staedtel] such a big tree should have grown over a few generations?"

One summer, Nanny went to another Silesian town named Schweidnitz where her daughter lived. She had been asked by her Dutch relations who tried to put together a family tree to provide information about all other Laqueurs. But at the end of her visit she wrote: "I discovered to my horror that the Schweidnitz Laqueurs are also related to us. As you know, one can pick one's friends but not one's relations. Louis Laqueur set up a place of ill repute producing and selling schnapps and thus provides grist on the mills of the local anti-Semites."

Nanny's reaction was interesting, she articulated what others were probably thinking but might have put more elegantly. Her information was out of date—Louis Laqueur had retired from business a long time ago, and had, in fact, died seven years earlier. Far from being the Al Capone of Schweidnitz he was a quiet sort of person who was never in conflict with the law, sold spirits to Semites and anti-Semites alike. The fact that he sold it to the wrong sort of people in a shop on market square, in the very center of town, was perhaps a thorn in the flesh of some of the local leaders.

By 1926, when Nanny visited Schweidnitz, the infamous shop belonged to Louis' son, my uncle Emil, who despite his small stature had served in the First World War (Iron Cross, second class), was a bit of a domestic tyrant, and the most law-abiding citizen I have ever known. I accompanied him sometimes on his evening constitutional; everyone seemed to know him—there was a constant exchange of "good evenings." His one bad habit was to play for hours on Sunday mornings Bach violin sonatas, unaccompanied. He was a passionate, but not very accomplished player. Once a week they made chamber music at his home—a local science teacher came, a police officer (or was he from the local Reichswehr garrison?) and some other persons of substance. It was all very peaceful and Hitler seemed far away.

But for Nanny Drewitz selling schnapps had become an embarrassment, and she forgot that her parents and grandparents had been peddling old clothes and some had also sold spirits. But it is not really fair to pick on her; European attitudes at the time were not those of America where a Bronfman became within a generation a pillar of society.

Nanny died in 1932, a year before Hitler came to power. She was a Jewess according to the Nuremberg laws, but her daughter in Schweidnitz was only half Jewish, her grandchildren one quarter Jewish, and her great-grandchildren—one eighth. This was a question of life and death in the Third Reich; they survived, even if they could not be promoted to positions of command. I have not followed in detail the subsequent careers of Nanny's descendants. I think most of them survived the war and I have been told the present minister of the interior in Bonn, born in Schweidnitz might or might not be a distant relation.

What became of the children of Uncle Emil? His only daughter managed to escape to Shanghai at the very last moment. She did not have a good war but survived and later on settled in California. Uncle Emil's granddaughter is a leading breeder (and international prize judge) of dalmatians, and his great-grandson, who came to dinner in Washington not long ago, is an ardent young ecologist and an all-American free-style wrestler—though he does not look the part. He very much wanted to come to the reunion, but could not afford it, looking for his first job after college. How far can one get from what were once considered undesirable Jewish occupations such as Uncle Emil's? And all these farmers and army officers at the reunion? Even a stern judge such as Nanny Drewitz would have approved.

After the victory of Nazism those who could, left Germany. In the standard Nazi works of reference Laqueur appears as a Jewish name despite the many conversions in previous generations. One such work claimed that Laqueur ("a derivation of Laquiedem") was one of the names Ahasver, the Eternal Jew went by. They forgot to mention that this genealogical information came from a novel (by Gustav Meyrink) some of whose books have again become fashionable in recent years. Since the Nazis thought that Meyrink was a Jew (for only a Jew would write a book called *Der Golem*) they could not give their source. Ironically, Meyrink was a pure Aryan.

But it was true that for the second time in two hundred years the Laqueurs had become wanderers not just moving from a village to a nearby town, but to faraway countries well beyond their past experience. The largest single contingent went to Palestine in the 1930s, others, after the war by way of Latin America to what is now Israel. Some found temporary shelter in Turkey, Yugoslavia and other Balkan countries. Several went to Britain, others had been living for years in Holland. There was also emigration to North and South America. One Laquer, the vitamin B chemist, arrived at Ellis Island in 1940 (and wrote an essay about this experience; today there are 49 descendants of this branch who recently had their own private reunion). Of those who went to Palestine most became agricultural laborers, at least for a while. One had trained as an electrical engineer and his expertise was soon in demand in the British and later the Israeli army. A few settled in Tel Aviv, others in or near Haifa, for a while there were none in Jerusalem.

Family ties which had been loose or nonexistent before 1933 suddenly became closer. It was a matter of life and death to have an uncle or second cousin who could support one's application for a foreign landing permit. If a substantial number managed to get out in time this was mainly owing to help rendered by distant relatives.

"*Familles, je vous hais,*" André Gide has written, "*foyers clos, portes refermeés, possessioms jalouses du bonheur.*" Fortunate André Gide, he had never had to run for his life; by the time the Laqueurs rediscovered the family, the *portes refermeés* were those of foreign countries, and the issue at stake was not the possession of *bonheur*, but physical survival.

This was also true in my case: my parents had no money; there were only nine months left before the outbreak of the war and the quickest, only feasible, way to leave the country quickly in my case was to obtain a student's visa for the Hebrew University; all other categories of visas were exhausted for years. An uncle gave the money needed—two years' tuition and some minimal living expenses for that period. This uncle, a medical doctor and a bachelor, happened to be in a state penitentiary at the time having fallen afoul of the Nuremberg laws—defilment of the Aryan race through sexual intercourse. But since he was a highly decorated (and injured) World War I officer, he was given some privileges including the right to dispose of his property even while he was in prison. But for him my departure from Germany—one day before the *Kristallnacht*, would have been impossible. In retrospect I have no regrets that I did not make use of this wonderful opportunity to educate myself, but became one of the first dropouts at what was then a very small institution. The uncle was released from prison after the outbreak of war on condition that he immediately leave Germany; he took the last train (the Transsiberian) from Berlin; little did it matter that it led him to an uncertain fate in China.

Much help for a number of relations was provided by the family in Holland. The pharmacologist succeeded in getting himself protected by the German Ministry of Economy; a branch of his big pharmaceutical laboratory existed in Latin America which the Germans very much wanted to acquire. This saved him and his wife, his children were deported later during the war , but most of them came back. He died soon after the war while extending first aid to the victims of a road accident in Switzerland.

Another second cousin, caught with his family in Holland at the outbreak of the war lived with his parents in a small attic, thought to be uninhabited. This kind of existence, known to a wider public from Anne Frank's diary was quite intolerable for a restless and adventurous boy and so he made his way in the middle of the war through occupied Belgium and France to Spain and ultimately to Palestine. The trip lasted almost a year, and involved work as a foreign laborer in a German army installation; the problems involved in this kind of existence have been depicted in *Europa, Europa.*

Yet another family member had a less heroic war; he seems to have survived because he worked for the Amsterdam *Judenrat.* He was in his twenties at the time, his position was a lowly one. Since I do not know the details, I find it difficult to adopt an Hannah Arendt-style posture.

Life in the country of adoption was invariably difficult. It meant acquiring fluency in a new language, adjustment to unfamiliar ways of life. Above all, it meant subsistence on very little. For the young, this process was easier than for the older ones who never really felt at home in the new country. It was a question of survival, of swimming or sinking, and this knowledge brought out inner resources that had not been needed by the generation of the parents and grandparents. They had to start from scratch, and such a new radical beginning has certain advantages.

Those who had survived in Turkey, half- or quarter-Jews according to the Nuremberg laws, returned to Germany after 1945; one of them became a career diplomat. I know little about the members of the family who survived inside Germany. Richard Laqueur had been a distinguished historian in Weimar Germany, for a while rector of one of the most prestigious German universities. His writings on Flavius Josephus and Hermann the Cheruscan are occasionally cited to this day. But Hitler came to power, neither his Protestant faith nor his conservative and patriotic convictions were of any help. During the war, in his sixties, he was washing dishes in Chicago, and after his return to Germany he did not even get his professorship back.

Those who had prepared the Givat Haim reunion envisaged a minimum of speeches. In Reb David's time there was a common language, but now, as the result of the dispersal of his descendants, simultaneous translation would have been needed and this would have been out of place at such an occasion. Those who attended the meeting were introduced at the beginning, and for the rest of the time, everyone was conversing with everyone else, a great deal of picture-taking went on and the small children played more or less peacefully.

There was no prime minister to welcome the guests as in the case of the Rothschilds, but then the Laqueurs could not have helped Mr. Kohl to make Frankfurt again Europe's financial center. There was a conflict of interest; the Israelis wanted to go home, those who had come from afar complained about the short duration of the meeting. In the end some more get-togethers were arranged as well as excursions during the days that followed.

There was a break for more tea or coffee in the middle of these unstructured proceedings, and I used it to wander off Bet Terezin where the reunion took place. Terezin had been the luxury ghetto, the fortress in northern Czechoslovakia that served during the war as a transit station to Auschwitz for many thousands of "privileged Jews"—elderly people, a few war veterans of World War I, Jews from Denmark and Norway and some other such categories. But for us that day the Holocaust was not the central event, there was the wish to look back even further into the past, to learn about forgotten people and places.

There had been quarrels in the family, and some skeletons in the cupboard, but tiny ones only. There were no Balzacian conflicts about legacies, usually someone had been snubbed by someone else.

Givat Haim is a good place for reflection on past quarrels. The kibbutz, founded in the 1920s had split in 1952 on a number of seemingly crucial ideological issues, including the politically correct attitude towards Stalinism. Old friendships had broken up, families split, and two separate settlements came into being, one on the left, the other to the right of the highroad traversing Emeq Hefer. Had they not split, Givat Haim would be the biggest kibbutz in the country with almost two thousand residents. Perhaps they are better off now living in two smaller settlements. But what a waste to split on issues that are no longer remembered except by the oldest residents of the two settlements and that, in any case, now seem altogether incomprehensible.

I walked back as the meeting was resumed and as I watched my kinsmen reentering the hall the obvious question occurred: what had these people in common other than the descent from Elieser from Staedtel— and what had made them come to Givat Haim?

The former question confronts students of kinship with problems of impossible complexity. This was obviously no longer a family, even not a joint or compound or extended family, however broadly interpreted. The biological connection was minimal. There were no common household nor other significant social links. Was it a clan or a tribe? Few of the findings of generations of anthropologists about consanguinity, unilinear descent groups and cognitive kin groups would be of much help for virtually none of the usual characteristics applied to this group of people, who for the most part had not even known of each other's existence until a few months earlier. But the anthropologists also discovered that fictive kinship can be as strong as biological. There is a phenomenon called pseudo-kinship and if the terms "father" and "mother" in the Catholic Church have not been taken literally, addressing a fellow member of the Laqueur tribe as a cousin is perhaps not that farfetched either. Anthropology offers no clue and one has to refer to a level of unconsciousness and instinct about which little is known and in which there are few certainties.

What made them come from afar to Givat Haim? Just to see and be seen? To discover at first hand a bit more about the past about a once common heritage, and how the various branches of the tree had grown and developed? Or was it just curiosity, idle and not so idle? There is nothing wrong with curiosity—without it there would be little science and no writing of history. Or was it perhaps a feeling of some satisfaction or defiance having survived after all a ghastly period in human history?

For a few moments a wholly fantastic scene obtruded itself: what if using a time machine Elieser and his three sons could have descended that afternoon on Givat Haim? The first reaction (I felt) would have been one of wonder at the seeming chaos, the absence of hierarchical structures - there was not even a head of the family (as the Rothschilds have to this day). How could one know according to clothing, bearing or language who were the people of substance, of importance? They seemed to address each other on the basis of equality irrespective of rank, sex, and even age—perhaps they were all equal...

I suspect the ancestors would have been proud of the tall and well-built young people (much taller than they had been) so prominent in the audience, many of whom spoke *lashon hakodesh* (Hebrew) much better than even the most learned people in Staedtel. Reb David , to be sure, would have been disappointed because there was not one superior chess player among them. Obviously, a price had to be paid for normalization. Coming to think of it, if dispersal was one key word at this reunion, normalization was the other.

Notes

1. B. Brilling, Die jüdischen Gemeinden Mittelschlesiens, Stuttgart, 1972, p. 179.
2. Walter Laqueur, Thursday's Child has far to go, New York 1993, chapter two.
3. *Aterkomster (Returning)* by Bo Persson and Joanna Helander. Staedtel has now perhaps two hundred inhabitants , it can be reached by a little local railway and a minor road from Pokoj (Carlsruhe) where the Dukes once resided.

Index